Punishment

Punishment
The Supposed Justifications Revisited

Ted Honderich

Pluto Press
LONDON • ANN ARBOR, MI

First published as *Punishment: The Supposed Justifications* by Hutchinson, 1969, second and third editions published by Penguin, 1971 and 1976, and fourth edition published by Polity Press, 1989.

This revised edition published 2006 by Pluto Press
345 Archway Road, London N6 5AA
and 839 Greene Street, Ann Arbor, MI 48106

www.plutobooks.com

British Library Cataloguing in Publication Data
A catalogue record for this book is available from the British Library

ISBN 0 7453 2132 1 hardback
ISBN 0 7453 2131 3 paperback

Library of Congress Cataloging in Publication Data applied for

10 9 8 7 6 5 4 3 2 1

Designed and produced for Pluto Press by
Chase Publishing Services, Fortescue, Sidmouth, EX10 9QG, England
Typeset from disk by Newgen Imaging Systems (P) Ltd, India
Printed and bound in the European Union by
Antony Rowe Ltd, Chippenham and Eastbourne, England

166869 34

To Ingrid, John and Kiaran

Contents

Introduction   1

1   Problem and Definition   4

The Need to Justify Punishment   4
The Definition of Punishment   8

2   Backward-Looking Theories   17

Retribution Theories in General   17
Legal, Circular, and Intrinsic-Good Retributivism   23
Distress–Culpability, Forfeited Rights, Indifference   29
Innocence System   35
Annulment, Offenders' Rights   41
Rational Contract   46
Consent to Loss of Immunity   48
Satisfactions-in-Acting   53

3   Grievance Satisfaction   58

An Actual Reason   58
System   65
Defences and Criticisms   69

4   Utilitarian Prevention Theory, etc.   74

Questions of Fact about Prevention   74
The Utilitarian Prevention Theory   86
The Victimization Objection   89
Utilitarians on Victimization   95
Justified and Unjustified Victimizations   104
Retrospect and Conclusion   109

5   Reform, Rehabilitation, Treatment   112

Punishment as Reformative   112
Illness and Treatment   118
Objections   125

6   Determinism   **130**

Punishment, Freedom, Responsibility   130
A Sketch of Determinism   133
Determinism Despite Quantum Theory   138
Compatibilism and Incompatibilism   144
Attitudinism   145
Arguments for Compatibilism
  and Incompatibilism   151
The Real Consequences of Determinism   155
Punishment   158

7   Compromise Theories   **163**

Retrospect, Separate Questions   163
Prevention and Retribution   170
Correct-Values Retributivism   176
Liberal-Community Retributivism   184

8   Non-Problem, Other Conclusions   **195**

The End of All Retributivism   195
The Decent Society   201
The Principle of Humanity   206
Our Societies   210
Our Unjustified Punishments   216

Acknowledgements   228

Notes   229

Index   245

Introduction

This book is philosophical, which is to say that its ambition is logic about a subject – logic in the most general sense. So it consists in an attempt to achieve a clarity that is rightly called analysis, and then consistency and validity, and then a completeness. It is true that disciplines and lines of life other than philosophy have some aim of this kind, which does not exclude commitment, but they cannot be so single-minded in it. Physical science has other aims to which it attends, obviously, and so do the humanities, say history. Something the same is true, even, of the works of jurisprudents and lawyers on the subject of the justification of punishment. They rightly give attention to a lot more than what at bottom is a question of logic in morality and thus in moral philosophy. So too do sociologists, criminologists, penologists and other social theorists have other concerns.

With punishment, then, there is a division of labour and has to be, a division according to the possession of different tools, ways of proceeding and the like. This is not at all peculiar. It is to be found with respect to other subjects, say the nature of consciousness, free will, time, reality in general, and terrorism. To think any of these can be treated wholly within science, for example, is inevitably to bungle them. Proofs surround us.

The somewhat grand intention of the original book of which this is a revision was to consider everything clear and at all persuasive by way of arguments or justifications for the practice of punishment, and also to pay attention to the main obscurities. That is still your author's intention. But it cannot now be carried forward by introducing a reader to just about all of what accredited philosophers and the like have put into print on those arguments. As your search engine on the web will demonstrate to you, there is now too much print. There is only a sample of it here. A relief to both of us, maybe.

You will gather that answers to the question of why we punish, the explanation, where that is not the question of what reasons we can give for punishing, but rather a question about causes, are not our concern. Nor is the *meaning* of punishment, which thing you may not have known it has, and which presumably is not either its explanation or its justification. The book is not sociology, social theory, social psychology or the like. It is not the sociology of punishment, where that is a descriptive account of the practice and also of its causes and effects in and on society and its history as well as its other relations to other social things.[1] Still, the book's realism and plain sense, if that is what they are, about retribution in punishment and the retribution theory of its justification, does contain part of an answer to the question of explanation. Is that not reassuring? Is our reason for something not likely to be the answer, now and then, to the question of why it exists?

The first chapter is a quick introduction to the problem of justification of punishment, in fact punishment by the state, and the matter of its definition. The second and third chapters together, and then the fourth and then the fifth, deal with traditional 'theories' of punishment – in fact three families of theories or arguments, sometimes with members whose membership is uncertain. Theories of the three sorts are not considered, however, because any of them is now much advanced on its own as a sufficient justification of punishment. Rather, the aim is to get clear about each of them by giving it separate consideration. This is a necessary prelude to considering almost all contemporary theories of punishment, which mix together the traditional ones in various ways.

The sixth chapter is about different assumptions of all theories of the three families and their combinations. It is thus about freedoms, holding people morally responsible for actions, and determinism, essentially the questions of the freedom and responsibility of offenders and the truth of determinism.[2] The seventh chapter is concerned with the contemporary doctrines mentioned – mixes, combinations and compromises. The eighth is conclusions. It certainly includes a different theory of punishment, and more than that.

It would be alarming for an author if a book written 35 years ago and revised 20 years ago seemed just as right now as it did then. It would not be reassuring to a reader either. Fortunately for its peace, and as you will have gathered, my mind has changed about things. If this additionally revised and enlarged edition is no recantation, but remains on the side of its predecessors and does not go over to any other side, it does take up a different position in the one it stays on. You could say there is more edge to its moral conviction. Is this partly because the world has changed? That, as is plain, punishment has become more punitive and there is more of it?[3] Or because the world has not changed? Because, that is, the political moralities of conservatism and liberalism do not change their spots, but keep their societies serving their interests, and because this has sunk in on the author?

As well as in moral conviction, the book is also very different in other contents and in organization. Certainly there was reason to change the title. Two chapters of the last edition, the first and last, about backward-looking theories of punishment, have become two different ones, the first and second. The sixth chapter, on determinism, freedoms, and ways of holding people morally responsible, entirely replaces the old one. It reflects my own progress, if that is what it has been, in thinking about these subjects on their own, the separate problem that is nearly as much a problem in the philosophy of mind as in moral philosophy.[4] The seventh chapter, on compromise theories, and the eighth, giving conclusions, are entirely new replacements of their predecessors. Throughout the book some mistakes have been put right. Some propositions are worked out more fully.

Another way of saying much of this is that the book remains true to a realism and plain sense, as it does indeed seem to me, about almost all talk of retribution, desert, proportionality and the like in punishment. That is a realism that has never endeared the book to a better class of readers, including some too self-respecting lawyers. But, to go back to differences, the book is now truer to the proposition that the subject of punishment is not to be treated without an actual consideration of the subject of *crime*, which is to say what a society or part of it deals with by means of punishment. That is also to say that the subject of punishment is not considered without actually considering and judging, if too briefly, what a society or some part of it takes to be rightly defended – indeed takes to be a decent society.

The book is also different in being aware of some late twentieth- and early twenty-first-century thinking and also of some empirical facts and other things that have become plainer, notably facts having to do with rehabilitative and deterrent hopes for punishment and also the subject of determinism and an interpretation of quantum theory. No really new doctrine of the justification of punishment has come into being since the book was first published.[5] But certainly there has been enlargement, modification and some admission of error with respect to the old doctrines, and also that wonderful intellectual progress that is terminological.

1
Problem and Definition

THE NEED TO JUSTIFY PUNISHMENT

The problem of punishment arises in the first place because the practice includes what traditionally has been called suffering. Whatever can be said for the practice, the need for it, it is an intentional infliction of suffering. Apologists used to say that it is an automatic reflex of society, like that of a living body to injury. This sort of thing was at best darkening metaphor, and any serious suggestion that punishment is wholly an ungoverned reaction would be absurd. It does not become less absurd when some of the sociology of punishment, in its uncertain moments, edges towards it.

Is it true that by comparison with penalties visited on offenders in the past, many of our present penalties are humane? Is it then inappropriate to describe contemporary penalties as giving rise to *suffering*? It was said by a philosophical defender of the practice in the middle of the twentieth century that

> most punishments nowadays are not inflictions of suffering, either physical or mental. They are the deprivation of a good. . . . Imprisonment and fine are deprivations of liberty and property. The death sentence is deprivation of life; and in this extreme case every attempt is made to exclude suffering. . . . We have taken the . . . important step of substituting the removal of something desired for the infliction of positive suffering.[1]

The distinction between deprivations and inflictions of suffering or pain was less than reassuring when it was made. Now, at the beginning of the twenty-first century, it seems to me not a good idea, either, for a good philosopher to sum up penalties as *what are generally regarded as unpleasant consequences* or as *burdensome sanctions*.[2] Our prisons are grim and usually hellish places. Some say it is right that they be so. Our reflections on punishment would be

4

improved by our knowing not only what men, women, boys and girls have done in order to get put into them, about which we read a great deal, but also knowing more of what drives them to suicide in them, say male-on-male rape.[3] We could learn something, too, of the fact that our prisoners with mental health disorders, a very large majority of all prisoners, have their disorders worsened by imprisonment.[4] It is unlikely to be disputed that penalties now imposed on offenders, whether or not they are to be described as causing suffering, or being more than burdensome, do raise a question of moral justification.

The question of justification would be raised correctly, however, even by a practice that did no more than deprive someone of their usual freedoms, or usual resources, in some protective, considerate and even kindly fashion. For us to be deprived of our voluntariness, that personal and bodily freedom, not to mention social, civil and political freedoms, is certainly our being deprived of a great good. Being locked up, however sensitively, is to experience an evil, have a bad life, whether or not for good reason.

To that needs to be added the fact that some men are imprisoned for a couple of decades, or have their lives taken from them barbarously in what prides itself as civilization, and turn out beyond doubt to have been innocent rather than guilty. Others suffer excessive punishments. Others bargain their way out of what would have been justice with respect to their guilt. It cannot be a requirement of a social institution that it is perfect. That it kills men without reason cannot be left out of consideration either.

The moral problem of punishment also arises, with respect to any system of punishment, as a consequence of a different fact. Others than those punished, some ordinary law-abiding members of society, are coerced by it. Their freedom is at least curtailed. One need not, in order to regard this as a consideration of importance, believe the laws of a society to be bad ones. There has been an inclination on the part of some philosophers to believe that to be forced to behave rightly is not to have one's freedom curtailed, but that involves a special and loaded conception of freedom.[5]

Does the moral problem also arise because the general quality of life in a society, the quality of its public and private institutions and relationships, is influenced by the existence of a central practice of an authoritarian and repressive nature? Are child-rearing, education, work and religion different than they could be? Is sex? Love? It is possible to think so. It is also possible to be trapped in the encompassing habit of a society, never think about it much, or raise such questions, and suppose nothing other than the society as it stands is reasonable.

Is the problem of the justification of punishment also raised by another consideration or two? Well, we have enough to be going on with.

In the past, single reasons have often been given for the rightness of punishment. One sort of reason is to the effect that what has happened in the past is in itself a reason for or a justification of punishment. The best-known instances of this backward-looking thinking or feeling, which may be characterized with deceptive simplicity, are to the effect that punishment is *deserved* by offenders for what they willingly did. Punishment is *retribution*. Other instances of looking to the past rather than to consequences of punishment have to do with past free *consenting* by individuals and other past states of affairs.

Another idea is historically associated with utilitarianism, whether or not this is an unfortunate fact, utilitarianism being the doctrine whose fundamental principle, the principle of utility, is that what makes an action, practice or institution right *is* only a judgement as to certain good consequences. What makes the action or whatever right, for utilitarianism, is more particularly the fact that it will probably give rise to a greater total of satisfaction or a lesser total of dissatisfaction than any other action or whatever. What we have often been told about punishment is that punishment serves this good end by the means of deterring people from offending. *Deterrence* consists in men being made fearful of breaking the law or made to keep it out of a self-concerned judgement of the possibility of punishment. When they actually consider offending, that is, they do not go ahead.

But the idea of deterrence is better made part of a family of claims, that punishment is justified because it *prevents* offences, thereby serving the end of utilitarianism or some different end, not necessarily by means of deterrence. For one thing, the punishment of imprisonment makes most offences impossible. It *incapacitates*. Prisoners do not decide not to break the law, but are made incapable of breaking it in ordinary ways by their being in prison. Death works better.

A third sort of reason for punishment is that it secures that fewer offences will be committed in the future but not through deterrence, understood as we just have, or incapacitation. Instead, men become law-abiding through what used to be called higher motives.

It was once the case, but is no longer, that all views of this third kind could be positively described as recommending the moral regeneration of individuals as an end in itself and also a means to the prevention of crime. We used to speak of *reform* and we now speak, sometimes, of *rehabilitation* or socialization. Well, some of us do. Other theorists raise a question about themselves of whether they should be included in this third category. They speak of punishment as *communication*. One is Robert Nozick, the defender and celebrator of private property rights at whatever cost to those without them. Also to be found here, without doubt, are the theories that propose that we should give up punishment, or give it up to some large extent, and engage instead in the treatment of offenders for their disorders.

Claims in these three families, as remarked already, have been known as 'theories' of the justification of punishment. This is so, perhaps, partly because it has been assumed that punishment or some closely related practice is an indubitable social necessity whose justification is beyond doubt. There is no question but that it is justified. Given this seeming fact, what is to be done is to provide a hypothesis in explanation, as one provides an explanatory theory about a fact of the physical or non-human world. Let us keep the usage for its usefulness, not for this implication. Assumption, conventionality, orthodoxy and piety about punishment are not useful, indeed not decent, in inquiring into it.

More recently, philosophers and others have contended that no attempted justification having to do with the past, or with prevention, or with rehabilitation or the like, taken by itself, is sufficient to justify punishment. Two or more are needed together. Sometimes a number of reasons are mentioned but one is accorded a very secondary importance. We are told that some retribution theory is correct, since punishment is justified because it is deserved in some sense for a past offence, and then we are reminded that punishment also has the recommendation that somehow it reduces offences. It may be that these are no more than the standard compromises just mentioned, variously disguised in an attempt to keep an old flag flying, or an old feeling respectable, or certain sentencing policy as tough or harsh as it is.

In order to clarify what is involved in each of the three original sorts of claims, and the later unions, I shall begin by looking at claims separately, quite a few of them. Each one will be regarded as historically it was regarded, and in several cases may still be, as sufficient by itself to establish the rightness of punishment. This procedure, as indicated earlier, will have the advantage of demonstrating why it has been thought, whether or not correctly, that no single claim is sufficient. More important, as I have said, it may bring into clarity each element of the ensuing compromises, show whether they can be necessary if not sufficient conditions of justification.

THE DEFINITION OF PUNISHMENT

There is one other preliminary matter. We need a definition of punishment. This is not a matter of choosing the one true description of punishment, as is sometimes supposed. What we need, rather, is to come to a conception of it that serves the purpose of inquiry and does not impede it, perhaps by going against ordinary usage, perhaps by begging a question in advance.

Punishment is not treatment, although some patients, like offenders, are subjected to deprivation or distress. Anything we describe as punishment *must* involve some such thing. At any rate it intends to cause deprivation or distress, which, indeed, is reasonably described as its aim. This remains true, although the aim is not the final end, when punishment is imposed to prevent or reduce offences by deterring or rehabilitating, and thought to be justified by this. Treatment, obviously, has no such aim but rather seeks to avoid distress whenever possible. It mostly does.

Punishment, secondly, is not revenge, although certain of its supposed justifications would go some way to justifying revenge as well, and some of those who punish share motivations and needs with those who take revenge. Punishment is not revenge because a man who has been injured by another and then revenges himself upon him is not *authorized* to act as he does. That is, he is not empowered by generally accepted rules, as a judge is empowered by the law, to fix and enforce penalties. If there are societies with practices that are governed and limited by generally accepted rules, where the injured man or his family exacts the penalty, these approach to being practices of punishment.[6]

Punishment, thirdly, is obviously not something done to a man chosen at random and without regard to his previous conduct. Punishment, or so we habitually think, is imposed on an *offender*, someone who has broken the law of a society – or maybe has just been found to have done so. An offending act for which someone is somehow responsible is a logically necessary condition of punishment – punishment for any reason.

Punishment may then seem, given these rudimentary differentiations, to be

> an authority's infliction of a penalty, something involving deprivation or distress, on an offender, someone who has freely and responsibly broken a law or rule, for that offence.

Is this tentative definition, a customary one, true of all practices that we are ordinarily willing to call practices of punishment? Is it true of punishment by the state, punishment by our judges, prosecutors, jailers and the like? Certainly it is ordinarily a good idea for a definition to be in some accordance with ordinary usage. If the tentative definition does not cover everything it might, this is so partly for the reason that, as we have noted, not all punishments take place within a society's ordinary legal and penal systems.

It may be said, against the definition, that punishments are not always the work of an *authority* – persons or groups of persons empowered to act by rules that have a general acceptance. 'War criminals' are said to be punished despite doubts as to whether the tribunals of the winning side count as authorities. Victor's justice, it may be said, is not justice. It may also be denied for a particular reason that punishment is always preceded by an *offence*, assuming an offence to be an action that went against a specific rule previously stipulated. A father is unlikely to have announced, before his son does some astonishing and unpredictable thing, that no one was to do *that*. Perhaps he may be taken as having announced something so general as that his son wasn't to behave in outrageous ways. Might there be similar cases which we would call cases of punishment and where the point was to teach a quite new rule?

If there are such cases as these latter ones, where there is some hope of arguing that there have not been offences, are these also cases where the person punished is not an *offender* – that is, someone who has freely and with responsibility broken a rule? So it seems. But there is also another matter having to do with offenders, more pressing. Anyone who sets out to define punishment faces a decision about defining ordinary offenders, those dealt with by our judges, prosecutors and jailers.

It is at least natural to say that someone who in fact has not broken the law – e.g. did not do the killing – is not the offender, not an offender. If you say this, then not all punishment is of offenders, as the tentative definition supposes. This will be so since mistakes are made by judges and juries, and hence some punishment is of non-offenders, innocent people. If, on the other hand, you define an offender as somebody who has been found guilty of breaking the law, whether or not he or she did so, you have a similar upshot. All or nearly all punishment is of offenders as defined, but since judges and juries make mistakes, not every offender is an offender in the other and more ordinary sense – somebody who in fact has broken the law by cheating or harming the customers, embezzling the funds, stealing the car, or committing the murder.

There is a tendency on the part of law-makers, lawyers and indeed newspapers to choose the definition by which an offender is someone found guilty. In my newspaper, anyway, somebody found guilty of murdering his wife is reported to have murdered his wife. Later on, when it turns out he didn't do it, the paper may have to call him the supposed murderer, the alleged offender, as indeed it does. Is it better, given the ordinary implications of the word, to take the more ordinary definition of an offender, as somebody who has in fact broken the law and not just been found to have done so?

That is not to say that finding someone to be an offender is not essential to punishment, as distinct from essential to somebody's being an offender. Should this not go into a definition of punishment? With respect to the finding, by the way, whether or not of a real offender, this has to be done by the judge and jury in good faith, and by way of certain procedures. A judge cannot find someone to have broken the law, in this sense of 'find', if he is convinced that he hasn't done so but pretends that he has. Nor can he find him to have broken the law if he does not investigate the matter in certain ways, look into the question of responsibility by certain methods. He must go through a certain process, follow the law on trials.[7]

Putting aside ordinary trials, it may also be suggested on the basis of quite different examples that punishment is not always of an offender, maybe even of somebody found to be an offender. There can be doubts in the case of war-crime trials so-called. We also speak of collective punishments of groups, such as classes in schools and villages in wars, some only of whose members have offended.

More importantly, to revert to ordinary punishment, American, English and other law is such that a supermarket that sells dangerous food, without anyone's intending to do so and without anyone's having been careless, may none the less be held legally responsible and be penalized. That it was not responsible in an ordinary sense, morally responsible, does not matter.[8] So may a motorist who without being negligent runs into a pedestrian under certain circumstances. A bartender who sells whisky to a man who is drunk already, without knowing the man's state or being careless about finding out, may be in the same position. It is also against the law under certain circumstances to take a girl to bed who is under 16, and remains so if the man made an honest mistake in thinking she was older. That he did not intend to break the law and took some care is not a defence. These are offences of *strict liability*. They are not a peripheral part of the law and may be more pervasive in the future.

There is also *vicarious liability*. The owners of a supermarket may be legally responsible under certain circumstances if an employee puts dangerous food on the shelves. The company that owns the truck with poor brakes, rather than the driver who didn't check them, can be legally responsible for negligence. So too may an insurance company be responsible when its salesman leads a customer into a disastrous policy improperly. Or so we are told. Employers generally may be legally responsible for certain acts of their employees. It may be said that none of these could be regarded as offenders in the ordinary sense.

What difficulties do these various cases raise for our tentative definition of punishment? Do they show we have not captured the ordinary notion of punishment? They are put forward as instances of punishment, instances of what we would be inclined to regard as punishment, and also as instances where some feature required in the given definition is missing. On further reflection, most people may be inclined to say of these cases either that they do possess the feature in question and are punishments, as ordinarily conceived, or that they lack it and should not be regarded as punishments. That is, the cases in question do not show a conflict between our definition and ordinary usage.

What is done to 'war criminals' may be taken to be punishment by those who *do* accept that the tribunals count as authorities. Those who do not accept this will give some other name or description to the practice, or to particular instances of it. So perhaps with the father-and-son case and the question of whether there was an offence – if it is accepted that there was *no* antecedent rule of a relevant character it will go against the grain to call the case one of punishment. One can deal in some related way, perhaps, with collective punishments. Strict and vicarious liability are much the same. Some people may, after reflection, be ready to name as punishment what is done in such cases, perhaps out of a kind of determined orthodoxy. Others will not be willing to regard what is done as punishment. They will give it another name. As for a court's *finding* someone to have offended, that surely *will* have to go into a final definition.

Fortunately, we need not set out to discover majority opinions. What we want is a definition of punishment convenient for our purposes. It must certainly be more or less in line with the ordinary understanding of the term, but over cases where there is no agreement, or where any existing agreement is not obvious, we may make our own decisions in order to facilitate our inquiry. As in the case of a definition of terrorism, say, despite the efforts of governments, nothing of a substantial nature follows from this with respect to the main question being considered. The matter of definitions, descriptions and names is not simple, but there is some point in saying that there are not false definitions, only definitions that complicate things or get in the way, maybe disastrously.

It will be convenient to take up a definition of punishment that allows us to use the term of cases of strict and vicarious liability, whatever may be true of ordinary usage. We need not worry about war tribunals, fathers and sons, and collective reprisals. We will henceforth be concerned only with ordinary punishment by a society, or rather by the power in it that is the state, of its citizens or those who live in the society. The definition we have, where punishment is an authority's infliction of a penalty on an offender for an offence, does not cover cases of strict and vicarious liability. What is to be done?

To linger a bit with strict liability, which will have some importance later, suppose we take it to be established beyond any doubt that a store's action in selling dangerous food in no way resulted from a relevant intention of anyone or even from negligence. In a certain sense it would be mistaken to say anybody broke a rule. This is the sense that carries the implication that the person who broke the rule was at fault or responsible – somehow morally responsible. It is the ordinary sense of the words, and precisely the sense of the words, that has entered into the tentative definition of an offender. Hence, it would be mistaken to regard the woman as an offender. There is something else to be noticed, however, of which we shall make use.

There is a different sense in which the store *did* break a rule. After all, you can break a rule unintentionally, unknowingly. You can do something without being morally responsible for doing so – that is, without there being any possibility of your being held morally responsible for doing so or being credited with responsibility for doing so. The store, then, may be understood to have broken a rule although not to have done so with intention or negligence, not with moral responsibility. Vicarious liability, however, is another matter. One could not without absurdity exhibit the owners of the trucking company or unfortunate employers generally as individuals who have broken rules in any way – if, that is, it is *really* true that they fully intended to have no trucks with poor brakes, were not at all careless, and so on. Maybe that is rare, but it is what we are talking about.

The tentative definition with which we began has another quite different disability. It specifies that punishment is *for an offence* and so may be taken to state or imply that the moral justification of punishing a man is that he deserves it for what he has done. If we were to use this definition, it might appear that we had so defined punishment that the principal question before us, 'What, if anything, justifies it morally?', was already answered by the definition, anyway in part. The answer might appear to be built in. Anyone who disputes it, or anyone else for that matter, might protest that the outcome of the inquiry could hardly be in doubt. That is not quite true – definitions do not determine the outcomes of inquiries – but is there anything to be said for the inclusion of the words 'for an offence'?

They are significant in two ways. They specify a necessary feature of what we normally count as punishment, not included in our tentative definition but subsequently mentioned, to the effect that a man must be found to have committed an offence. This, however, is already implied by the very mention of an *offender*. Secondly, as I have said, the words suggest an attitude to a man's having committed an offence. The words 'for an offence' suggest that the penalty is justified because he *deserves* it for the offence, or something of the sort.

This attitude is not itself a necessary feature of what we shall take to be punishment. We shall not regard something as other than punishment if the judge, who seems to be the relevant person, is a forward-looking fellow who does not hold the view that the penalty he imposes is morally justified because it is deserved. We shall not think that he is not engaged in punishment at all if he takes the view that the existence of an offence is important merely as an indication or proof that the man in front of him is one who is likely to offend in the future if he is not deterred or incapacitated.

It will be as well to make explicit something implicit in these thoughts. It is not the case, although it is sometimes supposed that it is, that a punishment follows on not merely an illegal but necessarily a *wrongful* act.[9] It would follow from making this stipulation that putting a man in jail for 30 years, or executing him, as a result of legislation, due process of law and so on, would not be a punishment if he had not behaved wrongly as distinct from illegally. The punishment would not be an unjust or vicious punishment, say, but rather not a punishment at all. That would be the view of those who thought the law against which he offended was wrong, maybe monstrous, and he was not wrong but right to break it.

There is no need to follow this line, tempting though it may be, and no advantage in doing so. It may well be that the justification of punishment depends on an act's having been wrong, but that is nothing to the point. Making punishment necessarily of a wrongful act, maybe an act said to be regarded as wrong by a society, is certainly not needed, in particular, in connection with distinguishing punishment under the criminal law from the awarding of damages against someone in civil law and so on. We might contemplate saying that punishments follow on illegal acts that 'officially' are wrong, and struggle to make that clear. But that is different and hardly in need of explicit mention.

Another point needs making about the tentative definition of punishment. It registers the fact, remarked on at the start, that punishment unlike treatment actually aims at deprivation or distress – for whatever purpose. The definition does this in saying that in punishment an authority inflicts deprivation or distress. Some have said that this by definition makes punishment 'retributive'. Does that mean that punishment by such a definition is justified at least in part by a proposition, some proposition or other, to the effect that offenders deserve it?

It does not. That punishment aims at distress or whatever, for whatever reason, is certainly not a proposition that punishment is deserved, or that it is right because deserved. Those who deny or dismiss exactly these propositions about desert also accept that punishment is aimed at distress, and may depend on this in connection with other propositions. They may justify punishment by an argument that has nothing to do with desert, probably to the effect that the distress is useful, something that reduces offences.

A historical remark is in place here. Over the last 30 years or so, in the United States and Britain, there has been an increasing emphasis on retribution in punishment, whatever retribution comes to.[10] This has been owed to or at any rate connected with a conservative trend in politics.[11] This is not at all our main business, which is the worth or logic of retributive and other theories of punishment rather than their connection with politics and social change. It is worth noting, however, that writing desert into a definition of punishment in the ways noticed prepares the way for a substantial conclusion in favour of desert in punishment.

The writing in, whether or not deliberately, influences the innocent or unwary. It does not serve our higher purposes to do this. This is a proper inquiry, or so I hope, not a vindication or a defence of the liberal society or the like. Nor would it serve our purpose to write in some influencing in the direction of any other theory, say a prevention theory that leaves out desert entirely. It would be easy and indeed natural enough to do so, but not a good idea from the point of view of inquiry.[12]

Given these considerations about 'for an offence' and the aim of distress, and the considerations about strict liability and vicarious liability, and the previous considerations, let us change our minds. Let us leave behind the tentative definition and define punishment as

> an authority's infliction of a penalty, something intended to cause distress or deprivation, on an offender or someone else found to have committed an offence, an action of the kind prohibited by the law

and understand that to be found to have offended is to be found to have

> actually broken a rule out of intention or negligence, somehow freely and responsibly, or broken certain rules without that, or have occupied such a position as employer with respect to a rule breaker in either of the preceding senses.

Our definition, so interpreted, is reasonably satisfactory for our purposes. Perhaps it does not fit everything that is ordinarily called punishment, whether by parents, teachers or irregular tribunals.

It does fit the subject in hand. That is a dominant practice of control, or *the* dominant practice of control, within our societies. The offences, of which more will be said in due course (p. 214), include crimes involving the property of others, such as theft and damage, crimes of violence to persons, such as murder and assault, crimes consisting of certain acts considered to be immoral, and certain crimes against the state and some of its institutions, including treason and the subversion of justice. The penalties are those fixed by law. In the main, the law sets down maximum penalties for offences. The choice in a particular case, fine or imprisonment or worse, is made by the judge or judges.

If the given definition is suitable for our purposes, it is also true that it departs somewhat from definitions provided by philosophers who have considered the question of punishment in the past. This is so for several reasons, one of them that many philosophers have attempted to capture the most common or ordinary notion. Many people do have the feeling, maybe have been got to have the feeling, that at least part of the justification of punishment is that it is deserved, and this attitude finds expression in their use of the term. Some such implication is thus present in many definitions, as it was in our earlier definition. Also, of course, given this genesis of definitions in ordinary life, and a want of awareness there of the existence of strict and vicarious liability, the definitions have excluded a part of their intended subject matter. This has issued, if not in clear mistakes, at least in an overlooking of things of relevance.

If the definition we have brings in a thing or two not made explicit in other fairly recent ones, and leaves out things they put in, it is not greatly different from them.[13] It might have included, say, a specification of the nature of the authority involved. What has been said seems to me sufficient for the arguments we will be considering.

2

Backward-Looking Theories

Entirely backward-looking theories of punishment are those that can be said somehow to find the justification of punishment wholly in the past. It is not that what they find in the past is evidence with respect to some benefit in the future that may be gained by punishment, which benefit is its justification. Rather, they look back to an offence committed, or something like an agreement made, or a certain state of affairs that existed, and find the justification of punishment there, or more particularly in a relation of the punishment itself to the past thing. So you can say, a little too neatly.[1]

More certainly, entirely backward-looking theories as we shall understand them divide into retribution or desert theories, and theories naturally spoken of as having to do with consent or contract, and theories having to do with satisfactions-in-acting. All of them are about some freedom and responsibility of offenders in their offences. All of them, for what it is worth, can be expressed in terms of rights, put into talk of rights. None of them pays attention, however important this may be, to offences of strict and vicarious liability.

A stark and influential statement of the place of retribution in punishment was given by Immanuel Kant, the greatest of German philosophers, in the eighteenth century. The following three passages, central if not entirely clear, are from his work *The Philosophy of Law*.[2]

> ... Punishment can never be administered merely as a means for promoting another Good, either with regard to the Criminal himself or to Civil Society, but must in all cases be imposed only because the individual on whom it is inflicted *has committed a Crime*. For one man ought never to be dealt with merely as a means subservient to the purpose of another, nor be mixed up with the subjects of Real Right

[i.e. goods or property]. Against such treatment his Inborn Personality has a Right to protect him, even although he may be condemned to lose his Civil Personality. He must first be found guilty and punishable, before there can be any thought of drawing from his punishment any benefit for himself or his fellow citizens.

. . . If Justice and Righteousness perish, human life would no longer have any value in the world. – What, then, is to be said of such a proposal as to keep a Criminal alive who has been condemned to death, on his being given to understand that if he agreed to certain dangerous experiments being performed on him, he would be allowed to survive if he came happily through them? . . . a Court of Justice would repudiate with scorn any proposal of this kind if made to it by the Medical Faculty: for Justice would cease to be Justice if it were bartered away for any consideration whatever.

Even if a Civil Society resolved to dissolve itself with the consent of all its members – as might be supposed in the case of a People inhabiting an island resolving to separate and scatter themselves through the whole world – the last Murderer lying in the prison ought to be executed before the resolution was carried out. This ought to be done in order that every one may realise the desert of his deeds, and the blood-guiltiness may not remain upon the people; for otherwise they might all be regarded as participators in the murder as a public violation of justice.

It is not said in these passages merely that we are justified in punishing an offender – that we may do so, that we have a moral right to do so but can without moral failing choose not to exercise it. Rather, we are told, we have a categorical obligation to impose a certain penalty – it would be wrong not to impose it. This is so, we are initially told, 'only because the individual on whom it is inflicted has committed a Crime'. These words, as well as other expressions of the supposed reason for punishment, may call up several ideas.

The words may be taken to amount to the claim, as on occasion they have been, that we as a society have a moral obligation to punish a man simply because his past act was against the criminal law as it stood, an offence. We all have an obligation to punish simply because of a past act contravening a law on the books, without taking into account the moral nature of the act or the law.

Or, as some have thought, a judge has a kind of moral obligation, presumably one that may be overridden by other moral obligations, to administer the law as it stands. He has undertaken to do this.

Or, as some have thought, what the words come to is that a judge may be *legally* obliged, or more likely, legally permitted, to punish a man simply because his act was against the criminal law. This is to say no more than that the law lays down certain possibilities for the judge in such cases. For him to be under a legal obligation, or for him to be legally enabled to act, is for there to be a covering law. The rest of us are legally obliged not to interfere in the course of justice in certain ways.

None of these three ideas comes close to resulting in the conclusion that we are morally justified in punishing offenders, let alone morally obliged to punish them. None of the three ideas is the principal one intended by Kant. But let us consider them briefly in order to have them set aside clearly.

It cannot be that a society is morally justified in punishing, or under an absolute obligation to punish, simply because of the existence of the society's enacted law making an act a criminal offence. It is notorious that there have been wrongful, vicious and indeed odious laws, including genocidal laws, and hence completely unjustified punishments. That, however, is not the main point.

Despite temptations and indeed some efforts by jurisprudents of certain kinds, the difference between mere legality and what is right has never been unclear for longer than a minute or two, either in thought or action. *Whenever* a man is punished under a law, however acceptable the law, a moral justification may be dependent upon the rightness of the law but not upon the fact that there *is* a law. It will not depend on the fact that a law-making procedure has been carried out by the correct authority, say politicians, priests, or indeed a dictator, and hence that a certain kind of act has become an offence.

Nor will a punishment be justified just by this legislative fact, or fact of legal precedence, plus the fact that a man has been found guilty of an offence according to the existing rules of procedure – by what is called due process and so on. No doubt a retribution theory requires that to be punished a man must be an offender – must have been found guilty – but that proposition is not a claim or theory of retribution. Rather, it is contained in any tolerable definition of punishment, as we have assumed in our own definition – which definition as you will remember leaves out any suggestions of justification by desert. Talk of desert, as we shall be seeing, can be put to many uses, but it is at least misleading to express the fact that a man has been found guilty by saying that it is the fact that he deserves a penalty. That a man must have been found guilty is required by theories of punishment that specifically *deny* that its justification is retribution.[3]

As for the second idea, the moral obligations of a judge are clearly insufficient to provide us with a justification of punishment or an obligation to engage in it. It cannot be that a judge is justified in punishing a man simply because in effect he has promised to do so. The law might be one that serves to send Jews to gas chambers, or one that permits or obliges soldiers to kill Palestinians in the aim of taking over more of their homeland, or a law permitting the torture of captives.

As for the third idea, it is obvious enough that the legal rather than the moral obligations of judges, and our legal obligations, do not result in the conclusion that anyone is morally permitted or obliged to punish. It just has to be remembered again, for a start, that there have been bodies of law binding judges and societies to do wholly unjust and awful things.

Kant's words, that we must punish a man only because he 'has committed a Crime' require another interpretation. Such an interpretation is suggested in several places, notably by the assertion in the third passage that we are obliged to support a man's punishment because he must have 'the desert of his deeds', what he deserves for his 'bloodguiltiness'. The point is that he has acted freely and wrongly or immorally in the past, as distinct from only illegally, which moral responsibility is somehow connected with his particular punishment.[4]

Notice again, before we set about considering more fully the possible meanings of what will be called desert claims, the nature of the supposed obligation. We are to observe, as we are elsewhere told explicitly, the *lex talionis* – 'an eye for an eye, a tooth for a tooth'. Contained in that idea, to which we shall come, is another one. A man *must* be punished if he has performed an act for which he deserves a penalty. It is not that we may rightly choose to punish him but are under no obligation. Rather, we do wrong if we do not punish him. Further, he must not be given a lesser penalty than he deserves for his action even if it is true, as sometimes it may be thought to be, that some lesser penalty will have the consequence of rehabilitating him or benefiting others while the penalty he deserves will make him a hardened criminal.

That is not the whole story of desert or retribution, however. The obligation of retributive justice is two-sided. A man who has obeyed the law must not be made to suffer even if this would have the good effect, for example, of keeping him from committing offences he is otherwise thought likely to commit. Further, given that every man must be treated exactly as he deserves, an offender's penalty must not be increased over what is deserved for his action even if it is believed that a more severe penalty is needed as an example to deter others from the same offence. He is not to be used to set an example, if that means he is to get a week more than he deserves in prison. This human, just or fair side of talk of desert, sometimes referred to as *negative* as against positive retributivism, is evidently of great importance in considering it.

Retribution theories, to come to a statement of them in accordance with Kant's convictions, are as follows.

> Legislators, who regulate the practice of punishment partly by fixing scales of penalties, are obliged to arrange that men get what they deserve for the wrongfulness of their actions, simply because they deserve it. Legislators are not to take into consideration, in this respect, the well-being of offenders or of society as a whole. Judges are to proceed similarly in the fixing of particular penalties, again because they are deserved. We, finally, are obliged to support our legislators and judges, again because that is what offenders deserve.

To some of us, maybe fewer than in the recent past, this is harsh and unrealistic. Could we be misunderstanding Kant? John Rawls, the distinguished elaborator of liberalism, was one philosopher who thought so. He asked: 'Does a person who advocates the retributive view necessarily advocate, as an institution, legal machinery whose essential purpose is to set up and preserve a correspondence between moral turpitude and suffering?' The answer given by Rawls was 'Surely not.' Rather, we are told, 'what retributionists have rightly insisted upon is that no man can be punished unless he is guilty, that is, unless he has broken the law'.[5] That is, presumably, since presumably Rawls would not have confused morality with legality, desert is a necessary condition of a justified punishment, but is not in itself a sufficient condition. Desert is needed, but is not enough by itself.

As we shall certainly come to see, not everyone who holds what he or she calls a retribution view of punishment advocates a practice whose sole and sufficient principle is to preserve some relation between immorality and suffering. Other things are added to produce what is really a combination or compromise view. But it would be strange indeed to suppose that Kant is of this outlook. It would be strange to suppose either that Kant's view in the quoted passages is not a retributive view or that it is that desert is only a necessary condition of justified punishment – let alone that his having acted illegally, merely, is what Kant has in mind. Certainly a prohibition on punishing individuals who do *not* deserve it is clear in the first passage. Equally certainly, there is the supposed obligation to act, to punish those who are said to deserve it, for that reason alone, and to punish them as much as they deserve. In other passages of the *Philosophy of Law*, maybe, one hears other notes, but I shall not consider them. Our concern is not really with Kantian scholarship but with the clarification and appraisal of one possible view about the justification of punishment. That it has been the view of many is to me a certainty and not something for which argument is needed.[6]

Talk of people deserving things, of their getting the desert of their deeds, may not be quite so ordinary or comfortable in general as once it was. Certainly 'he deserved it' is commonly said, but there may be a tendency with punishment to avoid talk of desert and to use other words instead. Certainly other terms *are* used. We hear of a penalty not that it is the deserved one for the offence, but that it is the one *equivalent* to the offence, or that it is the *proportional* or *commensurate* one. We hear of a penalty that it is the penalty that *corresponds to* the offence or is *according to it*, that it is the *reciprocal* or the *merited* penalty. We hear that it is the *retributive* penalty, *the retribution* for the offence, *the just penalty* or the penalty *required by justice*. We may hear that it is the penalty, given the offence, that is *according to our right*, or even *according to the offender's right*. Certainly we hear a good deal of colloquial stuff, such as that a particular penalty was what someone had coming to him.

It is or becomes pretty clear that all of these claims about desert, desert claims, are ways of saying one main thing, whatever it is. That some have slightly different implications does not much affect the fact. They are all ways of saying that a certain penalty or punishment stands in a certain relation to a past offence or something about a past offence, which relation makes the punishment right – morally obligatory or at least permissible. The relation is what is crucial and fundamental to retribution. Finding it must be our main business or at any rate a main part of our business.

I shall for the most part persist in speaking of a punishment being *deserved* for an offence. It is clear enough, however, and will be clearer, that everything said will be as true of talk and theories of punishment being *proportional* to an offence and so on. It may be that one way of speaking suits a particular intention a little better, but that will not affect the main line of inquiry and argument.

LEGAL, CIRCULAR, AND INTRINSIC-GOOD RETRIBUTIVISM

What does it mean, more particularly, to say a man deserves a particular penalty for what he has done? What reason for punishment is being given? That is our main question. There are a lot of answers that have been given or implied. We need to go through enough of them – look at some quickly, consider or study others. Each of them, in the sense of the words to be used here, is a particular retribution theory.[7] Do you still half-feel, by the way, that in effect we have already passed by or maybe unreasonably discarded one understanding of saying that a man deserves a punishment, that what it comes to is the following simplicity?

(1) He broke the law.

Well, you can certainly *say* that in explanation of the desert claim, if misleadingly. As we shall be seeing, talk of desert can be put to a lot of uses.[8] Talk of desert is loose. Count as a retribution theory, if you want, the proposition that punishment is right just because someone freely broke a law – whatever the law. You can also do that. Call it *legal retributivism*.

But it remains clear, without further ado, that we get nothing of what we are looking for here. We get no conceivable moral justification for punishment, no obligation or permission to punish, from the fact that an act was against a law, no matter how wrong or useless or disastrous the law, no matter the worth of the whole body of law of which it is part. And, to remember something already noted (pp. 14–15), any reason or supposed reason whatever for punishment, including a reason that has to do with the future rather than the past, is a reason for *punishment*, which we defined in an ordinary way as what is done to *offenders* and others who have been found to have broken the law. As noted, not all reasons for punishment are thereby converted into retributive reasons, reasons of desert as ordinarily understood.

Do you stubbornly persist, and say, a little differently, that the fact that somebody has been found guilty and sentenced according to law does make *some* contribution to a justification of punishing him? And that it can be called a fact of desert? Well, he is being treated as like offenders are being treated and differently from other offenders and of course non-offenders. That is not the fact exactly that what is done is according to law. But, you may be satisfied to hear, it does seem to me to be morally relevant, and we will be coming back to the matter, several times (pp. 35–41, 65–9, 96–100).

There are some other answers to the question of what desert claims come to that must also be dispatched quickly, whatever inclination may be felt in their direction. People say often enough that a man deserves something, say a punishment, and intend something that comes to very little indeed, the following thing.

(2) It is right that he gets the punishment.

To attempt to argue that a man's punishment is justified, by saying in this sense that he deserves it, is of course pointless. Any desert claim that reduces to the assertion that it is obligatory or permissible to impose a penalty cannot, of course, be offered as a reason for the proposition in dispute, that it is obligatory or permissible to impose the penalty. *Circular retributivism* is an instance of the fallacy where the supposed reason is identical with the supposed conclusion. It may sometimes be concealed, indeed concealed from its proponent, as we shall notice later. It has an effect, of course, only when concealed or not seen.

One philosopher objects that these true thoughts lead us into error and confusion. They lead us to miss something. We miss, indeed, what is standardly meant by those who use desert locutions in connection with punishment.[9] What they mean is something other than the circularity.

(3) There is intrinsic good in precisely the suffering of the guilty – as distinct from what causes it, the penalty.

More generally, when people talk of deserved penalties or punishment, they are to be taken as really not talking of jail sentences or fines and the like, punishment in that sense, but of suffering itself. And what they are saying is that there is intrinsic good in the suffering of the guilty. This *intrinsic-good retributivism*, though circular retributivism brings it to mind, needs more attention than that predecessor. What is to be said of it?

Well, it is pretty plainly false that desert locutions in connection with punishment never or rarely have to do with the penalty, as distinct from the resulting distress. More often than not they do. Nevertheless, let us grant that people sometimes have in mind what is suggested, having to do with only the suffering or distress. In this case, as certainly must be granted, they do escape circularity. To support the rightness of a punishment, they say something about desert, and mean nothing about the act of punishment itself, but only that there is intrinsic good in what is different, its effect, the suffering of the guilty.

Our philosopher of retribution informs us that there is no good argument against the judgement that the suffering of the guilty is intrinsically good, good in itself, and that there is a widespread inclination to believe it 'among the people whose moral intuitions constitute the main data we have for settling questions of value'. Hence it is 'very likely' that the judgement is 'true'.[10] Still, it is allowed that this reason for punishment might be outweighed by others, allowed that it is consistent with the judgement that we never ought to punish.

There is a prior question about the given reason for punishment, a question that is not raised or answered by its proponent but which certainly needs our attention. In fact it will arise, whether or not it is brought up, with every retributive theory of punishment and indeed every theory of punishment without exception. It is plain that what we are offered in the present case is an intrinsic good that consists in the suffering of someone who is guilty in the general sense of having committed a wrongful act, someone who can be held morally responsible for a certain act. There would be no intrinsic good in the subsequent suffering of someone who failed to call the police because, say, he was bound and gagged and hence not to be held morally responsible at all for what was going on.

In which case, what does the required freedom in the guilt of a guilty person come to? There can be two views about that. One results in the theory that there is intrinsic good in the suffering of someone whose wrongful action was free in the sense of being entirely his own, according to his own desires and nature, not an action he was compelled to do by someone else or something else. This is the sense in which someone bound and gagged is not free. Another view of freedom gives us the theory that there is intrinsic good in the suffering of someone whose wrongful action was free in that it was not caused or determined, but could have been otherwise even if everything in the past and at the time had been just as it was. Here the wrongful action is uncaused rather than uncompelled. What is absent is causation as against compulsion.

The first kind of freedom can be spoken of as *voluntariness*. The second kind can be spoken of as *origination*, or *free will* in a special and traditional sense of the term. As already remarked, we are not told which of the two resulting theories of punishment to consider. Are you inclined to suppose, as I am, that it is the free will theory that is intended or both together? We can keep both possibilities in mind and also the voluntariness theory. This can be our procedure with all of the theories of punishment we consider. When in due course we have considered the matters of determinism, freedom and ascriptions of responsibility more fully, we will indeed be able to look back on the various theories and draw some conclusions about them. One will be that retribution theories have generally been understood by their makers in terms of free will.

Intrinsic-good retributivism also raises several general issues in moral philosophy. If these are not to be finally settled here, it is nonetheless possible to come by way of them to a view of intrinsic-good retributivism. Before considering them, however, we need to remind ourselves of a few things.

First, it needs remembering that even if all mankind minus none were morally in favour of the suffering of the guilty, it would not follow that all or even any of them judged that suffering to be good in itself, good without reference to anything else whatever, including what may come most quickly to mind, some resulting change in the minds, hearts, social consciences, attitudes to the community or whatever of the guilty. All mankind might be in favour of the suffering, too, on account of some other effect of it, just the prevention of offences.

It needs noticing too that it is mere bluff to announce the existence of a strong argument based on the claim that most or many of some group of people, an authoritative group whose intuitions somehow settle questions of value for us, have intuitions that the suffering of the guilty is good in itself. Suppose such a group can be conceived in a tolerable way – of course in a way so not as to beg the question from the beginning. The group will surely or indeed undoubtedly include many who are morally opposed to or reluctant about justifying punishment by the suffering of the guilty taken by itself, which absolutely ineffectual suffering they properly characterize as pointless or useless or irrational. How, they traditionally ask, can two bads make a good, two wrongs a right? Those who reject intrinsic-good retributivism include even retributivists.[11]

To put aside this head-counting, and the hard questions of its relevance, we evidently can consider directly the question of whether the judgement that there is intrinsic good in the suffering of the guilty is 'true'. Or rather, to avoid the wholly unexplained assumption of, as it seems, an ordinary and simple objectivity had by moral judgements – their having truth values in the sense in which such ordinary factual claims as '2 + 2 = 4' and 'You are reading this book' have truth values – we can consider whether the judgement is acceptable or what weight it has or whether it has some other other truth (pp. 206–10).

It will be useful to compare the judgement that the suffering of the guilty is good in itself with two other judgements of intrinsic value, certainly different from one another. One judgement is the very general one that there is intrinsic badness in suffering. If I contemplate the possibility of an unknown person's suffering in itself, without introducing *any* further fact at all, anything whatever, I cannot but judge that it would be a bad thing, something I ought not to bring about. Consider someone who believes otherwise.

He believes that if he presses a button in front of him, this will cause another person to suffer. He has no further beliefs about the suffering. He has no beliefs as to the victim's previous actions, any deterrent effects of his suffering, any purifying or elevating effects on him of the suffering, any repentence, any relation of the victim's suffering to the lives of others, and so on. Nothing about any consequence. Nonetheless, he judges that he ought to press the button. He appears to understand what he maintains, is inclined to act on it, and shows the ordinary moral emotions in connection with his judgement. He isn't embarrassed. It comes to mind to say of him, if we suppose that he is not somehow dissembling, that he is *mad*, or at any rate that his nature is not human nature.[12] The general judgement that there is intrinsic badness in suffering, then, is of such a strength that its denial carries such a corollary.

Another judgement as to intrinsic value is that there is intrinsic good in arranging straight lines of Southern Californians. As with the judgement of intrinsic-good retributivism that there is intrinsic good in the suffering of the guilty, and the other general judgement of intrinsic value at which we have just glanced, this judgement has to do with no further facts. It is that arranging Southern Californians in straight lines is good in itself. To deny or doubt this bizarre judgement of intrinsic value, in a way chosen at random, is certainly not to be open to judgement in another sense oneself, or to be in danger of official action. It is any maker of this judgement of intrinsic good who would be at least puzzling and may be taken to be in need of restraint by society.

One point here is that while it may be open to anyone to judge anything whatever to have intrinsic value, it is only certain of these judgements that have weight. A second point is that if one actually succeeds in contemplating no more than precisely the suffering of the guilty, as distinct from anything else, a judgement of its intrinsic value is perhaps more of the weight of the judgement about lining up Southern Californians than the general one about the badness of suffering itself. Certainly the judgement about guilt is baffling, and it is not much like the general judgement. The latter judgement evidently may enter into resistance to the idea of the intrinsic goodness of the suffering of the guilty.[13]

Intrinsic-good retributivism in its assertion of its peculiar intrinsic good is strongly reminiscent of what seemed to have been put to rest, the doctrine of moral intuitionism, to the effect that there are moral properties of actions or experiences or whatever that are open to some kind of moral perception. It remains possible or anyway conceivable that it will be maintained that anyone who does not somehow see the intrinsic goodness of the suffering of the guilty is failing in moral perception, a victim of moral blindness. Presumably it will also be maintained that some of these other people, since they claim the existence of different intrinsic goods, maybe about forgiveness or mercy,[14] are in the grips of moral hallucination.

It will be necessary to maintain, incidentally, that those of us who are blind in the given way are not blind to one thing, but blind to a host of them. Intrinsic-good retributivism does not discover only one intrinsic good, but very many. It does not suppose, I trust, that there is intrinsic good in the rapist having just the suffering involved in a fine of £10, or of having his driver's licence endorsed. It does not suppose there is intrinsic good in the young bicycle thief having the distress of being tortured or imprisoned for life. This retributivism, presumably, discovers as many intrinsic goods, each involving a certain guilt and a certain suffering, as there are different guilts.

What is to be said briefly in reply to any supposition of the moral blindness of many of us is that there are great difficulties in *any* theory or account of moral perception or intuition, and hence of moral blindness, hallucination and so on.[15] It is important, of course that one feels no need of any such theory with respect to the judgement that suffering in itself is bad. Its foundation, whatever it is, does not bring in a curious faculty and its peculiar successes and failures.

Let us finish here, however, by retreating from what are discussable areas of moral philosophy generally. Let us come to firmer ground. The best that can be said of intrinsic-good retributivism, to my mind, is that it might as a result of further thought come to provide an *insubstantial and obscure* reason for punishment.[16] To come to a point to which we shall return several times, there surely is something solid in the retributivist or perhaps otherwise backward-looking tradition, something that can be made clear. It has in it an actual reason for action, one that moves ordinary men, men with an ordinary lack of what can be called moral sensitivity, anyway moral sensitivity as conceived by some of their betters and appointed thinkers. It must be an axiom of inquiry, surely, that anything so persistent and effectual as talk and feeling about desert, and anything with such a history as the retributive practice of punishment, has *some* sense in it at bottom, some clear sense.

We may not find a justification of punishment at the bottom of the retributivist tradition, but it cannot be that there is nothing substantial and clear there. The view we have been considering, about the intrinsic goodness of the suffering of the guilty, is therefore not the truth about retributivism. We can draw that conclusion, by the way, without exercising ourselves about the question of whether the guilty are to be taken as having acted freely in being voluntary or in originating an action or both, as having been uncompelled or uncaused or both.

DISTRESS–CULPABILITY, FORFEITED RIGHTS, INDIFFERENCE

What is meant or implied when it is said that a man deserves some particular penalty, as we have already assumed, is that there is some *relation* between it and something else. Can we not think of that in a simple way, simpler than in intrinsic-good retributivism?

People may once have meant that imposing the penalty would involve an action of the same kind as the man's action in his offence. This is one version, perhaps, of the *lex talionis*.[17] A murderer might in this sense be said to deserve execution. What a man who commits rape deserves, in this sense, or breach of promise, is a question which leaves room for reflection. A more important difficulty is that any retribution theory that is worth discussion will allow that certain justifications or excuses may be offered by an accused man. They are the very stuff of the law. They may include facts that his action was unintentional, that he was defending himself, or that he was grossly provoked. Such justifications and excuses having to do with responsibility would be entirely ruled out by the principle that a man is to be punished as he deserves, given the notion of desert in terms of same actions. All that would matter would be the kind of action he performed. This, *same-actions retributivism*, is easily discarded.

People may still mean something else in saying that a man deserves a certain penalty for an offence.

(4) The penalty would cause roughly as much distress to him as he caused to someone else by his offence.

This different contention about a relationship is in the neighbourhood of something, as you can instructively say, that deserves hardly more attention. As it stands, however, it could not be part of any tolerable retribution theory. The reason is the same as before. Two men who by their offences cause the same distress, one intentionally and one wholly accidentally, would be said in this sense to deserve the same penalty. No thinker has intended this *same-distress retributivism*.

To say that a man deserves a certain penalty may mean something else, very common indeed.

(5) There is a relationship of equivalence between the culpability of his behaviour and the distress of the proposed penalty.

The relationship of equivalence is or seems to be regarded as a relationship of fact, not so simple as but of the same category as the relationship between two men of the same height or women of the same age.

Whether it can sensibly be regarded in this factual or ordinarily true or false way depends on the terms of the relationship, which are the culpability and the distress. What is the first of these? The culpability of an offender in his offence, we may briefly say, depends on two things: the harm caused by his action and the extent to which he can be regarded as having been free and responsible in his action. Greater culpability attaches to violent assault than to pilfering, given agents who can be held equally responsible. Greater culpability attaches to intentional wounding as against accidental wounding.

Given some such understanding of culpability, it is pretty immediately clear that no penalty can be regarded as either *equivalent* or *not equivalent*, in any factual sense, to a man's culpability in his offence. This is so for a simple reason. The distress of a penalty and the culpability of an offender are not commensurable. If there are units for counting culpability and units for counting distress, both of which ideas at least face great difficulties, these certainly are not the same units. There simply are no common units of measurement. *Distress–culpability retributivism* so regarded is nonsense, anyway just loose talk.

Do you say that to object in this way to a common proposition about crime and punishment, a proposition uttered or implied more or less daily by judges, is to be too literal-minded? Do you say that it is not really a claim of fact that is intended by the judges? Well, you need to think about that. You need to remember that the judges are certainly offering a *reason* for a moral, attitudinal or somehow evaluative judgement. Reasons typically *are* claims of fact. Moral judgements get their force by being anchored in facts, don't they? Do judges think their propositions of equivalence state some facts or others?

You also need to keep in mind that if the reason of equivalence is demoted from a factual judgement into being a moral judgement itself, then we are at least in danger of pointlessness, of circularity. We are indeed in danger of asserting no more than that punishment is right because it is right. What needs to be added to those two thoughts, however, is that judges and others in talking of equivalence or the like may have in mind some other proposition to which we are coming. They may mean something else. We cannot pronounce a verdict on them just yet.

Another doctrine is not so common as distress–culpability retributivism, but is one of several that has in it claims of a kind increasingly common in contemporary moral and political philosophy and discourse.[18] These are claims as to *rights*. All of us, it is said, have rights – rights not to be injured, to keep possession of our property, and so on. A condition of our having such rights, we are told in this doctrine, is that we respect the rights of others. In general, rights of mine entail duties of mine to respect the rights of others. When an offender violates rights of someone else, he forfeits some of his own.

As a consequence, if his punishment were also to have a certain recommendation having to do with the prevention of offences, his punishment would be justified.[19] What this *forfeited-rights retributivism* comes to, it seems, is that to say that an offender deserves a penalty is to say something of the following sort.

(6) He has forfeited certain rights he would have if he had not freely offended.

As I say, we can consider this independently of the possibility of its being brought into conjunction with anything about prevention.

The argument does not suppose that an offender loses all of his rights. It is first said he keeps all the rights which he has respected in others – he loses just those of his rights which are the counterparts of the rights of another which he has violated. However, it has to be allowed to be impracticable to deprive him of exactly those rights – certainly it would be so, say, in the case of the right not to be defrauded – and so it is said the offender loses a set of rights equivalent to those he has violated. Or, again, there is not a prohibition on inflicting a harm on him equivalent to that involved in his violation of the rights of another. Here we have the problem we know about, of giving sense to talk of equivalence. It is certainly a recommendation of this doctrine that it provides a solution. That is not to say that it discovers commensurability, a method of common quantifying of culpability and distress. However, it can be said to achieve much the same end as would be achieved by commensurability.

The solution draws on the idea of what are called preference scales, essentially on the theoretically discoverable preferences of standard, average or normal persons, and above all on the theoretical discoverability of such persons being *indifferent* between certain options. We have on the one hand the loss or harm – say $L1$ – caused to the victim of an offence by violation of certain of his rights. On the other hand we have various losses or harms that may be caused to the offender by deprivation of certain of his rights, through punishment. One of these losses or harms in punishment – say $L2$ – is such that an average person would be indifferent between $L1$ and $L2$, preferring neither one to the other. We thus have a clear idea of equivalent rights, or equivalent harms or losses – which, indeed, could be detached from talk of rights and offered for use somehow on its own. We have a clear idea of what it is for a penalty to be deserved for or equivalent to an offence.

(7) Suffering the offence and suffering the penalty are such that people would be indifferent between the first and the second.

Certainly there are difficulties of several kinds about this *indifference retributivism*, some of them about the implicit specification of a standard person. As is said, however, they are difficulties common to all uses of preference scales. Let us take them as superable difficulties.

That is not to say that what we have in the combination of forfeited-rights retributivism and indifference retributivism is persuasive. What it comes to in its first part is that there is a reason for punishment, which itself is a denial of rights, in the proposition that an offender has violated certain rights of another. There are two objections, the first having to do with what is meant by saying that the offender has violated certain rights of another. For several reasons, one being the conclusion that is drawn, it is clear that moral rights are in question. Nothing else will do. We do not want the uncertainty or worse of legal retributivism. To repeat, then, what is meant by saying that the offender has violated certain moral rights of another person? What *are* moral rights? The question arises with more than the doctrine under discussion. It should be a matter of notoriety that so little attention is given to the question in a good deal of contemporary philosophy given over to talk and indeed declaration of rights.

To approach the matter by way of something else, consider the simple claim that the punishment of an offender is justified because of his culpability in his offence – he did what he ought not to have, failed in an obligation, did wrong. This sort of argument has not satisfied many reflective persons.[20] In general, retributivists find other things to say – as we shall continue to discover. Still, as we have seen, this sort of thing has found philosophical defenders. It can become what we know about, the idea of intrinsic-good retributivism, that there is intrinsic good in the suffering of the guilty. We could go back to that thinking now, or go on with the simple claim that punishment is right because of a man's culpability or wrong, and – this is the essential bit – we could do a certain thing. We could express any such doctrine in terms of moral rights. We could say what we have just been hearing, that an offender violates someone's moral rights.

But what, exactly, is the difference between the ordinary claim that a man has done what he ought not to have done to somebody else, failed in an obligation to somebody else, and the claim sounding more serious that he has violated moral rights of that person? The doctrine we are considering, like others, offers no explanation. Certainly there is *some* difference between the two claims. It is not hard to indicate what it is. The rights claim, as against the ordinary ought claim, makes reference to a supposedly established moral principle or to the existence of supposed support of another kind for the claim. The rights claim thus has a self-referring character – it relates itself to something else. That is the short story. Given some such analysis, there remains the question of how the rights claim can serve as a more effective reason for punishment than the ought claim. That it is wholly unlikely to do so seems clear for plain reasons.

Someone who says in the ordinary way that something ought not to have happened or was wrong does of course have a reason for his judgement. It is a general proposition, however explicit in his or her mind, that in such circumstances as this one, all circumstances relevantly like this one, something ought not to happen or is wrong. That is the fact of his having a certain principle. Someone who says that a man ought not to have done what he did to somebody else, that he failed in an obligation to him, has a kind of reason for what he says. That reason for his judgement is a generalization about such possible circumstances. It may be about all circumstances like this one, or more circumstances more widely described. He partly depends, in fact, on such a principle. Much can be said of the fact, one thing being that he would not have confidence in the particular case, or rather could not possibly have, without the principle. It makes for consistency, which is necessary to confidence.

The quick summary of these reflections, as you will anticipate, is that nothing significant is added to an ordinary line of argument by stating it in terms of moral rights. An ordinary ought claim needs to be defended by way of a reason that is a general principle. So too does a rights claim. The second is no nearer a good defence by bravely implying or referring to such a principle. What it is, really, is just a little pompous. A rights claim is just an ordinary moral claim given emphasis by an implicit reference to what it involves and in a way depends on.

If much more might have been said of the matter, no more is essential. The proposition that someone has done wrong, a proposition seemingly insufficient for certain purposes, does not become sufficient when it is put in terms of rights. The proposition that it is no longer the case that someone ought to be or must be treated in certain ways, no longer the case that we are obliged to do this, does not become more weighty by an ounce when it is put as the proposition that now we are not obliged to respect moral rights of his, that he has forfeited certain rights.

Now think a little bit about the other idea in the doctrine we are looking at. We have it that there is what can be called an equivalence of fact between offence and punishment. Here too we have a question that needs answering. There is the fact, we are supposing, that a standard or average preference scale would show indifference between being a victim of a certain offence and being an offender subjected to a certain punishment. But there is a question about the fact. Why is that fact in itself any reason for subjecting such an offender to such a punishment?

It needs to be granted, in line with what has been said or implied already of there being *something* in the tradition of retributivism, that there is force in citing *some* sort of equivalence in defence of punishment. But how is the particular equivalence that we now have before us a reason? The problem is that we can find innumerable equivalences of the given sort, between experiences of diverse kinds. There may be indifference, say, between someone's not getting a job and someone's not getting married. Such a fact supports no such claims as that my action in failing to give a man a job is a reason for someone's action of getting in the way of my proposed marriage. Some critics of retributivism have objected, as we have, to the want of clear sense in other talk of equivalence. They have failed to note what they might have, and need to have, that equivalences may be produced but not in themselves be reasons for action. That seems to be exactly the case with indifference retributivism.

INNOCENCE SYSTEM

We have not yet paid explicit attention to the idea that a deserved penalty has a lot to do, maybe everything, with a *system* of penalties. A deserved penalty is one to be found in a scale or scales of penalties matched to offences. This idea informs a great deal of jurisprudence – the theory or philosophy of law. Let us consider one working out of the idea by an eminent jurisprudent. It behoves us to be lawyer-like, to be diligent and attentive to detail, in considering this *system retributivism* or, as you could as well say, *jurisprudential retributivism*.

Our sample jurisprudent, Professor Gross, partly sets out to explain, as he says in the first sentence of a paper, why a punishment's being deserved is important to its being right.[21] We are to learn, as he also puts it, why the punishment's fitting the crime is something we ought to bother about. He does not set out, evidently, to explain why a punishment's being right is important to its being right. What we are to learn, evidently, is not why the punishment we ought to bother about is something we ought to bother about. He speaks too of proportion, which is said to be the key to talk of desert.[22] Certainly we need a key. What we are to learn is why proportion, whatever it may be, between crime and punishment, stands in some sort of justificatory relation to the punishment's being right. We are not to have instruction in the truism that the right relation between crime and punishment is in some justificatory relation to the punishment's being right.

So, as you well know already, it will be essential in what follows not to use the terms 'deserved punishment', 'fitting punishment', 'proportionate punishment' or any like terms in a quite natural way, to mean 'right punishment' or 'justified punishment'. If we do that we shall have no possibility of other than trivial argument from a premise about desert to a conclusion about justification. We shall indeed have fallen back into circular retributivism.

Something of less importance to be remembered is that it is false or at the least very misleading to say that all theorists of punishment almost certainly agree that punishment must be deserved.[23] What all of them almost certainly agree on is that an offence must have been committed and that the penalty must somehow take into account the nature of the offence. That is distinct from what is typically intended by the claim that punishment must be deserved.

The idea of desert, fittingness, or proportion, whatever it is, is attached to the idea of the seriousness of a crime. Our guide rightly sees difficulties here, having to do with what he calls scale, interval and pitch. They are difficulties which we are later told can be overcome. Our attention is now directed to what is said to determine the seriousness of crime, which is the culpability of the conduct in which the crime consists.[24] Culpability has as necessary conditions the conduct's being what is called controlled, which has to do with the offender's having had a responsibility for it, and its being harmful, dangerous, and not done by right.

It will be Professor Gross's contention that punishment has its essential justification in some proposition to the effect that it is according to the culpability of the relevant conduct, or, as we can as well say, a proposition to the effect that it is deserved, fitting, or proportionate. He approaches this contention by considering and rejecting three that are related to it, three other 'views of desert'. More plainly, we consider understandings of the claim that a man deserves a particular punishment for a particular offence, and whether these understandings give us a satisfactory ground for taking the punishment to be in some way justified.

First, we do not get an arguable ground in the proposition, which might be made true, or anyway *be* true, that his punishment causes him the same harm or as much harm or suffering as he caused to his victim. Certainly that is to be agreed. Second, we can understand the desert claim that a man deserves a particular punishment for a particular offence as expressing some proposition about the offender's state of mind in his offence, or about his character. Here too, in Professor Gross's view, we fail to get a ground for the rightness of punishment. Let us pass by this thought, to whose neighbourhood we will be returning.[25]

The third doctrine is said to abandon what has not yet been explained, the idea of a particular punishment's being *proportionate* to culpability of conduct. What we have is the idea that a man's offence might fall into some broad category of offences, and his penalty be the uniform one for all offences of that category. Professor Gross has interesting things to say about this. They have to do with punishment as preventive of offences, and indeed with a justification of punishment in terms of prevention. Let us leave aside the matter of how prevention figures in his own theory, if it does, and notice something else. He does not raise a certain fundamental question about this third retributive doctrine.

We are in fact giving our attention to a certain attempted justification of punishment. Despite the fact that it is said to abandon proportionality, it is a somewhat curious version of the claim that punishment is right because it is deserved for culpability of conduct. We come a bit closer to it by expressing it as the view that punishment is right when it is very roughly deserved, or within a certain desert category. That is, punishment is right when there is some or other relationship between it and the culpability of the offence. What relation is that? We no more have an answer to this than we have – so far – an answer to the question of what it is for a punishment to be strictly proportionate to culpability.

In effect we now come to the preferred understanding of desert claims, or the promise of one, including the general desert claim that *some conduct deserves punishment*, which general claim gives us some kind of justification for punishment.[26] We can as well express the general claim, which is to say not usefully, as the claim that some conduct can have proportionate punishment, or fitting punishment, or punishment such that there is parity between it and the offence. In the absence of analysis or at any rate clarification, all these locutions, if I may speak plainly, are useless. We need a proper understanding of the claim, however expressed. We need an understanding, further, as you have now heard a few times, that does not trivialize the claim by taking a proportionate punishment, say, to be a justified punishment.

It seems, first, that we are to grasp the preferred understanding of desert claims by reflecting on a way in which a punishment may be *undeserved*. It may be of a guilty man but in some sense excessive. Now of course if we do have explained to us in an adequate way what an excessive punishment is, in the relevant sense, we shall be able to divine the nature of a deserved punishment. What is an excessive punishment in the relevant sense? What is conveyed to us is that it is a punishment that does not reflect the offender's partial innocence. It does not reflect the fact that save for his offence, of which he may be wholly guilty, he is to be taken as innocent as the rest of us – no fallen angel, where a fallen angel is a creature who is guilty through and through, to the wing-tips.

What then is a deserved punishment? It seems the answer to the question of what it is for a penalty to be deserved can be brief.

(8) The penalty adequately reflects a degree of innocence.

But what is it for a punishment adequately to reflect a degree of innocence?

It is important, at this point, not to succumb to a certain confusion. All who have thought about punishment – the utilitarian Jeremy Bentham, the retributivist Immanuel Kant and all the rest – would no doubt say, of the punishments they take to be justified, that those punishments reflect degrees of innocence in the above sense. That is not to say that all have a single unexceptionable thought about retribution. Bentham would explain, sensibly enough, that his justified punishments are measures of prevention, whose need is judged partly on the basis of the intentions and character of the offender. We will be looking at all this in another chapter. Kant, and it seems Professor Gross, are of another mind when they give as a justification of a punishment that it reflects a degree of innocence. But they must tell us what they have in mind.

It seems, second, that we are to grasp the preferred understanding of desert claims by reflecting precisely on the man who is too leniently punished.[27] His punishment is less than deserved. What does that mean? What is said is that he gets away with something, that he enjoys benefits of the innocent, that he offends with impunity. Evidently what is being claimed is that there is a *want* of some relationship between his offence and his punishment. But what relationship is that? No amount of synonyms of the given kind for 'less than deserved' is going to add up to an analysis of the essential notion. What we have here, again, is mystery.

Consider the sentence – one of several – that might be taken to give the conclusion of this jurisprudential retributivism.

A person deserves to be punished according to the culpability of his criminal conduct because that measures exactly the extent to which his innocence has been lost.[28]

The first of three things to be said of this is that we must suppose that what is intended in saying a person deserves to be punished in a certain way is that it is right that he be punished in a certain way. I have no objection to this usage here – here it is not essential to use 'deserves' otherwise. The second thing to be said is that the fact of a certain loss of innocence is one and the same fact as a certain culpability in conduct. It is not as if some new justificatory fact has been discovered, over and above culpability, or underlying culpability. The sentence makes it sound as if some new thing had been espied, but none has. I doubt that our guide would claim otherwise.

The third and main matter is that of exactly what general ground is advanced for the rightness of a person's having a certain penalty. As is plain, it cannot be just that his conduct has been culpable, in some degree or other, no matter what. Precisely a certain penalty is claimed to be justified, by a given degree of culpability. The ground for the rightness of the punishment is that the particular penalty is in relation with just a certain culpability. But what relation? Our only source of light is the locution 'according to', but that is as dim as its many counterparts. It is as dim as the locution 'to the extent' which turns up in the two sentences immediately following.[29] Indeed, with respect to the principal question, none of these locutions gives any light at all.

Professor Gross, we may assume, does not go in for the proposals about desert we have already discarded – say distress–culpability retributivism. It is satisfactory that he avoids these proposals, but not satisfactory that he puts no sense in their place. This is my main complaint. To state it again, the burden of his paper is that some relationship between a crime and a punishment is of importance to the justification of that punishment. We need to be told what it is. We cannot be satisfied with a mystery. There is nothing worth the name of justification offered until we have an answer. We have no theory of punishment to argue about.

Is any light shed on the mysterious relationship in the remainder of what he has to say? This is, in part, that we can overcome difficulties in judging the seriousness of crimes. We can rank them, which is to say put them into an ordinal sequence. We can, further, not merely say that rape is more serious than shoplifting, but say by how much – we can get cardinality. We do this by looking at crimes in terms of culpability, which is to say harm, control, dangerousness, and rights. In addition to this, it is said, we can fix what punishment is to go with what crime. We can, in the preferred terminology, settle the pitch of the sequence of punishments. How do we do that?

Well, in line with what was said earlier, we fit a punishment to each crime such that partial innocence is not disregarded, and such that no one ever gets away with anything or enjoys undeserved impunity. It takes argument, care, trouble, and fine tuning, but it can be done. Professor Gross's principal sentence here is as follows.

> . . . once we determine the minimum that is necessary to avoid impunity, we have established the correspondence we seek with culpability.[30]

So, to take an example, we locate armed rape, somehow defined, in a scale of crimes. This we do by means of considerations of harm, control, dangerousness, and rights. By the same means we judge that armed rape is not only more serious than shoplifting but we judge that it is, say, nine times as serious, or we make a non-quantitative judgement somehow analogous. Whatever the truth about the possibility of this, I leave the matter undisputed. To come to the crucial point, we now determine or decide that a certain punishment, say five years, goes with armed rape. This determining or deciding – the ambiguous verbs are our guide's – is either the discovery of a truth or fact of some sort, that there exists some relationship between armed rape and five years, or somehow a matter of decision in another and somewhat more natural sense. Whichever it is, the relationship in question is a reason or ground for a certain conclusion – that it is right that armed rapists get five years.

Is the relationship a matter of *discovery* or *decision*? Return to the sentence which pertains to it: '. . . once we determine the minimum that is necessary to avoid impunity, we have established the correspondence we seek with culpability'. That is not pellucidly clear, but it might be taken to suggest what I have called decision rather than discovery.

If so, what is the decision? There is only one possibility. It is the decision that the *right* punishment for armed rape is five years. It is the justified punishment. It will also be dignified by philosophers as the *just* or *fair* punishment.[31] But this is a disaster of the kind of which we know, a disaster typical in retribution theories and anticipated above. The aim of the enterprise was to get an independent reason for the proposition that five years is the right or justified punishment for armed rape. The supposed independent reason we have come to is the beauty that five years is the right or justified punishment for armed rape. Here we do have the argument that in plain terms is precisely the circularity that a certain punishment's being deserved, which is to say right, proves that it is right.

There remains the other possibility. It is the possibility most favoured, as it seems, in the tradition of retributive thought about punishment. That is, some fact of relationship is presumed to exist between culpability and punishment. The one noticed above was same harm, or as much harm or suffering. Professor Gross provides no candidate whatever. He provides none at all, to repeat, by talk of a punishment's being exactly the one such that partial innocence is not disregarded, and such that the offender does not get away with anything. *Innocence-system retributivism*, to give it that name, leaves us in the dark.

That is not to say there is no more to say about punishment and a penalty system. We will be coming back to the subject again.

ANNULMENT, OFFENDERS' RIGHTS

Let us not give up. There are more retributive theories. We are obliged to punish, as a philosopher with a place in history says, since to do so 'is to annul the crime, which otherwise would have been held valid, and to restore the right'.[32] A punishment is an annulment, a cancellation or a return to a previous state of affairs. This alone is what justifies us in imposing it.

> If crime and its annulment . . . are treated as if they were unqualified evils, it must, of course, seem quite unreasonable to will an evil merely because 'another evil is there already'. To give punishment this superficial character of an evil is, amongst the various theories of punishment, the fundamental presupposition of those who regard it as a deterrent, a preventive, a threat, as reformative, etc. What on these theories is supposed to result from punishment is characterised equally superficially as a good. But it is not merely a question of an evil, or of this, that or the other good; the precise point at issue is wrong and the righting of it. If you adopt that superficial attitude to punishment, you brush aside the objective treatment of the righting of wrong, which is the primary and fundamental attitude in considering crime. . . .[33]

All this, of course, is obscure. It is by Hegel. It is also an expression of a common attitude of people not deep in speculative metaphysics. One's first reaction is that marriages, considered as contracts, can be annulled, but crimes cannot be, in any ordinary sense. My death or imprisonment, after I have killed a man, does not make things what they were before. In what way can my death or imprisonment be seen as an annulment? Hegel's argument begins from a conception of moral principles, such as the principle against taking another's life except, as we say, in certain circumstances. An act of murder is not merely a contravention of this principle but also a denial of its rightness. Such a denial is said to 'infringe' the principle. We must 'restore' it and this can be done only by punishing the offender. We are not to regard the crime as a harm done to someone, a mere 'evil', but rather as a denial of what is right. Nor do we 'restore' the principle because it is important for its effects in guiding conduct. We do what we do because the principle is right.

How are we to take Hegel's suggestion that offenders not only break moral principles but also freely and responsibly deny their rightness? They speak, perhaps, a language of action. But how are the principles thereby 'infringed'? Are we to understand that they become more open to question by them and other individuals? The argument would then be that because a principle is now differently regarded we are justified in doing some punishing. This would not be the argument that the new attitude to the principle may issue in certain effects, notably the commission of offences. It would not be tantamount to a version of the arguments from prevention or rehabilitation. It would be the argument that we are to punish *simply* because of a change of attitude. This is nonsense.

However, it is pretty clear that the supposed infringement of a principle has to do with more than individual attitudes. Hegel's intention, as distinct from those of some of his followers, is to be understood only by way of reflection on his view of moral principles. They are embodiments of *Spirit*, also know as the *Absolute*. So we are deep in metaphysics, or rather high in it – speculative metaphysics, free thinking and feeling about the nature of all reality, usually taken to be a spiritual or mental nature. It is at best elusive. Not a great deal of advantage can be had turning away from Hegel and consulting the related views of English metaphysicians who followed him. Bosanquet, for example, speaks of crime as having a bad effect on 'the general mind', which is not to be confused with even the collection of individual minds, mere 'atomic states of consciousness'.[34]

Anyway, we have another claim.

> (9) Punishment annuls an offence in that it restores a moral principle which itself has a kind of independent 'spiritual' reality.

No possible effects on human conduct or indeed human experience are part of this restoration. We might in reply question the truth, or more likely the meaning, of the metaphysical doctrines in question. The conclusion might be that punishment does not have the restorative consequences attributed to it, for there is no sense in talk of consequences of that kind.[35]

Another thing we can do is something more or less avoided until now, which is having recourse to some morality or other – or rather, to what is common to different moralities. To be quick about it, this is the proposition that what is right, like what is wrong, has to do with great goods desired by all of us, this being our human nature. They include enough to eat, freedom, relief from pain, and so on. What is right and wrong has to do with the satisfying or the frustrating of such fundamental desires or needs. Suppose we took the time to lay out such a morality. We could then come back to the matter of the restoration of a metaphysical moral principle and the question of whether that by itself could be something sufficient to justify the practice of punishment, that denial of great goods? It is difficult to bend one's mind to the question, but more will be said relevant to it later.

As you will have gathered, retribution theories are various, and, despite their basic nature, are like and unlike one another in different ways. To bring a first one together with a second, on account of a similarity, is to detach it from a third to which it is similar in another way. It is annoying, but there it is. So much by way of explanation of turning next to something else on *rights* – which is also some more thinking by Hegel.

He offers at least two lines of thought concerning not the right of victims of offences but the rights of offenders – rights to be punished. One line proceeds from the assumption that men are in some part of themselves rational. They recognize the supposed obligation to punish offenders, presumably the supposed obligation based on the need to restore a principle. They recognize this obligation even if they are offenders. So we are obliged to punish them for a particular reason.

> (10) Offenders themselves have a right to get the punishment that in their rationality they recognize they have an obligation to get.

This part of Hegel's doctrine, incidentally, like the earlier part about annulment, continued to find supporters into the twentieth century and very likely still does. 'If we respect personality', we are told, 'we must respect responsibility. If we respect responsibility, we must respect the right of offenders to be punished for their offences.'[36]

One's response to this *offenders' rights retributivism*, of course, is that a right that cannot be escaped is an odd right. Talk of someone's right to something usually presupposes that he or she has a choice about having the thing. Essays in the psychoanalysis of argument are not likely to more effective than other psychoanalysis, but it is hard to resist the feeling that someone's claiming of rights to punishment on behalf of others is as much in need of diagnosis as reply. Is it a matter of that person's own feelings of uncomfortableness about punishing people? But let us admit, for purposes of economy of thought, that offenders have such a right *if* there exists the supposed obligation. We have no argument for this. Until the obligation or permission is established, the argument about an offender's right to punishment comes to nothing. It can of course be stated quite as adequately, and less distractingly, without talk of rights at all. It is then the claim, in short, that offenders ought to be punished because they think they ought to be punished.

A second line of reflection about rights, sometimes confused with the first one, is mentioned by Hegel in the following passage.

> The injury [the penalty] which falls on the criminal is not merely implicitly just – as just, it is *eo ipso* his implicit will, . . . his right; on the contrary it is also a right established within the criminal himself, i.e. in his objectively embodied will, in his action. The reason for this is that his action is the action of a rational being and this implies that it is something universal and that by doing it the criminal has laid down a law which he had explicitly recognised in his action and under which in consequence he should be brought as under his right.[37]

The previous line of reflection was that the offender in his rational self accepts that his punishment is obligatory and demands the right to fulfil this obligation. The present line of reflection is that the offender in his offence explicitly establishes a certain principle: that it is right to injure others. In consistency, again since he is rational, he accepts that this principle should be observed even when it leads to himself being injured – by punishment.

In thinking about this *consistency retributivism*, we need not exercise ourselves over whether an offender can be supposed to assert such a principle. Nor need we wonder about what sense can be attached to the resultant demand that he be treated according to the principle. Let us suppose he makes the demand, or can be said to have a right. The question then arises of whether or not we ought to meet the demand or act on the right. We do not act on all rights. We do not act on all claims that something ought to be the case. We do not respect all principles supporting ought judgements. We need not do so when to do so would be injurious to the holder of the right. That we ought to has not been shown.

It is worth noting, finally, that one Hegelian scholar has presented yet another interpretation of the arguments said to be about rights, an interpretation which might indeed be extended to cover the previous argument about annulment.[38] It is that an offender may be reformed by punishment, and that he claims this reformation as his right. It is not that punishment, perhaps imprisonment, provides authorities with an opportunity to reform a man by one means or another. It is that punishment itself, the experience of suffering or deprivation, has a reforming effect. This interpretation of Hegel has often been accepted. Certainly it requires a curious reading of the first passage quoted above as well as others. It produces a supposed justification of punishment to be considered in due course. It is not of a backward-looking kind.

RATIONAL CONTRACT

Not all attempts to justify punishment in terms of past facts are retribution theories – theories of which it is natural to say that they justify punishment by the claim that it is deserved. Rather, there are backward-looking theories that attend to the fact that an offender has somehow freely consented to his punishment. It is possible but not natural to say of these theories that they justify punishment by desert or retribution. One is related to but different from the idea (9) of rationality issuing in an offender's right to punishment in terms of a contract.[39] The theory begins rather as do the others. The utilitarians, we may be told, are committed to using men as means to a social good, not treating them in accord with their dignity as persons, not recognizing that as persons they have rights. More particularly, the utilitarians do not show what is necessary, that punishment treats a man as an end and in accord with his dignity and rights, where that is *respecting his own will or decision, having his own consent.* This is just as necessary with perfectly ordinary punishment as it would be with awful acts of victimization taken to have some preventive value. While the prevention of offences must evidently be a part of the justification of punishment, there is also something else that is absolutely essential.

One typical way in which others coerce us without infringing our rights, we are told, is by our own ordinary consent. If I make a serious request, on the evening before an important day of ours, that my wife should not let us drink more than a bottle of wine, then she does not violate a right of mine later when I want another bottle, but only thwarts a desire. To come to the rights of offenders, it may be that they are not violated by punishment. This is so, we are told, despite the fact that they have not in the same ordinary way consented to be punished.

In considering this view, as becomes apparent even in its original presentation, there is again no need whatever to have things obscured by the rhetoric of *rights*. The essential claim is quite independent of it. It is that that justification of a punishment requires that the offender in some way consents to it, and offenders do in fact do this.

To continue, we can get some help in understanding how they do it from Kant, who writes that when a debtor is forced to pay up, 'this is entirely in accord with everyone's freedom, including the freedom of the debtor, in accordance with universal laws'.[40] What does this mean? Well, that in a certain conceivable but not actual situation the debtor 'would have been rational to adopt a Rule of Law'.[41] Kant is not much less explicit than his successors, notably John Rawls, in asserting that this is not the idea of any *actual* social contract, past or present, explicit or implicit. He writes that 'the contract is a mere idea of reason which has undoubted practical reality; namely to oblige every legislator to give us laws in such a manner that the laws could have originated from the united will of the entire people . . . '.[42] To assert in the given way that an offender consents to his punishment is to assert that if he had been in a certain conceivable situation in which a social agreement was being made, and if he had been in a sense rational, he would have agreed to social arrangements which have the consequence that as an actual offender he is to be punished.

It is worthwhile distinguishing this claim about consent by *an offender* from something else, with which it is likely to be confused. That is the argument that a certain actual social arrangement, an actual society in accordance with some conception of justice, is right or justified because it would have been agreed upon *by certain imaginable contractors*, or by contractors in an imaginable situation. The situation, because it would exclude certain influences on the contractors' choices, would confer a recommendation on what was chosen.

It is *not* part of this argument that the actual members of the actual society, influenced as they are, have ever made such an agreement, or indeed that they have in any diminished sense consented to anything. The actual members are not in any way identified with the contractors. Their obligation to support their society has to do with its goodness, which goodness is established by the proposition about imaginable contractors. Here too we have an argument for the rightness of punishment in a society, but not one that has to do with consent of actual members. Having had my say elsewhere[43] about what seems to me the particular futility of this form of hypothetical contract theory as a method of establishing substantive conclusions, I shall say nothing here.

The different claim we are considering is weaker – as it seems to me, yet weaker. It is, to repeat, that an offender's punishment is justified, at least in part, by *his* consenting to it, in a special sense, which in short is to say the following thing.

(11) If he had earlier considered the matter of punishment, and if he had been rational, he would have agreed to the social arrangements under which he is now being punished.

What is it to say that he would have made a contract *if he had been rational*? The short answer is this: he would have agreed if he had had the approving view of some given social arrangements had by a philosopher engaged in defending the institution of punishment.

Once this *rational contract theory* is made clear, it is not easy to think of a weaker moral reason for imprisoning a man. The reason given is that he would, if he had had certain views, views which no doubt he does not now have, and may never have had, and may always have disagreed with or hated – if he had had such views, he would have consented to something. It is exactly as true that if he had had *other* views he would not have consented to the thing, and hence could *not* be said to consent to his punishment in the special sense. His punishment is being credited *to him* by way of an arbitrarily chosen counterfactual statement about him.

The difference between what is given as a reason for an offender's punishment and an ordinary and actual consent as a reason for someone's doing something is immense. It is important not to drift into considering the supposition that the offender *did* have views of the requisite kind. If this were the supposition in question, rational contract theory could not hope to offer a satisfactorily *general* justification of punishment. It would leave quite unjustified the punishment of offenders without the requisite views.

Let me end here with the same remark as before. The backward-looking practice and tradition with respect to punishment has not persisted because it has been this ineffectual line of thought. This is not the truth of backward-looking punishment and thought about it.

CONSENT TO LOSS OF IMMUNITY

There is also a more clear-headed and less speculative theory about offenders consenting to their punishment – in my opinion a theory needing more attention than others.[44] It also begins from what is presented as a single objection to the utilitarian theory of punishment – that punishment is justified when it produces a greater total of satisfaction than not punishing or any other alternative. In fact it is best regarded as two objections. One is that if the utilitarian defence were the only justification of punishment, then all or a very great deal of punishment would be unjustified because it would involve an *unfair or inequitable or inegalitarian distribution of burdens* in a society. The rational aim of punishment is indeed the prevention or reduction of offences, or more precisely burdens of a certain kind, those borne by the victims of offences. The aim is pursued by imposing penalties, burdens of another kind, on offenders. But why can we use these persons, in particular, in pursuing our aim? The resulting distribution of burdens would on balance have to be judged unfair or the like to offenders if no more could be offered than the utilitarian defence of punishment.

The other objection is that if only the utilitarian defence could be given, then all of punishment would be unjustified, because it would involve treating all offenders merely as means and not also as ends. The Kantian maxim, I take it, is used in this objection in a commendably clear if not wholly explicit way. That is, not to treat men *as ends* is not to *recognize their own ends*.[45] Punishment considered merely as preventive does not consider the ends of offenders, presumably at least including their desires not to be punished. It treats them only as means to the end of the prevention of offences. It regards them only from the point of view of others' desires.

It transpires, if all goes well, that the view of punishment which meets the second objection also meets the first. If we satisfy the Kantian maxim, we also deal with the problem of distributive justice. What is required for a justification of punishment is an addition to a proposition about its preventing offences. What is required is *consensualism*, which is the truth behind the historical absurdity that offenders want to be punished. It has to do essentially with what is called *fairness owed to consent*. Punishment must be fair in that it is among other things a product of the will of the person who suffers it, something which respects his own freedom or autonomy in some sense. The matter is approached and clarified by way of five propositions about ordinary contracts in law.

(i) Consent here can be shown or given by any voluntary act done with the knowledge that the act has as a consequence a certain duty or responsibility. I consent to pay the taxi-driver merely by getting into his taxi and giving an address. I do not need to say that I agree to pay. (ii) Giving my consent, in so far as the law of contract is concerned, is not, then, dependent on my attitudes to what it is that I consent to do, or certain of my beliefs about it. I have consented even if I dislike the prospect of paying up, or am against it all things considered, or intend not to pay up, or believe that any obligation to do so can be avoided or will not be enforced. Nor is it true that I did not consent if, when the time comes to pay up, I do not want to do so, and so on. (iii) However, in all cases of contractual consent, there is the requirement that the relevant laws be in some sense just: 'the justification of particular distributions based on the free choice of the parties presupposes the fairness of the legal framework within which those choices are made'.[46] (iv) If I do give my consent, thereby entering into a contract, this gives others at least a prima facie moral justification for enforcing it. (v) Finally, if doing what I have consented to do will issue in an unfair or inequitable or inegalitarian distribution of burdens, it does not follow that I have not consented. It does not matter if the taxi-driver is a secret millionaire, etc. Nor does it follow, therefore, that there cannot be the mentioned moral justification for enforcing the contract, despite the resulting distribution. This is the fairness owed to consent.

To come round to punishment, *an offence itself* constitutes a certain consent on the part of the offender.

> (12) The offender consents to give up his immunity to punishment, which is to say to the gaining of a power by officers of the society.

To offend is to consent to be used as a means to the prevention of offences. Here we have five counterpart propositions.

(*i*) The consent is owed to the fact that an offence is a free act done with the knowledge that it has a certain *legal* consequence, the loss of the offender's immunity to punishment. (*ii*) The consent again is unaffected by certain attitudes and beliefs of the offender. It does not matter that he is against his punishment and intends not to be punished. Moreover, his consent does not depend on any explicit or implicit acceptance by him of the criminal law to which his punishment is attached. (*iii*) However, the law to which a punishment is attached, even if the offender need not accept it, must in fact *be* in some sense just – 'it should not be, for instance, discriminatory and should not proscribe actions that people have the moral right to do'.[47] Again, it must be that if keeping the law involves a burden, liability or obligation, these things are somehow justified. (*iv*) Given the fact of the offender's consent, the authorities have at least a prima facie moral justification for exercising their legal power to punish him. (*v*) Finally, none of the foregoing propositions is put into question by the offender's punishment issuing in an unfair or inequitable or inegalitarian distribution of burdens in the society. There is fairness owed to consent.

Consensualism, for the good reason that it could not, does not rest on the proposition that an offender consents to his *punishment*.

The general idea of consent in question is the idea that a person, whatever his mixed feelings and disinclinations, is to be taken to consent to all the necessary consequences of his action of which he knows. In this sense he could not be said to consent to his punishment, since his punishment, unlike the loss of his legal liability to punishment, is not necessarily a consequence of his offence. There is no necessity about it. The fact of the matter may well be that he will not be punished. Moreover, if the theory did require its kind of consent to punishment itself, it could provide *no* reason for punishment where an offender actually does believe that he will not be punished. What the offender is said to consent to, then, is no more than the loss of his legal immunity. More precisely, what he consents to can be expressed as a certain conditional proposition: if he is caught, and if the authorities make no mistakes, he will not be regarded as having a legal immunity to punishment.

That leaves us with something further that it is essential to keep clearly in mind, the fact about virtually all offenders that they do *not* consent to being punished. They do not consent to it in the sense of believing it to be a necessary consequence of their action, and moreover they do not consent to it in a more standard sense. They do not consent to it in a sense, difficult to specify fully, where they can be said to desire all or more of that which that they are said to consent to. On the contrary, they are wholly against their punishment, struggle to evade it, and so on. Rather than consent, they *refuse* or *dissent*.

But then the situation, to keep all of it in mind, includes the offender's consenting in the consensual theory's sense to a certain legal consequence, his losing his immunity to punishment, and his dissenting in every sense to his punishment. There is not much to be gained by asking if the first consent is 'really consent'. Let us rather ask what conclusions follow, given that the situation is as described.

First, to remember the two objections to utilitarianism from which we began, does it follow from what we have, whatever else may be said for punishing the offender, that the resulting distribution of burdens in the society cannot be resisted as unfair, inequitable, or inegalitarian? Secondly, does it follow from what we have that his own end is being recognized if he is punished? Is his moral autonomy respected? Does it follow in turn, thirdly, that the authorities have prima facie moral justification for punishing him?

It seems to me impossible to accept the first two inferences, on which the third rests. It is not at all persuasive to say that the resulting distribution of burdens cannot be open to objections of the given kind since, to speak differently, we have on hand fairness owed to consent. What we have is the offender consenting in a secondary sense to a necessary condition of his punishment, and not consenting, in any sense, to his punishment. As for the second inference, how *can* it be said with any force that the offender's own end is being recognized? What we do, and what raises the entire problem, which is to say our punishing of him, is what he does not consent to, despite the fact that he has in a sense consented to a necessary condition of it. It is, with respect to what is important, quite false to say that the agent has 'consciously acquiesced'.[48]

As it seems to me, one can be much moved by this doctrine only by having something other than it before the mind's eye. If one is in fact supposing that all offenders consent to their punishments, or their situations, in some fuller way than specified, it is possible to think one has a strong reason for punishment. But such a proposition is not being maintained, and is in fact false.

It may be objected, against this, that consent in the specified sense is sufficient for an ordinary contract in law, and that there it gives rise to a moral justification for enforcing the contract. If such consent will work there, why will it not work with punishment? Much might be replied here, about the nature of the law in general and its safeguards, and in particular its safeguards with respect to persons who will lie about their past acceptances. Let me make only a remark on something else.

Suppose I get into a taxi and give an address. I also tell the driver that I intend *not* to pay for the ride, and in the end succeed in overcoming his incredulity. He believes me. Still, for whatever reason, he delivers me to the right number in darkest Ritson Road. We need not take legal advice before concluding that it is far from certain that a contract was made. It is far from certain, too, whatever else is said, that *what happened at the beginning of the ride* issues in a moral justification for my paying a fare.

This suggests that while consent with respect to the law's contracts does not require proof of a certain intention, it is also true that a statement of the wrong intention, so to speak, gets in the way of consent and contract. What is of most relevance, however, is this: the commission of an offence is in closer analogy to this very odd taxi case than to the ordinary case where the passenger does not say he intends not to pay. The consensual theorist points to a certain act, the offence, and claims it to be analogous to giving a taxi-driver an address. But the offender will also give every evidence of not intending the upshot having to do with punishment. It follows that if we begin with an offence, and find a close analogy of it that might turn up in civil law, we do not find anything remotely like a clear case of consent and contract.

There are three other things to be remarked quickly about consensualism. First, there is a certain amount of tension between parts of it. One of its propositions is that an offence is a certain consent to a punishment only if the law in question is somehow just, or if the burden of keeping to the law is a justified one. Another of its propositions, put one way, is that consent in the special sense can justify a distribution of burdens that is in a sense unfair or whatever. These two propositions, if they are not clear enough to be inconsistent, do not come together easily. Secondly, the view does indeed depend on the first proposition – the law's being just, its burdens being justified. Since this requirement is not clarified, and since it is not shown that it is met, the view is at least incomplete.[49] Thirdly, although it needs to be admitted, in line with a necessary realism about what can be done in moral and political philosophy, that consensualism has not been *refuted* by me, it clearly does not provide a substantial and clear reason for punishment. It is unclear with respect to the requirement of justice just mentioned. The tradition of backward-looking thinking and feeling, above all its practices and institutions, has more in it. The consensual theory is not the truth of it.

SATISFACTIONS-IN-ACTING

It was allowed at the start of this survey that it is a little too neat to say that backward-looking theories of punishment do take into account nothing but the past in justifying it. The last theory at which we shall look is the main reason for this hesitation. It is, you can say, about restoration.[50] It is run together with consensual, contractarian and like ideas, but clearly it can be separated from them. To my mind, it is thereby improved. We begin again with classical utilitarianism. It is not only that it may issue in awful acts of victimization, but that it leaves out a consideration which is essential to the justification of ordinary punishment. Admittedly it is part of the justification of punishment that it is preventive, but it is also or as much a part that it involves a certain *equality, fairness, justice, rationality, equilibrium, balance, reciprocity, debt payment*, or *order*.

To try to become clearer about this, we are invited to consider the nature or function of the law. It legitimates certain activities for an individual and proscribes other activities. I am permitted to inherit a car, but not to drive it while drunk; I can in general forbid entry to my house, but not to a policeman with a search warrant; I can buy food or medicines, but not steal them. The law, then, as well as allowing me to do things, to indulge myself in certain ways, places a vast array of what are again called burdens on me, but seemingly not burdens of the kind we have lately been considering. The present ones, rather, are *burdens of self-denial*. The law forbids to me certain choices, certain self-indulgences, certain exercises of my will, certain followings of my own inclinations. Each member of my society is subject to an array of burdens of self-denial. The general result is a distribution of the burdens of self-denial that is equal, fair, just, balanced, ordered or whatever.

What an offender does is freely to put down one of his burdens. As he should not, he chooses for himself, indulges himself, exercises his will, follows his inclination. This constitutes a departure or a further departure from the society's distribution of these burdens, a distribution that is tolerably equal, fair or the like. The essential recommendation of punishment, over and above its preventive recommendation, is that it restores equality, fairness or whatever, or is a move in that restorative direction. It does this, essentially, by *enforcing* a burden. The man who is punished is essentially a man whose desires, will or inclinations are restrained, not by himself but by others. The result is that the maldistribution of burdens which he has produced is corrected. Things are in a specific way put back to what they were. The punishment also encourages others to stick to the legitimate distribution.

It is important to be clear about the goods involved in the original distribution, in the ensuing maldistribution produced by offences, and in the distribution reasserted through punishment. As already implied, and despite an uncertainty in some statements of the view, these are not material goods, say food, houses, painkillers, and so on. It is persistently asserted by one defender of the view[51] that they are not, and of course they cannot be such. If the goods in question were material goods, we would be offered nothing like a *general* reason for punishment. We would have no reason for punishing attempted crimes which produce *no* material gain for offenders, because of failure or because no material gain was attempted, as in many offences of violence.

Also, if the goods in question were material goods, it would be absurd to say the law produces an *equal* distribution of them, and any description of the distribution as *fair* or *just* or the like would require further argument. Finally, it cannot be that material goods are what is in question since the unfairness of an offence is specifically said not to be an unfairness only to the victim – say the man who loses his car – but an unfairness to *all* the law-abiding members of the society.

Material goods, as I have been speaking of them, are certain things in the world. There are other things closely related to them which also cannot be the goods that are in question with this view. I mean the satisfactions in large part owed to material goods. These satisfactions, rightly called the great goods or the objects of our fundamental desires, cannot be what is in question. There are the same reasons for saying these are not the goods of this retributivism. It can be added that these goods also do not include the satisfactions of which one thinks in connection with offences not aimed at material gain, say certain offences of violence. The satisfactions of vengeance got by a murderer are not goods in the right class, it seems, since one can think of murders where they are missing but to which this retributivism must apply.

It becomes clear that the goods or benefits in question can perhaps be described as *satisfactions-in-acting*. They are the goods of indulging one's will, or, to speak informally, of *letting go*, whether legally or illegally. They are those goods that one does not have, precisely and only, as the product of obeying or forbearing, of denying or restraining oneself or reining oneself in. Instead, here, one may have the burden of *dissatisfactions-in-not-acting*. The car thief presumably enjoys satisfaction-in-acting above all at the moment when he breaks the side window, although it makes sense to say he also enjoys it later, when he self-indulgently doesn't submit to the idea of returning the car or turning himself in. In sum, then, for present purposes, the law legitimates certain satisfactions-in-acting and it proscribes others, which is to say it enjoins certain dissatisfactions-in-not-acting.

> (13) Offenders choose to put down a burden, take a proscribed satisfaction-in-acting. Punishment puts such a burden on them, thereby reasserting a distribution of such burdens and benefits.

Various questions arise about the very nature of these burdens and benefits, and their relation to other dissatisfactions and satisfactions.

These we must pass by. The first of two questions not to be passed by is this one: are the burdens which we now have more or less in view anything like *equally* distributed in our societies? Better, are they somehow rightly distributed? That they are is suggested by a good deal of what is said in this doctrine of restoration or satisfactions-in-acting. Well, one cannot avoid the thought that the burdens of self-restraint or dissatisfaction-in-not-acting defined by law are lighter for the man who has everything as against the man who has nothing. I refer to the having or not having of material goods and their satisfactions.

As I have already indicated, it is notable that one gets a veritable welter of descriptions of the distribution that is fundamental to this view. If it is sometimes said to be or to involve equality, it is also said to be *fair, just, balanced, reciprocal*, and so on. However, we are not much helped by abandoning equality for this justice, since this justice goes unexplained. The particular distribution in question goes undefended. It evidently needs to be defended if the view is to be complete. The view, if it is not taken as involving an *equal* distribution, is vague. To glance back at the interpretation in terms of equality, incidentally, we would also need to know why *that* is a good thing. Is *any* equal distribution, at whatever level, a good thing, and better than any unequal distribution?

One final thought in connection with the nature of the distribution. What some of the advocates of this view take the law to produce is perhaps not an ordering or order of burdens which has some *further* recommendation – equality or justice or some such. What the law is taken to produce, and what the offender disturbs, is order *simpliciter*: that is, a situation in which self-denials and self-indulgences are *subject to rule*, whether the rule is good, bad or indifferent. It is a popular idea among those who benefit from rules, as distinct from those who do not, that there is a great recommendation in any old rules. That needs arguing, and any argument this produces will be a small one.

A second question about the satisfactions-in-acting view has to do with the relative importance of specifically the goods with which it is concerned, and with the fact that the commitment of the doctrine is to distributive justice somehow conceived. To speak quickly, surely *having* money or food, and the satisfactions got from them, are of greater importance than specifically the benefits we have in view, satisfactions-in-acting. Surely *not having* money or food or medical care, and the ensuing dissatisfactions, are of greater importance than the burdens of self-denial with respect to them, dissatisfactions-in-not-acting. Thus, if one sets out to justify punishment by considerations of distributive justice, it is bizarre to leave out the former benefits and burdens – benefits of possession and burdens of lack or deprivation. It might well be, from the point of view of distribution, that a gain secured by punishment in terms of the distribution of self-indulgence and self-denial was outweighed by a loss secured by punishment in terms of what we can call the benefits and burdens of possession.

This doctrine, to my mind, does little to justify punishment in our societies. It is necessary to say that this is a conclusion in a way shared and strongly defended by one advocate of the doctrine.[52] He takes it that the injustice of our societies makes the doctrine inapplicable to them. He also maintains, to my mind mistakenly, that the doctrine, at least with contractarian ideas added, is the best justification of punishment, and that it would justify punishment in a just society. On the contrary, punishment there could not be justified simply by reference to burdens of the specified kind, with or without the addition of contractarianism.

Of what else can be said against the doctrine, let me say only that at best it provides only an insubstantial and obscure ground for punishment. This argument, like its predecessors, is not the truth of backward-looking theories of punishment. We have not found that truth either in looking at the tradition of retributivism, but it is more likely to be found there.

It needs to be added that our sampling of backward-looking theories will be carried further in later chapters, including the one on mixed, compromise or combination theories of punishment. It will in effect also be carried a little further in connection with the subject to which we now turn. It is what seems to me to be the real truth of retributivism and of supposedly backward-looking theories generally.

3
Grievance Satisfaction

AN ACTUAL REASON

Such contentions as we have now considered about desert as the justification of punishment were also considered by John Mackie, a philosopher as acute as any in Oxford towards the end of the twentieth century.[1] The particular verdicts we reached differ somewhat from his, but there is no mistaking a similarity in general upshot. He drew a general conclusion. It was that no retributive principle of punishment can be 'explained or developed within a reasonable system of moral thought', that all the main lines of retributivist thought are signal failures, that we cannot make moral sense of them.[2]

He also had another conviction, however. It was that a retributive principle 'cannot be eliminated from our moral thinking', that retributive ideas which in one way or another are unsatisfactory, from what can be called the point of view of reason, are none the less deeply ingrained, a part of our lives.[3] The proposition that retributivism cannot be made decent sense of, and the proposition that it is inescapable – these comprise what Mackie calls the paradox of retributivism.

He offers what he calls a resolution of the paradox, of which the first step is the proposition from David Hume that moral distinctions, such as the distinction between the deserved and the undeserved, are founded not on reason but on feeling or sentiment. What is in question with retributivism, fundamentally, is what Mackie calls *retributive emotion*. Of this, he offers a persuasive biological explanation, in terms of standard evolutionary theory. It begins with the advantage to species and individuals of retaliatory behaviour and feeling, and hence their natural selection; it proceeds by way of the socializing or moralizing of retributive emotion; and ends with such items as the theories of punishment in terms of rational contract or a consent to give up immunity. I have no doubt that the explanation is at least in principle correct.

Nevertheless, this view of the tradition of retributivism seems not to deal with a main problem. It is not enough to grant that retributivism is entrenched. It is not enough to lay out a good explanation of the thing, as one might lay out such an explanation of someone's *true* belief or *valid* argument – which sort of explanation, as Mackie was of course aware, does not preclude truth or validity or other cogency. What must also be granted, surely, as I have already maintained, is that retributivism and indeed backward-looking theories generally somehow *make sense*.

On reflection, surely, it is a remarkable supposition that a *tide* of ordinary moral thought and language over centuries, and, larger than that, at least a major part of a tide of institutions in societies, should rest, as Mackie supposes, in so far as rational rather than causal grounds are concerned, on incoherence or on what is without rational content. Certainly there are difficulties or questions here, but it is surely impossible to suppose that in establishing, defending and developing retributivist institutions, punishment above all, men have not aimed at and secured something that is capable of clear expression or description. There has been *some* gain in it all, gain that can be discerned and put into an argument.

More particularly, it seems impossible that *no* contentful argument attaches to a basic fact of this unremitting sequence of institutions, the fact that they rest on an array of relations or connections between particular offences and particular penalties, and give these relations or connections as the justification of the penalties. It cannot be that all that can be said of the law's 'deserved' or 'fitting' penalties is that they derive from a confused image of actual measurement of things that in fact are incommensurable or some other equally unacceptable notion, or that they derive from a clear notion of equivalence but one that has no argumentative force at all, or that they are owed only to inflated stuff about rights that does not survive reflection.

Let us start again, with judges. It is notable that what is said for punishment by those who are engaged in meting it out is often enough of a very different character from the sorts of thing so far considered by us. When judges declare in one way and another that the coming distress of offenders is deserved, they are at least allowing the implication that it will give satisfactions to others. Consider what used to be the most entrenched of judicial utterances, no doubt given more colloquial expression now, that offenders must pay their debt, or pay their debt to society. What is it to pay a debt?

When a debt is paid, does somebody not *get* something? How very odd it would be if no one did. Necessarily, someone does get something.

I shall take it that what lies behind such claims, although disavowals may be expected, is the argument *that a man is rightly punished because his punishment brings satisfactions to others*. In particular, but certainly not exclusively, and not always most importantly, and not necessarily, it satisfies desires of the person or persons he has freely offended against. For a number of reasons that we need not delay us, some having to do with a kind of morality having got into the conventions of a culture, this argument has not often been made explicit in philosophical, jurisprudential or other high company. To ignore it is none the less to ignore what has given force to the retribution theory.[4]

The truth of retributivism, a little more fully, is as follows.

First, harmful actions give rise to what can be labelled *grievances*, which is to say desires for exactly the distress of the agents, desires whose only and full satisfaction is in the belief that the agents are being distressed or made to suffer. Grievances in this sense are not causes of complaints, real or imagined unfairnesses, injuries and the like. Rather, they are results of these – the ensuing emotions and feelings. Whatever else is to be said of grievances, one certainty is that they exist.

A second proposition, no doubt disagreeable, is that the existence of these desires is an argument for their satisfaction. As it seems to me, it cannot be left out. There cannot be any argument for not contemplating or not counting certain desires at all. There cannot be any argument for actually dismissing certain desires from consideration that is nearly so strong as the argument that their existence is reason for their satisfaction. A desire, whatever else is to be said about it, or hurries or rushes to be said about it, is itself an argument for its satisfaction. The proposition is familiar, of course, in the context of our desires for great goods, fundamental things we all desire – to live, to be without pain, to be free, and so on. In short, there would be a fundamental inconsistency in counting grievance desires as nothing.

Thirdly, such desires can be less than satisfied or more than satisfied. Above all, they can be just satisfied. This again is a fact of life. Who can doubt it? Also, clear judgements as to these things are possible. As it well known, there are behavioural criteria for these states of affairs, in particular for what is just enough to satisfy a desire.

It is worth adding, fourthly, that grievance desires are of course often bound up with feelings and judgements of condemnation of offenders. So too is the satisfaction bound up with such feelings and judgements, as it is with traditional retribution theories. Words and images mingle with the satisfaction. That is not to say, however, that what we are considering is any traditional retributive justification whatever of punishment to the effect that the offender was culpable in his offence or whatever – say intrinsic-good retributivism. What justifies punishment on the present understanding is precisely and only people getting what they desire, not suffering a frustration.

The truth of the retributivist tradition, again, is that it seeks to justify punishment partly or wholly by the clear reason that punishment, whatever other feelings it evokes, satisfies the grievances created by offences, through causing distress to offenders responsible for the offences, and that it considers penalties to be unsatisfactory if they do less than satisfy grievances or do more than that, and satisfactory if they just satisfy it. Here, the plain sense of saying that a penalty P is deserved for person A's offence O is that P will just satisfy the grievance to which A has given rise by O.

Further and importantly, and also convincingly, the requirement of an equivalent penalty, in this sense, is a direct consequence of the fundamental contention – that punishment is justified partly or wholly by grievance satisfactions. To do less than satisfy it would simply conflict with the fundamental contention. To do more would be to cause distress that would fail to have the given justification of being a satisfaction. There is nothing unconnected or ad hoc or unreasoned about the place of this idea of equivalence in the thinking and feeling in question. Compare, for example, intrinsic-good retributivism, or the addition of indifference retributivism to forfeited-rights retributivism, or innocence-system retributivism.

For a summary, then, the claim that punishment is deserved comes down to a notably clear thing. The penalty satisfies grievances owed to the offence, and does neither less nor more than satisfy these grievances. We do have a reason for punishment here, although, as you may want to keep saying, a reason that may be outweighed by others. That is true of very nearly all reasons, of course.[5]

The summary is somewhat premature. For one thing, it needs to be understood in a large way. What is in question is importantly the grievance of victims but not only that. There is indeed a public acceptance that a mother and father should have the peace of mind that comes with the conviction and imprisonment of the beast, idiot or drunk who killed their son. That is but a large beginning in the matter of satisfactions, however.

There are those in the rest of society who share, enter into, sympathize with or understand the grievance desires of victims. That they might not do so in the same way in the absence of the great and resolute institution in society for dealing with crime, an institution that can be taken as ratifying their feelings, is nothing to the point. Here too there are wants or at least real inclinations. The matter of satisfactions, however, also has more to it than this second thing. It includes what does not have to do with victims of offences in so focussed a way.

A full account of punishment and social emotion – shared emotion in a society – cannot be attempted here, but let me offer some of what surely are only reminders. One is that to have a general fear or apprehension with respect to crime, as many do, is to want the reassurance of punishment of offenders. That desired reassurance is not itself the fact of crime prevention, but an anticipatory satisfaction having to do with the fact or idea. If you can punish men in order to try to make them behave better, you can also punish them to make others feel better about the future – reassured by the prospect of the better behaviour. If this is not exactly grievance satisfaction, it goes with it and supports it.

Another reminder of social emotion is that to be among those who are called the privileged members of a society, the possessors of things, is to have a stronger desire and indeed passion owed to that good fortune. Many have the desire, and it is not simply a desire for order. It is a desire for a particular order, the one that is bound up with or produces certain privileges. Privileged persons, perhaps humanly enough, have different and stronger desires for the distress of those who can be regarded as having the privileged in their sights, even if they offend or also offend against the unprivileged. For example, many of them take themselves to have played by the rules, and resent those who do not. To which can be added that there are also those, among the underprivileged or the less privileged, who take themselves to have played by the rules and who therefore resent those who do not.

To these sorts of grievance desires and supportive accompaniments can be added others that have a less arguable or indeed a confused or irrational content. We contemplated 13 backward-looking arguments for punishment before coming to the present one. Fault was found with all those arguments, sometimes easily found. That does not affect the fact that they have had a hold on or have kinds of support in our societies. This is true, in fact, of the high metaphysics as well as the plainer propositions. A newspaper of the people is well able to find a spokesman to declare that a man is indeed to be locked up for life *because that is right*, where the declaration, on examination, is close enough to those of Kant or an intrinsic-good retributivist.

The arguments and beliefs in question give rise to what are plainly desires for the punishment of offenders. These are desires that have as contents the arguments in question – that a punishment be given that is factually equivalent to an offence and so on. Those desires are themselves arguments, and seen to be such. There is a difference between (a) defending what is done to someone by saying that he chose to break the law or that the penalty will cause roughly as much distress to him as he caused to someone else by his offence and (b) defending what is done to someone by pointing to desires informed by those objectionable arguments. To offer the second defence is to try to defend the penalty by reference to satisfaction. To offer the first defence is not. No doubt we should take care about encouraging desires based on confusion or mistake, but that is not to count them as nothing.

Since first being pushed into the idea that grievance satisfaction is the reality of retributive punishment and the retribution theory, I have learned of philosophical and jurisprudential passages that are relevant. Hermann Lotze, who has a place in nineteenth-century German philosophy, speaks of the vindictive satisfactions given to individuals, particularly the victims of offences, by punishment. He then continues.

> Were these persons all so organized that they were incapable of feeling pleasure and pain, then it is self-evident that there would no longer exist . . . any right of punishment. . . . It is only the unhappy condition of feeling which takes place in the soul of the injured person that explains and forms the basis for new actions which aim to obviate the same.[6]

James Fitzjames Stephen, the renowned Victorian judge, has a wider view. He writes as follows.

> The punishment of common crimes, the gross forms of force and fraud, is no doubt ambiguous. It may be justified on the principles of

self-protection, and apart from any question as to their moral character. It is not, however, difficult to show that these acts have in fact been forbidden and subjected to punishment not only because they are dangerous to society, and so ought to be prevented, but also for the sake of gratifying the feeling of hatred – call it revenge, resentment, or what you will – which the contemplation of such conduct excites in healthily constituted minds. If this can be shown, it will follow that criminal law is in the nature of a persecution of the grosser forms of vice, and an emphatic assertion of the principle that the feeling of hatred and the desire of vengeance above-mentioned are important elements of human nature which ought in such cases to be satisfied in a regular public and legal manner.[7]

Still, to construe desert claims in the proposed way still runs contrary to a prevailing orthodoxy and indeed an argument. Discussions of the retribution theory or rather retribution theories have defined them as doctrines that find justification for punishing a man wholly in his past action and a relationship between that and the penalty in so far as it affects him. If anything else is in question, it is said, such as the effect of the penalty on others, a doctrine is not a retribution theory. So grievance satisfaction cannot be the stuff of any retribution theory.

This is to fall under the thrall of a definition and into misdescription. It is to misdescribe the attitudes and arguments of retributivists. They cannot much protest because they have not been self-aware or explicit. Their unawareness or reticence, whatever is finally to be said of their argument, is misplaced. There is no reason for ruling out of discussion the claim that a course of action will lead to the satisfaction of desires. There is no reason for keeping it dark. The consequence of doing so is that a theory becomes mystery, a doctrine whose central proposition about equivalence, if not construed in such a way as to call out for dismissal, evokes little more than wonderment. Whatever the explanation of this state of affairs, allow me to repeat that it is surely unbelievable that the persistence of a powerful doctrine has had *no* basis in intelligible argument.

Mackie had a view of the retributivist tradition, consistent with the evolutionary explanation that he gives of it, that excluded the possibility that grievance satisfaction is its sense. He took the tradition to consist in institutions such that we cannot look, for whatever value they have, to the effects of the distress of penalties. The reason for doing so, as remarked, is essentially a respect for what most apologists for the tradition, notably moral philosophers and jurisprudents, have said of it. They have said that it depends on a reason for punishment that does not mention the effects of the distress of offenders, notably the satisfaction it gives. There would be call for respect of this declaration if they were successful in providing the supposed reason.

Objections have of course been made to taking desert claims to reduce to grievance satisfactions of the various kinds. One is the idea that the proposition is obviously false because it reduces to this: 'that a judge ought to sentence because the people outside in the street are baying for blood'.[8] It reduces to nothing of the sort. The fact of punishment's being informed and defended by grievance satisfactions is a fact shaped by considerations of consistency, precedent, the law's fundamental ideas of the reasonable, and so on. In this connection James Fitzjames Stephen also made the often quoted remark that 'the criminal law stands to the passion of revenge in much the same relation as marriage to the sexual appetite'.[9] The remark, I take it, expresses the view to which we have come of the truth of retributivism, and the consistent fact that retributive punishment is not ungoverned vengeance.

It has been objected, similarly, that the view reduces the retributivist tradition to 'just a primitive bit of intuitive vindictiveness'.[10] Part of what can be said in reply is along the same lines, that the view in no way conflicts with the fact that the criminal law and punishment constitute a developed institution – authoritative and rule-governed. That the view finds a basis for punishment that can be characterized mistakenly as 'primitive' seems to me a recommendation of it. That it finds a basis which is 'intuitive', in one pejorative use of that word, which suggests want of clarity, is false.

SYSTEM

It was remarked at the end of our considerable sampling of backward-looking theories of punishment that a little more would be said. It is that in saying that a particular penalty is the deserved one, people may have in mind that it stands in relation to others, that it is in accordance with a certain *system* of penalties – of which no more is said or implied. This system is the scale of penalties for offences of different seriousness in the criminal law. We thus get another understanding of the claim that a penalty is deserved.

(14) The penalty is according to a system connecting different penalties with different offences.

This is not already the idea that the penalty is according to any desert system, say a system that reflects degrees of innocence, or a system that is recommended on any other such ground. Rather, the argument is that imposing a particular penalty is consistent with what has been and will be done to others. Imposing the penalty is according to precedent, principle and the like. It is in this way reasonable.

It is not easy to say what this *bare-system reason* for punishment is worth in general. It is clear for a start that to say only and no more than that some action is according to a rule or a structure of rules may be no recommendation or a small or a secondary recommendation. The racist murderer who points out the fact of a perfect consistency in his choice of victims does himself no favour thereby. Nor is his situation improved by his having worked out a system of pieces of racism, from murder down to incidental insults or conveyings of his own racial superiority. Obviously to defend an action by citing a rule is to raise and have to answer the question of the worth of the rule or system, which may be no worth at all.

Take another case, where you are likely to allow that consistency *is* a recommendation, and to be spoken of as fairness. If food is to be distributed to a group of people, some of whom are very hungry and some of whom are slightly hungry, we are likely to give a larger amount to each of those who are very hungry and a smaller amount to each of those who are slightly hungry. Still, this consistency is a secondary recommendation. That we do anything at all, and that we feel that we ought to distribute any food, is not to be explained by the fact that all the members of one sub-group are in one state and all the members of the other in a different state. It is that they are all hungry. Suppose that there is a reason why all of the people in question should not eat for a given period. All of them are going to have surgical operations. We would not give them food, or feel we ought to, although some were very hungry and others slightly hungry.

A retributivist who advances a desert claim having to do with a system that connects different penalties with different offences, then, must indeed explain what is to be said for that system. He must do better than some exponents and defenders of the criminal law. They defend the rightness of a particular penalty by noting that it is according to a system which they assume, without further ado, to be a morally justified system. What a retributivist may try to do, if pressed, is to make use of one or more of the understandings of desert claims noticed earlier. He may explain, for example, that a penalty is right because it is according to a system of offences and penalties such that the distress of each penalty is equivalent to the culpability of the offence. A retributivist cannot leave us in the dark, as does Professor Gross. Plainly the worth of the argument for a particular penalty in a system depends on the worth of the idea that guided the construction of the system. This may be no idea worth the name.

It remains true, despite these propositions, that consistency in such matters as punishment may indeed have a recommendation, perhaps great. 'One person one vote' is a practice that evidently has a large recommendation. A retributivist theory of punishment based on grievance satisfaction can have in it something very useful about a penalty system. It will be a penalty system constructed by way of this intelligible notion of equivalence between penalty and offence.

To begin in constructing or more likely judging or defending such a system, a retributivist may reflect on actions of considerable harmfulness. The grievance to which they may be regarded as giving rise, however, will be seen as a function not only of their harmfulness but also of the extent to which the agents involved are responsible for their actions. Hence the retributivist initially fixes or confirms a particular penalty for actions of a particular harm and responsibility, say killing for which the agents can be held wholly responsible. He then fixes or confirms lesser penalties for actions of this harm where the agents are to a lesser extent responsible. In each case, the intention is to have a penalty whose distress brings satisfactions to others roughly equivalent to the grievance they have been caused. What this means, of course, is that the penalty does satisfy, and does no more than satisfy, the grievance. The process continues by way of comparison with actions of other harms and degrees of responsibility.

A number of objections may be raised against this sketch or indication of the construction and defence of a penalty system.

It may be objected that it assumes an assessment of grievance desires and satisfactions and there can be no 'objective' measure that can be used. In reply it can be said that the construction or the like involves, centrally, the picturing of a situation involving (i) a certain offence, generally considered, (ii) the grievance to which it gives rise, and (iii) the penalty that would satisfy the grievance. Let us take these in turn.

The offence is identified, as remarked, by way of the harm caused and the degree of freedom and hence responsibility of the agent. To say someone has been harmed in some way is to describe his state and also to do something like express an attitude of disapproval. 'Objectivity' objections, such as they are, are in place at this particular point. That a man's car has been taken away is as 'objective' a fact as that he is now on a bus. But has he been harmed? This is in part a question of attitude, however shared the attitude, and one that must be answered. Retributivists facing such questions, however, can say they are no worse off than their critics and the holders of other theories.

As for what can be called judgements about responsibility, they may be described as in part factual. We recognize a considerable range of conditions which may reduce a man's responsibility for a particular action. He may be compelled to do the thing, perhaps in such a way that what he does barely counts as a case of action at all. He may do a thing without intending it, or fully intending it. He may act only after having been subjected to extreme provocation, or as a consequence of illness or disability. There are many more such excusing conditions and we can order them as to their excusing capacity. Needless to say, it will not be a simple list.

Behind it lurks a larger question, that of determinism. Are our decisions and actions merely effects? Are they effects in such a way that some general question of our being held responsible for them is a real one? We will be coming back to this question, which, as you have heard, arises for all theories of punishment or at least is very relevant to them. All of them presuppose that offenders were voluntary in their decisions and actions or else originated them – or that both things were true (pp. 25–6). They presuppose this rightly with all offences save those of strict and vicarious liability – which they tend to overlook.

The point that seems likely to emerge from these reflections is that there is no insuperable difficulty, of the sort envisaged by an objector, in the specification of an offence. Perhaps he would do better to think about determinism. The specification of an offence is not in any unusual sense a procedure of 'subjectivity'. If we turn now to (ii) the estimation, in general, of the grievance caused by an identified offence, there again seems to be no such serious difficulty. That a man has a certain response to the disappearance of his car is a consequence, in part, of attitudes. What response he does have, what grievance he feels, is a question of fact. It is a difficult question but not an attitudinal one. It is partly to be answered, and this brings us to item (iii) above, by consideration of what satisfies him, what puts an end to his grievance. Here again, in judging satisfactions, we have what is fundamentally a question of fact, or at least can be. So too, finally, is our question of equivalence: whether a penalty satisfies, fails to satisfy, or more than satisfies a grievance.[11]

One reminder here. Our actual practice of punishment is undeniably governed by a certain system of rules. These rules in some manner or other connect particular offences with particular penalties and may be classified in various ways. The description and justification of these rules, unlike their existence, is a matter of question. A retributivist may indeed regard them as the outcomes of a construction of the sort just suggested, or at any rate he should. A very different account, as we shall see in due course, may be given by proponents of another theory of punishment.

To come to a summary and conclusion, the truth of retribution theories of punishment consists in a certain proposition. All of them, on the evidence we have, boil down to this understanding of the claim that a punishment is deserved for an offence.

> (15) The penalty satisfies grievances owed to the offence, and does neither less nor more than satisfy these grievances, and in so doing it is in accordance with a system that connects penalties with offences by way of grievances.

DEFENCES AND CRITICISMS

If the desert argument in terms of grievance satisfaction is worth some consideration as it stands, can it be strengthened? Is there more to be said for it? Might it be the case, as no doubt retributivists have supposed, that it has the support of some very general moral principle, presumably something called a principle of justice? You might think that the more general principle is that equals are to be treated equally and unequals unequally. Does the desert argument in terms of grievance satisfaction not rest on the judgement that those who offend in the same way should be treated equally, and differently from others, including those who have not offended at all?

It may, since those who deserve punishment are different in given ways from others. Does it provide support for the claim that those who deserve punishment should be punished and those who do not deserve it should not? It does not. The mentioned general principle would be satisfied, equally well, if we were to punish those who do not deserve it and not punish those who do. The principle would also be satisfied if we did no punishing at all and, say, repeated three times to ourselves the names of those who do not deserve punishment. All that the stated principle requires is that individuals who are equal in some respect should be treated equally and in a way that is different from others.

That is just the beginning of an inquiry into the idea that there is a useful general principle that can be taken to underlie the argument that people are to get penalties because this provides grievance satisfaction. The useful general principle would have as much to do with getting good things as bad ones. That is, it would cover various kinds of reward, including high salaries and bonuses. The principle, you can easily say, in anticipation, will be to the effect that each individual is to get what he or she deserves on account of personal qualities or actions and activities.

For an inquiry into the possibility of such a principle, you will have to look elsewhere, to a treatise on the nature of the political tradition of conservatism.[12] But perhaps enough can be said here, quickly, to enable us to go forward. The first remark is that we have just completed a pretty adequate survey of talk of desert with respect to punishment. If there is a useful general principle of desert, should it not have come into view at some point? Should we not have got a glimpse of the thing? We didn't.

A second comment is that talk of desert, so to speak, can go in any direction. You can seem to rely on some general principle of desert in *opposing* retribution theories. You can say, indeed, and be understood, that men do not deserve to be put in prison for 20 years to give grievance satisfaction to people. You can say that what we all deserve is an institution of punishment that succeeds in the aim of preventing offences. These possibilities are no indication that there is a general principle of desert that is of use to the theorists of retribution.

Passing by some other cautionary or disappointing thoughts, there is a certain conclusion. There *is* a general principle you can come upon when you are thinking of these matters. It is something like this: what people are and what they do are to count in connection with what they get and what is done for them and to them. No doubt that is true, in fact a truism, with respect to much or most of the natures of people and their actions. Does this piece of sanity give support to the proposition that the punishment of some people is right because it gives grievance satisfaction? There is no hope of that. The piece of sanity, it seems, and as will certainly be claimed, can be put to about as much use by those who were in view earlier – those who think and feel that it is degrading and wrong to take account of low desires for just the distress of another person. So too can the piece of sanity be used in other ways against retribution theories generally.

So much for what else might be said for the desert argument in terms of grievance satisfaction. What can be said *against* this retribution theory to which we have come? Well, some will think of a common objection to or inclination against any retribution theory. Is it not inconsistent, they ask, to condemn one man for injuring another and then to claim that society is morally correct to injure the offender in turn? Both the offender's act and the act of punishing him, it may be said, are contraventions of some principle, perhaps one of benevolence. The fact that the victim, in the case of punishment, has himself freely injured somebody else should not be regarded as making a sufficient difference between the two cases. If the first action was wrong, so is the second. Nor is there a sufficient difference to be found in the fact that in one case the injury is the work of a private individual and in the other the work of officers of a society acting in accordance with the law. Given this fact, punishment is not revenge. But if it can be defended only by considerations of desert then it, like revenge, is unjustified.[13]

A retributivist can oppose this argument in a number of ways. He or she may insist that there is a fundamental difference between a private action of one individual and the lawful actions of society. He need not but might introduce principles of democracy into the argument. He may say, further, that there is a fundamental difference between striking and striking back.[14] One may think a little or a lot of these considerations. What cannot be disputed is that the retributivist can rebut any charge of inconsistency. His principle of benevolence, he may say, includes a distinction between private actions and those of a society's authorities. Or, he includes in his principles, in addition to one having to do with benevolence, another having to do with desert. Injuries are wrong except in certain circumstances when they are in a specified sense deserved. Here there is no inconsistency.

If the objection of inconsistency to the grievance-satisfaction theory of retribution is not much use, neither is something else.

We cannot object, as we can to all other retribution theories, that men and women must not be made to suffer, or be deprived, if no good comes of it. We cannot say that what is proposed is useless suffering. Rather, this retribution theory *does* recommend punishment on the basis of good consequences. That they are consequences different from crime prevention, or in some sense more connected to punishment, does not make them other than consequences or other than good consequences.

We can ask, as we shall, if the theory is vulnerable on account of its evident assumption of the freedom of offenders in their guilty actions. We can object now to the theory, however, and indeed come to a conclusion. It is that the retribution theory of grievance satisfaction is mistaken, indeed intolerable or worse, because it proposes that a certain good be gained at far too great a cost. It is in this sense irrational. It is essential in thinking about the matter to keep in view exactly and thus no more than the argument we are considering. It has nothing to do with punishment having the effect of preventing or reducing offences. It has nothing to do with prevention by means of rehabilitation or reform, or even with punishment as an announcement that certain things are wrong. The view we have is just that punishment is justified because it satisfies grievances, puts an end to dissatisfactions.

In the course of our inquiry so far, we have several times touched on the subject of *great* goods, fundamental things we desire as a result of our human nature. These are conceived of or categorized differently by different people, but most conceptions and lists converge to a great extent. One good list of the great goods begins, as indicated already, with the three great goods of a decent length of life, material or bodily well-being, and freedom and power. To those are added respect and self-respect, the goods of relationship, and the goods of culture. More will be said of these, and of what issues from reflection on them, a certain general moral principle, the foundation or summary of a morality.

What needs to be said now is only that punishment is a denial of great goods to men and women, those punished and some of those related to them, and that it must be wholly wrong to punish them if all that results from the punishment is grievance satisfaction. I take it that almost all of us can agree on that, and also that we will not be much troubled by anyone who disagrees. Punishment, if that is what justifies it, is not far enough from cutting off someone else's arm in order to improve your sleep. This conclusion, surely, does not actually need the articulation of the mentioned moral principle. It is closer to truth that the principle derives from such convictions.

Still, more will be said of the principle. More will be said, too, of the nature of the collection of retribution theories of punishment (1) to (14). A little more will be said of the fundamental idea of reducing desert claims to a matter of grievance satisfaction and more of how the analysis of those theories into grievance satisfaction is buttressed, strongly supported from the side, by general facts of our holding people morally responsible for actions (pp. 144–5, Chapter 8). More will be said as well of what was called the human side of retribution theories – their prohibition on doing to the innocent what we do to the guilty, and also their prohibition on over-punishing the guilty.

None of this will qualify what we do now in this inquiry. We give up on retribution theories by themselves as justifications of punishment. We give up on a commitment that has grown stronger since about 1975 in theorizing about punishment and indeed in punishing.[15] The commitment seems to be owed to something other than a good reason for it. We turn instead to the second of the supposed sorts of justification of punishment.

4
Utilitarian Prevention Theory, etc.

QUESTIONS OF FACT ABOUT PREVENTION

The retribution theory, that family of theories, has traditionally been understood as giving a justification of punishment that looks only to the past. It has been contrasted in this with the prevention theory, again a family of theories, and also reform theories, which look to the future. The retribution theory as we have finally conceived it, however, is at least principally the contention that an offender's punishment provides grievance satisfactions. It must be so taken if we are to make sense, as we need to, of a strong and persisting attitude to offenders and their punishment. Given this, retribution theories as rightly understood are in a way similar to the theory or theories maintaining that what justifies punishment is its prevention of crime, which realistically is taken to mean reduction of crime. Retribution theories do rest on supposed consequences of punishment. Both retribution and prevention theories are members of the large category of moralities and moral theories spoken of as consequentialisms.[1]

The two differ in their attitude to the past offence. For prevention theories the past offence is evidence, perhaps an overwhelming case, for action now and in the future. It is safe enough to say, however, that the attitude of typical prevention theorists is more a matter of dismay or horror with respect to the offence than hatred with respect to the offender, despite the existence of feelings about the offender. Is the offence something for which the offender is held responsible in a different way from the one in which retribution theorists and retribution seekers hold him responsible?[2] We shall be thinking about that. The offence issues in a different kind of resolution for the prevention theorist and seeker, if sometimes as iron a resolution, and one that can issue in *more* severe penalties.

It would be of interest, and probably of value in argument, to inquire further into the attitudinal differences. We will be doing some of that at later stages, first in connection with the general question of freedom and responsibility, and subsequently in connection with differences in social attitudes generally between, say, the traditions of conservatism and liberalism in politics.[3] But a more direct approach to our subject is possible and required.

> General prevention ought to be the chief end of punishment as it is its real justification. If we could consider an offence that has been committed as an isolated fact, the like of which would never recur, punishment would be useless. It would be only adding one evil to another. But when we consider that an unpunished crime leaves the path of crime open, not only to the same delinquent but also to all those who may have the same motives and opportunities for entering upon it, we perceive that punishment inflicted on the individual becomes a source of security to all. That punishment which considered in itself appeared base and repugnant to all generous sentiments is elevated to the first rank of benefits when it is regarded not as an act of wrath or vengeance against a guilty or unfortunate individual who has given way to mischievous inclinations, but as an indispensable sacrifice to the common safety.[4]

The writer is Jeremy Bentham, the founder of utilitarianism – and the designer of a prison that would not have been soft on crime. He goes on to suggest that punishment prevents or may prevent the occurrence of offences in three ways. Punishment can make it impossible for an offender to break the law again, at least with respect to people outside prisons. It also deters or may deter both punished offenders and also others from offences. Thirdly, it provides an opportunity for the reforming of offenders.

Some but not all punishments prevent offences in the first way, by incapacitation. Imprisonment of a man pretty well rules out the possibility of offences by him against the general public for a time, but of course not against fellow inmates. The death penalty incapacitates absolutely. Fines incapacitate least. The second way of prevention, deterrence, is also a distinct kind of prevention. It is the making of individuals less likely to offend again or to offend a first time because of fear or prudence – because of something of this sort rather than what may still be called a moral motive. As for the third way of prevention, punishment may be a means to changing a man's character, personality or attitudes, so that out of some motivation like moral consideration for others or a new entry into or identification with a society's feelings about crime or an identification with them, he obeys the law.

Our concern now is with only the first two reasons for punishment, incapacitation and deterrence. We will look at them, as anticipated, as being sufficient by themselves to justify punishment. The two of them together will be taken as making up the prevention or crime-reduction theory. Or rather, to speak more carefully, our concern now is with ways of preventing offences other than the reformation or rehabilitation of offenders. As we shall see, there are more other ways of prevention than incapacitation and prevention as defined, indeed as ordinarily defined. So the prevention theory, to repeat, has to do with all ways other than reform or rehabilitation of reducing offences by punishment.

The retribution theory as traditionally understood has seemed not to depend very much on facts – ordinary or empirical claims about which questions can arise. This is so partly because it has generally gone together with a certain assumption, that in general offenders have been morally responsible in some way for their offences. Very differently, if not always seen clearly, the retribution theory does indeed for a particular reason have less dependence on facts than might be supposed – because it is mistaken to suppose that it can depend at bottom on legal facts. It *does* depend, however, as we have understood it, on facts of grievance satisfaction and of a penalty doing no more and no less than satisfy grievance desires.

Still, the prevention theory is certainly different with respect to factual presuppositions – both in what they are and to what extent they are true. As all agree, it depends on whether large thoughts about prevention are clear and true. In general, does punishment prevent offences? Does it, that is, reduce the number of offences sufficiently? That question, in the absence of a definition of sufficiency, is evidently not at all precise, but a kind of gesture. Nor are the questions satisfactory that we can put in its place, about both incapacitation and prevention. But let us proceed with them in a tentative way.

A first question, about whether punishment incapacitates, has a short answer, which is yes. Certain punishments do this. Execution does. Imprisonment has at least a significant incapacitating effect with respect to the world outside prisons. That proposition is not made small by another one, presumably, but it does have to be brought together with it. This is that with some crime, imprisonment has something like a *capacitating* effect. Imprisonment as we have it provides rather than takes away opportunity. More precisely, it gives rise to desires which it then gives men an opportunity to fulfil. In the United States outside of prisons in a recent year, there were about 90,000 male-on-female rapes. An estimate of the number of male-on-male rapes in prisons was 240,000. This was sufficient to get a bill on prison rape put before Congress. It got more of a hearing because in prisons the incidence of AIDS, sexually transmitted and with a probability of being fatal, is about ten times the level outside.[5]

There are other capacitating effects, as they can be called. To be among criminals is to learn the possibility of certain attitudes. It is also to learn more resentment, maybe resentment wtih reason. It may be to acquire a depravity that makes possible actions that were not possible before. But this is plain enough. There is also a prior matter about incapacitation.

The question of whether and to what extent prison incapacitates criminals with respect to offences in the outside or public world, as it is possible to forget, is not the main factual question about this incapacitation. Incapacitation can be a fact without having the importance unreflectively assigned to it, anyway all the importance. The main question here, a difficult one that does not prompt a general answer, is whether prisoners would in fact have offended if they had not been in prison and incapacitated. Would some of them not have offended because they would have been *deterred* by the experience of previous punishment, maybe imprisonment, or in some other way deterred by the large fact of the institution of punishment?

A rather young mugger, tax cheat or pension-fund shark may be imprisoned and incapacitated for two years, and in the second year, because of deterrence owed to his first year, would not have offended if he had been able. There are other such possibilities. Plainly there is the question of whether an executed man would have been deterred from offences if alive. The answer to the question of whether incapacitation is necessary to the prevention of offences thus depends in part on answers to other factual questions, including the next one on our list, about deterrence. Both questions, incidentally, as we need to remember, precede and do not settle the attitudinal or moral question of whether kinds of prevention actually do justify punishment.

To come to deterrence, is it the case, or rather to what extent is it the case, that men, women, boys and some girls by their own experience of being punished are led not to choose to offend again because of an aversion to more punishment or a judgement that the gain from an offence would not be worth the probable or possible price of more punishment? In short, are those who are actually punished deterred from reoffending? We can take this question together with a third one.

Is it the case that many individuals who have never been punished or accused are deterred from offending? Are they deterred from an offence by the fact of punishment, by what they believe or know of the experience of others of the practice? More particularly, to remember what deterrence is, are many individuals such that when they think of, contemplate, consider or start to plan a first offence, they are put off by what they believe or know of police, courts and prisons? As in the case of people who have already been punished, these individuals are not only persons contemplating a crime in advance, but also persons who find themselves in situations they did not anticipate or intend, perhaps situations in which they are subjected to provocation or attacked.

Towards the end of the twentieth century and the start of this one, there was a growing resistance to reliance on the idea of deterrence of either kind as a justification of punishment. There was a recourse to ideas of retribution, of which we know, and also ideas of incapacitation. The trend was said to be owed in large part to such facts as those that emerged from the largest study of recidivism ever conducted in the United States.[6]

The summary of the research was that more than two-thirds of those released from state prisons in the United States committed at least one serious new crime – some serious crime or other – within three years. Nearly half of them did so within six months. More than half of those released were in fact back in prison within the three years. Of those imprisoned for larceny, 79 per cent somehow offended again. With burglars and robbers, 74 per cent and 70 per cent did so. Those least likely somehow to offend again were murderers (41 per cent) and rapists (46 per cent). Of those released after being imprisoned for murder, about 1 per cent were arrested for murder in three years. Of those imprisoned for rape, about 2 per cent were arrested again for rape.

The figures touch on the idea noted above that part of an incapacitating punishment or a second such punishment may in fact not be needed for an upshot that it guarantees. But the figures are mainly important for what they say about exactly deterrence as a justification for punishment. If it is in general true that about one-third of prisoners do not offend again in three years, is that few or many? The question is on the way to the question of whether the amount of deterrence is a justification for punishment or not.

Nearly half of the imprisoned rapists, it seems, decide not to re-offend. Let us suppose for a minute this is because they are deterred by the punishment they have had. If so, would that be sufficient to justify the punishment? Societies do engage in policies, no doubt, where the success rate in a clear sense is just one-third or a great deal less. This can be true of public-health policies, or policies for the prevention of tax criminality, or transport or education policies. Come to think of it, the crime-prevention policy of *having police to catch offenders* is a policy that has nowhere near the success of catching one-third of those who commit crimes. But leave this complication with deterrence for a while and consider another one.

Crime is predominantly the work of young adults or near-adults, about four in five of them male. In the United Kingdom in a recent year, the ages of persons found guilty of indictable offences, or officially cautioned for very good reason but not prosecuted, was fairly typical of many or all societies, certainly all Western societies.[7] The peak age for proven offending by males was 18, and by females 16. The percentage of male offenders in the group aged 10 was below 1 per cent. For the 18-year-old males it was about 7 per cent. For 25-year-olds it was about 4 per cent, for 30-year-olds about 2 per cent, and for 40-year-olds about 1 per cent. In the United States, to consider only murder, 18- to 24-year-old males have traditionally had the highest offending rates. From 1975 to 2000, there were in that age group of 18- to 24-year-olds about 25 to 40 convicted murderers per 100,000 of the population. For 25- to 34-year-olds, there were about 10 to 30 per 100,000 population. For 35- to 49-year-olds there were about 5 to 10.[8]

What is to be said of these sets of statistics? Well, we do have the mentioned problem, with the American recidivism statistics, that it is not obvious what to say about the fact that about two-thirds of prisoners, only about two-thirds, reoffend again in three years. A deterrence theorist can point out that this is a lot better than *all* of the prisoners reoffending – better by hundreds of thousands or a few million offences. But, as already indicated, the figures have also been taken by others as proof of the failure of the attempt to deter by punishment.

As for the general fact of numbers of offenders reducing with age, it can truly be said, of course, that implicit in it is that *very* large numbers of individuals do not come back to the attention of the courts after either having been punished or having been made particularly aware of the prospect – offically warned by policemen or other officials. Several other propositions or speculations, however, are consistent with this truth about one thing coming after another.

The figures are for those found guilty or warned, not for all men and boys who actually committed indictable offences. It might be said that the figures are consistent with the supposition that many offenders, as they grow older, continue to break the law but avoid apprehension or conviction. One reply to this is that while older individuals may be more capable of avoiding apprehension and conviction, those who are younger are often not charged or officially warned at all, but dealt with in other ways.

Certainly the figures do not establish what proportion of offenders become law-abiding as they grow older *because* of the experience of punishment, or of having been made particularly aware of the possibility. The figures are consistent with the supposition that a large proportion of young offenders become law-abiding adults because of something else having nothing to do with punishment. That we *grow up*, of course, is a fact of life as large as any. Is there a process of maturation that leads to law-abiding behaviour and would do so as effectively without punishment or a heightened awareness of it? We lack statistics, I take it, on boys who break the law but are never convicted or warned. What is *their* later behaviour?

If we stick with the statistics we have, our response to them must depend on the conviction that is carried by alternative explanations of them. The explanations open to the prevention theorist, the propositions about punishment deterring to some sufficient extent, are not obvious losers from the beginning. The boys in question, he may say, are by their experiences made more fearful of or averse to punishment, or more prudent. They get to hear of prison rape, want things like cars, like having a job and a place in the world, hope for careers, get a girlfriend, and so on.

It has long been replied that such explanations, or some of them, involve a fallacious assumption, 'that we are rational beings, who make a careful calculation of possible gains and losses before deciding upon our actions'. It is fallaciously assumed, 'in the Benthamite phrase, . . . that we always act in accordance with our own "enlightened self-interest" '.[9] On the contrary, it is said, individuals do not approach the law as such rational calculators. Some commit offences for the excitement, and it is not a surprising fact given the quality of their lives. Many others, in varying ways antisocial, abnormal, retarded, mentally ill or disabled, or mad, are equally far from any prudential consideration of possible consequences of their actions. Only one-third of discovered murderers are sentenced as mentally normal, it may be said, and of these a large number act in conditions or situations where 'rationality' is anything but likely.

Finally, it may be added, it is a truism that people do not choose between possible courses of action in a prudential way if the possible consequences of one course are distant in time and the consequences of the other immediate. A penalty is a distant possibility while the gain from an offence is usually immediate. Also there is a larger truth that many offences have a low probability of detection and conviction, and thus that the extent of the deterrence is much smaller than it would otherwise be.

All this is confusion if intended, as it sometimes seems to be, as a reply to all the explanations of the prevention theorist. He can admit without reluctance that some or indeed many of those who commit offences are for one reason or another not influenced by the possibility of punishment. That leaves many who are. Also, it certainly does not follow that those who do obey the law are not deterred by the punishment of others. It can hardly be claimed that the possibility of punishment must be as uninfluential in the consciousness of many who obey the law as it is, in different ways and degrees, in the conduct of the minority who do not. The fact that non-rational factors govern the behaviour of some individuals is not good evidence that they govern the behaviour of all or many others. It is open to the deterrence theorist to remark that if a decent or tolerable practical means of dealing with a problem required overwhelming success, there would be few or no decent or tolerable means of dealing with problems.

To revert to thinking about a process of maturation in place of deterrence by punishment, this is similarly unhelpful. Doubtless, something of this sort does occur, but would it occur as it does in the absence of punishment? Would it have the supposed consequence, obedience to law out of fear or prudence, in the absence of an institution of punishment? In the absence of an adequate and wholly independent alternative explanation, it is difficult to resist the belief that many young offenders are affected by their experience. It is also difficult to resist the belief that individuals who never offend are influenced in a related way. They watch television. I myself am certainly inclined to such propositions about deterrence. They require qualification, however, as we know. As they stand, they are too general.

As implied earlier, the argument would be improved if a positive correlation could be shown between youthful lawbreaking, without apprehension, and more lawbreaking later. One should not expect, given the deterrence supposition, a strikingly high correlation. The supposition is in part that the practice of punishment has a deterring effect on individuals other than those convicted of offences. It is reasonable to suppose that this effect is also a function of such things already mentioned as expectations, obligations and settled wants, which increase in strength and number during early life. None the less, one would expect some correlation of the kind mentioned – more lawbreaking by the unapprehended and unpunished.

There are bits of evidence of a different kind for deterrence. In Iraq, after the second attack on it and the occupation of it by American and British forces, there apparently was some increase in ordinary crime as distinct from resistance to the invaders and those Iraqis who collaborated with them. Some of it was the robbing of museums, some of it kidnapping for ransom. This increase, it was said, was the result of no effective police force and no threat of punishment. There have been other such historical episodes, one often cited.

> A unique opportunity for making an evaluation of the deterrent approach to crime was presented by Danish experience during the war. In 1944, the German occupying forces deported the Danish police, and for some time the country had only a local guard force invested with police authority. There followed an immense rise in the number of robberies, thefts, frauds, etc., but no comparable increase in murder or sexual crimes. While this experience does show that crime is reduced very considerably by the prospect of detection and presumably punishment, it suggests that deterrent methods are of less value in reducing the incidence of those crimes in which strong passions or deep psychological problems are involved.[10]

One can raise questions about both the Iraqi and the Danish cases, which are of behaviour in an abnormal situation, the occupation of a country in wartime, not merely the absence of a police force. One might also resist any implication that it is only rarely that robberies, thefts, frauds, and other 'ordinary' offences are the product of 'strong passions or deep psychological problems'. None the less, there presumably is *some* support to be had here for the contention that the prospect of punishment has a considerable deterrent effect with respect to many offences. That it does not have this effect with respect to other offences, as already allowed, is a probability as well supported by general beliefs of a more or less sensible and empirical kind.

We have so far looked at the institution of punishment's prevention of offences by way of incapacitation, deterrence of persons punished, and deterrence of persons not punished. One other way has been remarked on by prevention theorists. It is said that many people who do in fact commit certain offences are restrained from more serious offences because of the greater possible penalties. That is, as always with deterrence, they have in mind and approach certain possibilities, and then retreat from them, in this case to lesser offences. This is out of fear or aversion or some other such feeling with respect to possible or probable punishment, or else a prudential judgement or calculation, in fact an exercise of rationality in a fundamental sense. This is the rationality that consists in choosing only effective and economical means to your end.

No doubt it would be worthwhile looking into whatever statistical evidence exists. It has long been said that some or many burglars and robbers go about their business unarmed, or at any rate without a gun, to avoid the possibility of committing murder and being severely punished or even executed for it. This fourth possible way of prevention, although worth some attention, is in fact implicit in the previous two about prevention. Let us turn to a larger matter.

It is in general true, I think, and invariably so in my experience, that consideration and discussion of the preventive effect of the institution of punishment is limited to the propositions we have now considered – incapacitation, two kinds of deterrence, and deterrence from greater as against lesser offences in particular. Do we need to add something important, having to do with a way of prevention as important as any so far considered?

It concerns a very large class of people, seemingly the largest class of people relevant to our considerations. These are people who live their lives without seriously considering serious infractions of the criminal law. They are not the class of individuals noted earlier, those who mature in the sense that out of fear or prudence they do not offend when they seriously think of doing so. The people now in question do not ever in any serious way think of, contemplate, consider or start to plan a serious criminal offence. Of course a good deal of philosophical and psychological effort might be put into further distinguishing this class of people from, and comparing it with, the class of people who *do* seriously consider serious offences – and therefore in contrast are candidates for deterrence by punishment. But the distinction between people who do not and people who do seriously think of breaking the criminal law seriously is good enough for our purposes.

Turn your attention now, as briefly, to a related and larger subject. What are the elements in an adequate explanation of what happens in societies like ours, the course of life as we know it, and particularly the consciousness of individuals with respect to ranges of possible behaviour, things that they might do? You may mention the explanatory elements that are education, kinds of family life, kinds of government, economic organization, profit seeking, public ignorance and information, possibly religion. Your additions to the list of explanatory elements, to my mind, could not possibly leave out something else – the *law* of the society, and in particular criminal law and punishment.

Nothing of interest, let alone a large fact of behaviour, has a single or simple explanation. Nothing is owed to another single thing in any ordinary sense. All things are owed to *causal circumstances* that have in them various different conditions, perhaps one of them spoken of as *the cause* despite that all the conditions are necessary to the effect and in other fundamental ways alike.[11] This is the case, certainly, with respect to something we are now considering, which can have the name of being *unreflective law-abidingness*. To come to the main proposition, it is inconceivable that the institution of punishment, in itself and in what goes with it, which includes some of customary morality, does not play a major or large role in explaining the existence of unreflective law-abidingness. In the causal circumstance for law-abidingness, punishment has great weight. So punishment prevents offences in a further way, different from incapacitation and the two kinds of deterrence.

Let me not labour the point, or begin to try to clarify and elaborate a proposition that is the business of a line of life other than the philosophical one. It presumably turns up in the subject of social psychology. What needs to be added is only a reminder of the size of the effect of unreflective law-abidingness. Return to a sample of statistics, the sample having to do with ages of offenders. The percentage of British 18-year-olds who were *not* known offenders was 93 per cent. The percentage of 30-year-olds was 98 per cent. I take it that these immense majorities included a very large number of unreflective law-abiders. What we have then is the proposition that punishment can be regarded as having a further preventive effect, a very large one.

To be a little more verdictive, let me say that it seems entirely mistaken to minimize the preventive effects of punishment other than incapacitation. It is entirely mistaken to suppose that the possible justifications of punishment are in terms of incapacitation and retribution. It seems possible to speculate about this current habit in a certain way. What comes to mind is that it would be difficult to make this mistake except in the grips of some desire, or out of some distorting commitment or ideological or other cause. Might such a desire, commitment or cause have to do with the retribution theory and its satisfactions? And with a desire for more of them? Might advocates of retribution want to leave the field more to their own policy in order, so to speak, to have more of it?

There is one other very general point. We have been contemplating the question of whether or to what extent punishment *reduces the number of offences*. There is another question, seemingly not hard to answer, that of whether punishment has a larger effect, which effect is nothing less than *the existence of law in a society*. What is law in this sense? It is not request, instruction, exhortation, or even demand. It is not moral law either, or moral convention, or only social conventions. Whatever else the law of a society may be, it is the threat of punishment. Law as we have it is something in which sanctions are integral. There is no law of this kind without the measures of coercion essential and fundamental to it. In brief, punishment is necessary to law, indeed a thing that is constitutive with respect to it.

This large fact, different from the nostrum that the law will not be respected in the absence of punishment, needs consideration. It needs somehow to be added to prevention theories of punishment. It is at least more naturally added to them than to other theories of punishment. The whole subject is no easy one, however. It is plainly not the case that *any* body of law is better than none. There is no need to imagine horrific bodies of law in horrific societies. The historical record, including the recent historical record, contains examples. We will be coming back to the matter of *what* law a society may keep in existence by punishment – and, indeed, the prior question of *what* offences are to be prevented by punishment.

A little more will be said of relevance to the main idea that we have been considering, that punishment does prevent offences in the various ways. Theories of punishment in terms of rehabilitation and reform have to do with prevention by other means. My inclination, in which I shall persist, is that there are adequate grounds for supposing that the practice of punishment does sufficiently reduce offences in the ways we have been considering, a large group of offences if not all of them. To say that it sufficiently reduces offences is to say at least this, that it reduces them enough to make further inquiry into the prevention theory of punishment reasonable.[12]

THE UTILITARIAN PREVENTION THEORY

In effect, what we have been considering so far, despite the attention given to Jeremy Bentham, has been prevention theories in general. What has been said pertains to *any* prevention theory that is likely to come to mind. But what we proceed with now is one prevention theory in particular, the utilitarian one, and also theories related to it that are much less explicit and much more common. The latter theories are of more practical importance, indeed of some large importance, in the running of our societies. But it will be useful to conduct our inquiry in terms of the utilitarian theory. Given its clarity, we will know where we are.

Redescribed, the utilitarian prevention theory is that punishment is right or justified when probably it will issue in a certain consequence. Right punishment is an instance of what is right in general, which has to do with amounts of happiness, fulfilment, anxiety, deprivation, misery, suffering – the states of experience that can be summed up as satisfaction and dissatisfaction. Our general moral principle, according to utilitarianism, is to be as follows.

> What is right in general is the action, activity, policy, practice, institution, kind of society or whatever which when compared with other possibilities is the one that probably will result in *the greatest total balance of all kinds of satisfaction* – on the assumption that all the possibilities result in both satisfaction and dissatisfaction, the greatest balance of satisfaction over dissatisfaction or the least balance of dissatisfaction over satisfaction.

Punishment is right, in accordance with this principle of utilitarianism, when it so prevents offences as to make probable the greatest total of all kinds of satisfaction. To say this is to provide the reminder that utilitarianism, for a start, may not justify all of our punishments in our societies.

This doctrine of punishment and the greatest happiness principle of rightness are not greatly in favour in contemporary moral and political philosophy. This has something to do with utilitarianism's recent philosophical gravediggers, even if they have not dug nearly so well as some of their predecessors.[13] But in a way utilitarianism is not at all abandoned. It has survived elsewhere than in moral and political philosophy, survived on the large stage of ordinary reflective life and in social policy and politics. A lot of utterance by politicians and planners, not to mention civil servants, administrators, economists and doctors, is close enough to the principle of utilitarianism.

What are in favour are doctrines of the public good or the public interest or the general well-being or the good of the community. Institutions and practices are commonly defended as serving these things. These ends are more vague than the utilitarian one, but not so vague as in the case of the political tradition of liberalism – which will get some attention in a later stage of this inquiry. The doctrines, if they are not free from political and other pressure, distortion and contrivance, and run the danger of being watered down into a defence of the status quo, are like utilitarianism in being directed, at any rate more or less directed, to increasing what can vaguely be called well-being, indeed to maximizing it.

We can consider them more effectively by considering what remains their exemplar. Utilitarianism throws light on them. It is clear, wonderfully clear by certain comparisons, and so enables us to look into certain questions efficiently, one in particular. To which can be added another thing. Utilitarianism serves as a good introduction to something better, a different theory to which we shall come eventually.

That punishment cannot be justified by prevention serving the utilitarian end is the conclusion of a number of moral rather than factual arguments, to the effect that punishment governed only by the intention to deter will be unfair, unjust, inhuman, or the like. Despite its notoriety, some say, the retribution theory is superior in this way or ways. In the past, some of this criticism has derived from taking into consideration a parody of the utilitarian prevention theory. It has been derived from supposing that what is being claimed by Bentham, John Stuart Mill and their successors is that *any* punishment is justified if it serves to keep the offender and possibly others from committing offences in the future. It was said that this is the prevention principle per se, and that if we acted only on it we would be perfectly justified in attaching savage penalties to certain minor offences if such penalties were required in order to prevent potential offenders from offending.

It was remarked, for example, that the principle would justify flogging a man for a parking offence, since flogging would certainly have the effect of deterring him and others from parking their cars in the wrong places.[14] It is patently true that such repugnant consequences follow from the simple principle that *any* punishment is justified if it prevents offences. No one would regard this as a defensible principle, however, and it would be absurd to suppose that Bentham, for example, puts it forward. The idea that it can be correctly described as the prevention principle per se need not detain us.

Bentham's view, whether or not it is open to a related objection, is not so simple. It is, partly, that a penalty may be justified only when the distress it causes to the offender and others stands in an acceptable comparison to the distress that would result if he and others were not prevented from offending in the future. Punishment is an 'evil' because it causes pain both to those who suffer it and to others, and also because it limits the freedom of those who obey the law because of it. Offences, obviously, are an evil to the victims. Both evils, that of the punishment and that of the kind of offence in question, must always be considered. 'If the evil of the punishment exceed the evil of the offence, the punishment will be unprofitable: the legislator will have produced more suffering than he has prevented; he will have purchased exemption from one evil at the expense of another.'[15]

We then have it that punishing a man is justified if it is preventive and if the resulting total balance of satisfaction is greater than that which would result if he were not punished. One addition is desirable, and in fact obvious. It may be true that any of a number of possible punishments would deter and in so doing cause less distress than would otherwise occur. If this is the case, of course, only that particular punishment is justified that causes the least distress.

We thus have a principle of punishment.

A man's punishment for an offence is morally justified if (1) it does indeed reduce offences, (2) despite causing dissatisfaction to the offender, it gives rise to a greater total balance of all kinds of satisfaction than would occur as a result of offences if it were not imposed, and (3) there is no other punishment that would prevent the offences as effectively at a cost of less distress.

Punishments that satisfy these conditions are spoken of as those that prevent offences *economically*. The usage, of course, does not have to do with the economics, in the sense of financial cost and profit, of punishments. It has to do, rather, with cost and profit in terms of satisfaction, what can as well be called well-being and was first called happiness.

It may be of use to reiterate, in anticipation of later arguments, that punishments may fail to satisfy the given conditions in several ways. If they may cause too much distress to the offender, they may also cause too much to persons other than the offender who are affected by the fact of his punishment. The connection, as we shall see, may be very indirect. It is also to be noticed that the conditions have other consequences. Penalties must be sufficiently severe to prevent offences effectively. They may have to be more severe than what is said to be deserved. It has sometimes been true that offenders regarded penalties for their offences as like licences – an unavoidable feature of conduct of a certain kind and not so undesirable as to be a preventative. Such penalties, on the view we are considering, have no justification.

Something else is worth noting about the utilitarian theory. It has a clear recommendation that may be lacked by other prevention theories, and perhaps by some theories that justify punishment by prevention along with something else. The recommendation is that it does not leave it uncertain what reduction in offences is sufficient to justify punishment – to what extent punishment must prevent offences for it to be justified. The utilitarian answer is given by part (2) of the theory. A justified punishment, to put it one way, must be likely to prevent more distress than would occur without it.

THE VICTIMIZATION OBJECTION

Of the pertinent criticisms of the utilitarian prevention view, a resonant but vague one owed to Kant is often given pride of place. It can also be used against the related doctrines of the public good. It is that to punish a man simply because this will deter him and others from offences in the future is to treat him, as Kant is renowned for saying, only as a means and not as an end. This might be taken to refer to several supposed moral errors and it is important to distinguish them.

To treat all men as ends and not merely as means may be to take into account, in any particular situation, the personal welfare of each and every individual involved. We should, that is, consider the interests of each individual affected by a different possible course of action before coming to any decision. Count everybody. Under this interpretation of the rule that all men are to be treated as ends, it is at least arguable that the prevention theory observes it. According to the theory, certainly, the degree of suffering caused to the offender is indubitably relevant to the question of whether or not his punishment is justified. No one's interests are put aside, not considered.

What may be intended, however, by a critic who employs Kant's rule, is that the prevention theory does not give *enough* attention to the interests of the offender. Such a claim has sometimes been advanced, in particular, by some of those who argue for a justification of punishment in terms of a supposed reformative function. They suppose that punishment protects the interests of others by reducing the number of offences, and serves the interests of the offender by reforming him. Punishment is not justified simply by the prevention of offences. We are not yet in a position to assess the claim about means and ends when so interpreted. It amounts to a version of the reform or rehabilitation theory.

Sometimes, thirdly, the rule about treating men as ends is at least partly intended to convey the injunction that men are to be treated as free and responsible moral agents, which they are supposed to be. What is recommended here is a general attitude, difficult to encapsulate, that takes as supremely important the supposed fact that men make free decisions for which they are accountable and which place limits of a certain nature on our treatment of them. This attitude is taken to issue naturally in support for the retribution theory of punishment and in particular criticisms of the prevention theory. These and other criticisms will now be made clearer and considered in more detail. There is little to be gained by retaining Kant's terminology.

The criticisms attempt to display the utilitarian prevention theory, even in its reasonable form, as having entirely unacceptable consequences. Unusual and well-worn cases are produced where punishments that may seem *unjustified*, given our ordinary moral convictions, appear to be justified by the principle of economical prevention.

We have been asked to suppose, often, that on a particular occasion a judge knows or reasonable believes that the man before him is actually innocent of the offence with which he has been charged. He knows too that there is no possibility of apprehending the actual offender. Finally, he knows that the offence that has been committed will be followed by others of the same kind unless the potential offenders are deterred – unless, that is, someone thought to be guilty is punished for the offence that has been committed.

Given all this, we are invited to conclude that the judge would be justified by the stated principle in pretending or assuming that the man before him was the actual offender and imposing a penalty on him. Why not punish him? This would, we suppose, have the effect of preventing other offences, which would involve more distress than that caused to the innocent man by his punishment. This effect would follow from the belief on the part of others that justice had been done. That the man was not really guilty would be irrelevant to this fact.[16]

In short, if one maintains that punishment is justified by utilitarian prevention alone one seems committed to the immorality of punishing the innocent. It seems that one is committed to denying the rule that only the guilty may be punished. Surely, then, the prevention theory is unacceptable.

This traditional and stark counter-example of the lying or assuming judge can of course be replaced by more realistic ones. We can think of a judge who succeeds in acting honestly and within the law, but according to a law that opens the way to punishing the innocent. We can also think of a government that holds men without trial for three years, justifying this by declarations of uncertain content, but seeming to consist in exactly the argument of a need for economical prevention. I refer to the United Kingdom and the New Labour government of Blair and Brown, and its grim treatment of merely suspected terrorists or terrorist supporters or terrorist sympathizers in Belmarsh Prison up to at least 2005. This New Labour government's activities, of course described by it in terms of moral necessity and plain realism and the like as well as something like economical prevention, happened to be condemned by the highest bench of English judges on the day this sentence was written.[17] They regained a little of the lost authority of English law.

But let us proceed in terms of the traditional argument, which raises the same problem. In persisting with the traditional argument, we are less likely to be distracted by irrelevancies or unduly influenced by ideology or mere politicians. The traditional utilitarian rejoinder to the traditional criticism was that imposing a penalty on an innocent man, first appearances to the contrary, would not result in economical prevention. We shall consider this, but let us first look at two other attempts to dismiss the criticism summarily.

The first, made by the stout and graceful philosopher Lord Quinton, amounts to the reminder that the prevention principle of punishment is about punishment and that it attempts to justify this and nothing else.[18] That is, the principle is about an authority's infliction of distress on someone found by a certain process to be an offender. The principle, it is said, simply does not apply to the case imagined, where a man known to be or believed to be wholly innocent is made to suffer. Since the man is not thought to be an offender by the judge it is quite mistaken to suppose that this is a case of punishment.

In calling it such, we have been forgetful of the definition of punishment given above in the first chapter, one of a kind stipulated by defenders of the prevention theory. We might better say, although the term may have some misleading connotations, that the imagined case is one of *victimization*. The prevention principle has nothing to say about victimization. It is not the principle that imposing a penalty on *anyone*, if it prevents offences economically, is justified. It is that punishment, the imposing of a penalty on a man who has been found to be an offender, is justified if it prevents offences economically.

This forceful reply has been thought inadequate by a number of philosophers, although they have not done much to despatch it. We are told, for example, that the given reply prevents us from considering the question of whether the prevention theory does justify the imprisonment of innocent men. So it does, and for a given reason that must be considered. It is true that the prevention principle as ordinarily expressed does not appear to commit one to sending innocent men to prison when this would serve the end of prevention. This seems odd. One expects that it is at least a possibility, if no more, that the prevention theory has such a consequence. Can it be that the contrary seems true only because the view has been expressed in a particular way? That this is so can be shown.

According to the theory, punishment is justified by the fact that it prevents offences economically *and for no other reason*. The anticipated result, a state of affairs involving fewer offences, secured at a certain cost of distress, is by itself a sufficient justification. It is not the case that the means to this end, punishment by itself, has any separate and additional justification. The contrary is explicitly said to be true by the utilitarian defenders of the theory, for the simple reason that punishment consists in the causing of distress to offenders. Punishment is valuable only as a means to a desirable end. If one keeps these facts in mind, it becomes apparent that the following formulation, 'Punishment is justified when it deters economically', is misleading as a formulation of the utilitarian prevention theory. By referring only to punishment, which necessarily is of people found to be offenders, it implies a falsehood.

That falsehood is that this prevention theory taken by itself has some feature such that its holders could not possibly be committed to acts of victimization. There is no such feature. All that is relevantly impossible is that they are committed to acts or practices that do not serve as economical deterrents. The theory can be formulated in a way that overtly excludes this false implication. For all that has been said so far, there can be no objection to expressing it in the following more general way: 'A society's practices or actions in dealing with criminal behaviour are justified if they deter economically.' So expressed, it is at least a possibility that acceptance of the view commits one to victimization in certain circumstances. If it can be established that certain victimizations would be preventive, and if we accept that such preventions are not morally justified, the conclusion follows that the view that sanctions them is unacceptable.

This argument may give rise to an uneasiness, one which can be dispelled. It may be thought that there is an arbitrariness about the reformulation of the prevention theory. Might it not be defensible for a proponent of the theory simply to persist in his own formulation, that *punishment* is justified only by the consideration that it prevents offences economically? This and only this, he says, is what he means.

He may do this, but without gain. His intention is to give a justification of punishment but evidently he is bringing to light only part of what he counts as its justification. It is impossible to avoid the conclusion that he takes punishments as justified not only because they prevent offences but also for some other reason having to do with the fact that those who suffer them have in fact been found to have committed offences. If this were not the case, then certain victimizations too would be acceptable to him. It must be that he refuses to defend them because they lack a feature had by punishments. He has implicitly abandoned a utilitarian prevention account for something else. He can *either* take up a compromise view of the justification of punishment, one that includes some requirement having to do with guilt or whatever, and so avoid accepting the possibility of certain justified victimizations, *or* he can take up the utilitarian prevention view and accept the possibility of such consequences. Our present concern is with the latter view.

Let us now consider a second attempt to deal summarily with the speculations about victimization to which the critic of the prevention theory has recourse. One cannot but feel a certain suspicion, touched on already, about the producing of cases where it is claimed that judges, according to the theory, would be committed to secret acts of victimization. The suspicion, misidentified, may issue in the comment that if we are to keep in touch with social realities, something better must be found by way of criticism. What might better be offered, it may be suggested, are descriptions of social practices that might actually be established in the usual way.

John Rawls thus asks a question. Might we have 'an institution . . . which is such that the officials set up by it have authority to arrange a trial for the condemnation of an innocent man whenever they are of the opinion that doing so would be in the best interests of society'?[19] The officials might be judges of the higher courts together with police authorities, the minister of justice, and members of the legislature. But, we are told by Rawls, when we consider the possibility of such an institution, which would be established by law and a matter of public knowledge, we see that it would involve very great dangers. There would be the possibility of abuse of power and the creation of a general insecurity among members of the society. It cannot seriously be supposed that someone who defends punishment by the argument that it is an economical deterrent would be committed to the institution we have imagined. It is entirely too likely that the losses would exceed the gains.

Rawls asked and answered his question before the terrorism of 11 September 2001 and afterwards. Thus he did his thinking before an advance by the New Labour government in Britain. It was certainly the case that Britain then had a practice, perhaps as well called an institution, such that the officials set up by it had the authority to arrange that *no* trial be allowed to a possibly innocent man for three years and that he be driven mad by a kind of imprisonment.[20] The officials were indeed the judges of higher courts together with police authorities, the minister of justice, and members of the legislature. It was unclear what response would be made by the government in question to condemnation by Britain's highest court already mentioned, belated condemnation owed importantly to public feeling. The government was not subject to the court in the way that the American government is subject to the Supreme Court.

Still, we need not complicate matters by this sort of thing in order to proceed with the traditional objection to the prevention theory. That objection does not involve, or need to involve, the specification of some social institution different from punishment. There is no reason why the objection should proceed by specifying some possible publicly known practice and by arguing that such a practice would have a justification given the prevention theory. All that is required is that the objection isolate some possible action and relate it to the prevention theory. The logic of the argument does not even require that the action in question be one by an officer or officers of a society.

We are told by the prevention theorist that the one and only, and a sufficient, justification of punishment is that it prevents offences economically. There are no other justifying features. If so, any action or practice that does deter economically must be morally acceptable. If it is not, then a question arises about the claim that punishment is justified *solely* in virtue of being preventive in the given way. The simplicity of the objection reflects the simplicity of the theory. What I am maintaining, then, is that in criticizing the prevention theory one is in a way free to choose one's counter-examples. One need not initially meet any demand but that they be examples involving victimizations which might be of an economical kind. *Reductio ad absurdum* arguments are not essays in social theory.

Certainly this is but the first step of the argument. One must go on to establish that in the examples in question it *would* be true that victimization would, so to speak, prevent more distress than would otherwise occur. The traditional position of those who hold the utilitarian prevention theory, to which we now turn, is that this cannot be shown. The suspicion one does feel about the cases in question is that in the end the suggested victimizations would not be economical. This suspicion, we are told, is not merely reasonable but very well founded.

UTILITARIANS ON VICTIMIZATION

We have on the one hand defenders of the utilitarian theory, who have maintained that it does not in fact ever issue in victimization. They almost all agree, however, that victimization would never or nearly never be morally acceptable. The same is true of defenders of the less clear doctrines of the public good. We have on the other hand the critics, mainly retributivist critics, who maintain that the theory does or would in certain circumstances justify victimization. They declare, of course, that victimization is not and would not ever be morally acceptable. Their reason for the latter belief, whether or not it is the right reason, has traditionally been that victimizing a man is treating him in a way that he does not deserve. Are both defenders and these critics in error – defenders with respect to both of their propositions, critics in supposing that it is absolutely impossible that a victimization should be morally justified and in their general ground of opposition to victimization?

Our practice of punishment, as we know, is taken to be governed by certain rules, such as the rule that those found guilty but not the innocent are to be penalized or may be penalized. Other rules are to the effect that offenders of greater culpability are to receive greater penalties. Grievous assault carries a heavier penalty than petty theft, injury that is fully intentional a heavier penalty than inadvertent injury. For the retributivist, as we have seen in some detail, the point of these rules about harm and responsibility is that they secure that men are treated as they deserve. The rules are taken to comprise a penalty system of the kind whose construction was sketched in the last chapter. To the traditional prevention theorist their point is quite otherwise. They are rules whose observance secures that we prevent offences economically. To depart from them, in one direction, is to engage in what we have been calling victimization. Victimization, according to the argument, is never justified by the prevention theory because it is never economically preventive of offences.

Let us look at the details. With respect to the general rule about punishing only the guilty, those who have somehow freely offended, one insufficient claim has its origin in the truth that if we are to prevent offences by punishment we must direct our efforts toward the right individuals, those likely to offend in the future. One kind of evidence that a man is likely to break the law in the future, in general the best evidence, is that he has done so already – of course freely, somehow of his own nature. To act on this evidence in picking out potential offenders is to obey the rule about punishing only those found guilty. It may also be added that it is by punishing those we believe to have already performed certain actions that we affirm or reaffirm to others what actions are offences and thus to be avoided. These considerations may serve to give an explanation of why in many cases we should abide by the rule in question. But let us return to the first case of possible victimization mentioned above.

Here, a judge reasonably believes that victimizing an innocent man is necessary if other individuals are to be prevented from offending. We assume he has good grounds for thinking they will commit the offence in question, perhaps one of racial hatred, perhaps race murder, unless prevented. Admittedly, there may be no good evidence that the defendant needs deterring or the like, but that cannot settle the question. A standard rejoinder by the prevention theorist is that such an act of victimization is unlikely to have good results on the whole, despite the possibility or even the certainty that sentencing the man might in the short term deter a number of potential offenders.

Sentencing the man would be to take an exceedingly dangerous step, one whose distant consequences are all too unpredictable. It might happen that one victimization would lead to others, and it might become known that innocent men were being punished for offences committed by men never apprehended. It might then be supposed that actual offenders escaped punishment with considerable regularity. One upshot would be that potential offenders of all kinds would cease to be prevented from offending to the same extent as before by the possibility of punishment. A man is certainly the less deterred the less certain it seems that he will be punished for an offence.

Another result, one of several, might be that the law would be brought into disrespect. This claim, never long forgotten in this context by defenders of prevention, is in part that people respect the law because they believe it deals somehow fairly with individuals. This respect would be lessened by a belief in the existence of victimizations. Who can say what the consequences of such a lesser respect for the law might be? All these are no more than speculations, certainly. But who, we are asked, could be reasonably certain that developments of this sort would not follow from the judge's action in breaking the rule that only the guilty are to be punished? If one could not be reasonably certain, one could not accept that such an action would in the end make for economical prevention. This is little more than a sketch for an argument, obviously. The processes by which victimization might issue in the supposed consequences would be complex.

Let us suspend judgement for a time and consider something else. Penalizing the wholly innocent is but one possible kind of victimization. Other kinds involve infractions of the other rules of punishment. These can be divided, artificially, into two groups. There are the rules that preserve heavier penalties for offences involving greater harms, for example, grievous assault against petty theft. Here, the prevention theorist explains, economy is obviously the justification and infractions of the rules would be uneconomical and hence not justified by his theory. The other rules, which may be roughly described as having to do with the responsibility of agents, have been divided into three kinds.[21]

There are those, first, that allow that in certain circumstances a man is justified in a kind of action that in other circumstances would be criminal, and so is not to be punished at all. Killing in self-defence is sometimes an example. Secondly, there are rules that specify that a man is to be excused in certain circumstances and not punished at all – he may be excused if his action was in some way quite involuntary or unintentional. Finally, there are rules, also having to do with responsibility, specifying that a man's punishment is to be mitigated under certain circumstances. If he can establish, for example, that he was subjected to extreme provocation, he may receive a lesser penalty. In choosing the particular penalty from the range fixed by statute for offences of the kind in question, a judge is to take into account provocation.

The explanation and justification of these three kinds of rules, according to the prevention theorist, is also that observing them serves the end of economical prevention. That is what they are about. Their explanation and justification has nothing to do with desert or anything else. Breaking the rules, he says, would not be sanctioned by his theory, for various reasons.

A man who injures another only in self-defence on one occasion gives no evidence that he is likely to injure others again unless he must do so to defend himself. He is no more a danger to the community than most other men. If it does happen that he is attacked again, then he will be justified in defending himself – we do not take the view that he should be deterred from doing so. The same is true of anyone else who is attacked. Thus there would be no point whatever, on the prevention view, in punishing the man on this occasion. In general, to follow rules of justification is to act in accordance with the principle of prevention. Somewhat similar considerations apply to actions covered by rules of excuse. A man who injures another by an entirely unlikely accident gives no indication of being a generally dangerous character. He did not choose to do the thing. Nor would punishment on this occasion prevent either him or others, obviously, from causing accidental injuries in the future.

There is no point in punishment, given the prevention view, where rules of excuse apply.

As for the rule of mitigation having to do with provocation, a man who retaliates only under extreme provocation is unlikely to offend again, since extreme provocations are few. There is some possibility, nevertheless, that he will be provoked in the same way again. What is required to make it likely that he will resist this future provocation, if it occurs, is no more than a lighter penalty on the present occasion. We suppose, that is, that a man who has resisted a good deal of provocation before succumbing on the first occasion will need only a slight additional motive derived from a relatively mild punishment in order to resist a bit more in the future. Thus there is no need for a heavier penalty on the first occasion – it would be wrong to impose it since it would cause more distress than is necessary.

One can present much the same argument, such as it is, with respect to other potential offenders, who must also be considered. One supposes that they are unlikely to be subjected to such a provocation. In general, the danger is small. If they are so provoked, one supposes that they will be deterred from giving in if they have been influenced by no more than the example of a relatively mild punishment. If we are to deter economically, then, we must not victimize by breaking rules of extenuation.

Such considerations go some way to showing that abiding by rules of the three kinds is in accord with the utilitarian prevention theory. Nevertheless, they have a general and considerable weakness.[22] Consider the argument that observing a rule about provocation is a necessity if we are to prevent offences economically. It hangs together, or appears to, only because certain of the future possibilities and not others are considered. This can be brought out by way of an example.

Brown injures a neighbour who has provoked him by kicking his dog. Brown's penalty is reduced, according to the prevention argument, partly because there is little danger of his offending again. People are unlikely, we suppose, to be kicking his dog very often, or to be doing things that are similarly provocative. We suppose, furthermore, that Brown will not need very much by way of a new motive to keep him from repeating his offence if the same sort of occasion arises again. Looking to other possible offenders, they are unlikely to be provoked to the same extent in the future, since such provocations are relatively rare. If they are so provoked, they will not succumb to the provocation if they know Brown has been lightly penalized – if, that is, they are as self-controlled as Brown.

But what if we look to other possibilities in the future? What if Brown's flowers are trampled? Perhaps he would resist the tempta-tion to retaliate by inflicting a serious injury if in the past he had been given a heavier rather than a lighter penalty for injuring some-one who kicked his dog. What of other potential offenders who are not as self-controlled as Brown? Suppose one of them was to see his dog being kicked or was provoked to about the same extent. Perhaps he would retaliate even if he knew Brown had been given a relatively light penalty but would not do so if he knew Brown had been given a heavier one.

When we consider such possibilities, and there is no reason for ignoring them, it is not at all clear that sticking to the rule of mitigation in question is called for by considerations of economical prevention. Indeed, it seems that the principle in question might demand infractions of the rule. It is equally arguable that if preven-tion is our only guide we might be committed to breaking rules of excuse, to punishing a man who injured another by accident. Our severity might well have the effect of preventing possible offences in the future. It might serve to prevent intentional offences and to make avoidable accidents more rare. Something of the same sort may be argued in connection with some offences covered by rules of justification.

Are there effective rejoinders to argument of this kind? In the case of the first imagined rule infraction, that of penalizing a wholly innocent man, it was open to the defenders of the prevention view to argue that such a victimization might in the long run issue in more rather than fewer offences. Our present cases are different. We suppose, for example, that a judge believes on good grounds that potential offenders will be prevented from offending only if he makes a striking example of a man, which involves breaking the rule about mitigation. Here it is not so open to holders of the prevention view to suggest that the outcome, in the long term, may be more rather than fewer offences. We cannot readily suppose that if the judge's action becomes known, potential offenders will be the less deterred. On the contrary, they may be more deterred by the fact of the judge's rule infraction. However, we may still worry about the possibility of disrespect for the law.

There is another argument to which the utilitarian prevention theorist can retreat. Rules of excuse and mitigation, aside from those of them having to do with certain special classes of offenders such as children, have the effect of excusing, wholly or partly, actions that are less than wholly free, voluntary, deliberate, intentional or the like. This means that to a considerable extent the possibility of a man's being penalized, or heavily penalized, depends on his some-how free actions, those over which he has some control. He thus can be reasonably confident, if he wishes to be, that his life will not be disrupted by judges. Precisely this security would be endangered if the rules of excuse in particular were sometimes suspended. The danger, although distant, would exist. It could come about that a man could no longer be reasonably confident of an undisrupted existence if his choice and intention were to obey the law. Accidents happen. It can thus be argued that while breaking the rules of excuse and mitigation might sometimes have a greater deterrent effect than keeping them, the cost in anxiety or some-thing like it which might result from breaking them would out-weigh the profit.

Such an argument, which is also relevant to our earlier case of a wholly innocent man, is open to anyone who takes up the position that punishment is justified when it prevents offences economically, although it has sometimes been suggested otherwise. It has been supposed, perhaps, that anyone who makes use of it must be appeal-ing to retributivist considerations. It has been supposed that the argument is rooted in a principle of justice or fair play. Quite obvi-ously, an argument could be presented that would begin from exactly the premise that each man should get what he deserves and proceed to the conclusion that the rules ought to be observed. But this would be quite distinct from what has been presented.[23]

Despite everything that has now been said on behalf of the pre-vention theory, it seems that in the end a certain admission is nec-essary. It is that we can at least *conceive* of a case of a very special nature where a judge or government or society would be committed by the utilitarian prevention principle to an act of victimization. It can be one involving a wholly innocent man or one involving a disregard for the rules of justice we have been discussing. Indeed, the conceivability of such a case has occasionally been allowed by prevention theorists. All that we require is an imagined case that has such peculiar features as to rule out the possibility of all the long-term dangers we have considered. In this case, for a start, there will for some reason be no possibility whatever of its becoming known that a man has been victimized.

If the conceivability of such a case has occasionally been admitted, it has also been maintained by the strong philosopher and metaphysician Timothy Sprigge that it is entirely unlikely that there will ever be an actual case that satisfies the imagined conditions. This latter fact has then been used in an attempt to escape the argument. We are told that

> ... if one considers ... fantastic situations ... one does of course consider them as a person with certain moral sentiments, the strength of which, in society as it is, is an important utilitarian good. These sentiments are offended. A utilitarian will see no point in trying to imagine oneself looking with approval on the imaginary situation, since this is likely to weaken the feelings while not serving as a preparation for any actual situation. If in fact punishing the innocent (say) always is and always will be harmful, it is likewise harmful to dwell on fanciful situations in which it would be beneficial, thus weakening one's aversion to such courses. Thus the utilitarian shares (quite consistently so) in the unease produced by these examples. Although he may admit that in such a situation punishment of the innocent would be right, he still regards favourably the distaste which is aroused at the idea of its being called right.
>
> Certainly if one imagines the world as other than it is, one may find oneself imagining a world in which utilitarianism implies moral judgements which shock our moral sentiments. But if these moral sentiments are quite appropriate to the only world there is, the real world, the utilitarian is glad that moral judgements in opposition to them seem repugnant. He sees no need for moral acrobatics relevant only to situations which in fact are quite out of the question.[24]

The objection to the prevention theory that we are considering involves three considerations that I shall state in order to comment on the quoted rejoinder. They are:

> (1) the proposition that in a certain conceivable case victimization would prevent offences economically, (2) the consequence that such a victimization would be called for and justified by the principle of economical prevention, (3) the acceptance that such a victimization would not be morally acceptable.

How does the argument in the quoted passage function? Does it attempt to call into question (1), (2), or (3)? One might think, confusedly, that (1) is the object of the argument. But it is not being maintained that in such a case victimization would not prevent offences economically. It is simply being claimed that to accept now that such a victimization would prevent offences economically may have bad effects. Given a commitment to the prevention theory, one would have to accept that the imagined victimization would be right. Accepting this, it is supposed, might weaken one's general aversion to victimization, which aversion is perfectly in place with respect to actual cases. The speculation may be that one might be led not to disapprove of victimizations in actual cases, where they are not economical.

We can accept all this without comment. It leaves undisturbed the hypothesis that in a conceivable case the action of victimizing a man would prevent offences economically. We can suppose, if with reservations, that a utilitarian judge who contemplates our conceivable case comes thereby to approve of or to bring about victimizations that do not prevent offences economically. This does not matter. We can still conceive of the case we want.

Can it then be that the argument is intended to falsify (2), that the principle of economical prevention would justify the conceivable victimization? The argument cannot possibly succeed in showing this to be false. There is a logical connection between the principle, the specification of the case, and a conclusion that victimization would be justified by the principle. Finally, can it be supposed that the argument is aimed at (3), that the imagined victimization would be wrong? On the contrary, it is accepted that the victimization in question would be without moral justification.

There is one further possibility. It might be thought that while the argument does not disturb any of (1), (2), or (3), there is implicit in it another forceful criticism. Is the objection to the prevention theory in a way toothless? All that it establishes, it might be said, is that in a case that is unlikely ever to obtain, the principle of prevention would give us a consequence we regard as unacceptable. This, it may be said, should not trouble us. The principle remains acceptable, for all that has been said, for the real world, and that is what we are concerned with.

The reply is that we are indeed concerned with the real world and in particular with our practice of punishment. The objection against the prevention theory, involving a merely conceivable case, appears to tell us something about a possible justification of that practice. It is that the practice cannot be justified by considerations of economical prevention alone. We have been offered the principle that our practice has no justification whatever other than that it prevents offences at a certain cost of distress. This by itself, none the less, is said to be sufficient. If this were true, then a certain conceivable case of victimization would be justified. If we do not accept this, and do accept that punishment may be justified, then it must have more to recommend it than merely that it prevents offences economically. It should be clear that the fact that this argument rests on a conceivable rather than a likely or an actual case is of no importance. What is important is the specification of the case and the moral view that is taken of it.

JUSTIFIED AND UNJUSTIFIED VICTIMIZATIONS

We have now surveyed, in something like its own terms, a persistent dispute. Sadly enough, it ignores certain very relevant facts. As has been pointed out by others,[25] we already have within the law what are regarded by many as justified victimizations. That they are not spoken of as victimizations, and indeed that our own use of the term is a special one, does not affect the matter. What it comes to is that we have departures from rules about responsibility and guilt.

In particular we have departures from rules of excuse and mitigation. Precisely what is true of a defendant charged under a strict-liability statute is that he is not excused because he did not intend to commit an offence and was not careless. The supermarket that sells dangerous meat, in complete ignorance of the fact and despite having taken reasonable care to avoid doing so, cannot offer this as a defence. The rationale that is given for this, of course, is that the dangers of rotten meat are so considerable that they must be avoided even at the cost of certain victimizations. Some of those who regard rules of excuse as essentially rules for securing that men get their deserts and only their deserts would claim that the dangers are so considerable that they must be avoided at the cost of treating some men in a way that they do not deserve. Convictions where defendants are vicariously liable are defended in the same and other ways.

Quite as important, we are familiar with victimizations where strict and vicarious liability are not in question. They are, indeed, absolutely common. Defendants who have been found guilty of certain offences are given penalties that judges announce to be 'exemplary' ones, penalties calculated to satisfy what is taken to be a considerable need for prevention. In England cases involving the treachery of spying and the killing of police officers provide out-standing examples. More everyday examples result from vandalism and drunken loutishness by yobbos lower down rather than higher up the social scale. It would be a work of benighted piety to argue that the penalties that are imposed are in general precisely those called for by the rules of justice ordinarily thought to govern our practice of punishment.

Two things can be said now about these facts. The first is that it is arguable that we do here have actual victimizations that *do* prevent offences economically. The last persuasive objection to their being such cases, it may be recalled, was that victimizations would give rise to a general insecurity and anxiety that would make them, in the end, uneconomical. This has not been the effect of the creation of offences of strict and vicarious liability. Nor has it been an effect of exemplary penalties.

The second thing to be said is that it is arguable that some of these victimizations *do* have a moral justification. With respect to exemplary penalties, it is at least sometimes true that they are not much greater than the penalties that would be imposed given a strict adherence to the rules. Also, the need for prevention may be regarded as substantial. Many of the penalties imposed under statutes of strict and vicarious liability are relatively small ones, or relatively easily borne by the defendants. As I have said, the total of the dangers to be avoided may be regarded as great.

Given these circumstances, obviously, the argument against the utilitarian prevention theory and related theories must take a different form. The defenders of the utilitarian theory need not labour to maintain that any conceivable victimization would be uneconomical. If certain victimizations would be economical, but also have a moral justification, they constitute no objection to the theory. Critics of the theory, on the other hand, must do more than show that certain victimizations would be economical. They must establish, as we so far have not, that these lack moral justification. Is it possible to produce such cases?

We can proceed to an answer by seeing more clearly what it is that makes certain victimizations at least possibly justified. With respect to at least some strict-liability offences, it can be said that there exists not only a great danger in total sum but also a great danger to each of a considerable number of individuals. Offences of selling rotten food are an example. Also, the penalty imposed on the store is certainly such as to cause its owner or manager less distress than would be caused to each of a number of individuals by his selling more bad meat. When a man is given an exemplary penalty, once again, it can be argued that there exists a great danger to each of a considerable number of individuals. Also, it may be argued, the additional distress caused to the offender, over and above what he may be said to deserve, is usually relatively small.

There is also something else to be kept in mind. It is not essential that for a possibly justified victimization the penalty in question must be a relatively small one. Utilitarians in their zeal to avoid the traditional objection to their prevention theory have not seen one clear possibility of defence. In that objection, as we have seen, it is vaguely said that in a certain case a judge *would* be justified in the secret victimization of an innocent man. Instead of hurrying to reply that this would be uneconomical in the long run, the utilitarian might reasonably demand a further specification of the case.

Could it turn out to be one where the judge may literally be said to *know* that a considerable number of offences will be committed unless there is a preventive example? Is it certain too that nothing else would work? The answers must be in the affirmative, it may be said, if the objection is to be coercive. Let us also suppose that the penalty imposed on the innocent man would cause him great or extreme distress – but something like the same distress as would be caused to each of the victims if the potential offenders were not prevented from offending. If this is what we are to consider, we have a situation in which there exists a choice between very considerable distress for one innocent individual or roughly the same distress for each of a considerable number of innocent individuals. The commendable response of most people, given such a situation, is to look for some other option. If there is no other option, however, it seems undeniable that the victimization of the defendant would be morally preferable. We have not got an economical victimization that is morally indefensible.

What brings us, however unwillingly, to admit the possibility of justification in all these cases is that (a) there is a considerable danger to *each* of a group of individuals to be avoided, and (b) the distress that would be caused to the victimized individual is relatively small or no greater than that which would be caused, if there were no victimization, to each of the group of individuals.

Obviously we *can* conceive of a different case of victimization without these saving features, a case of very unfair, unequal or inhuman treatment. It will be one where there is a great danger to be avoided, and which can be avoided only by a victimization involving very great distress to the individual in question. Most important, it will be one where the distress that would occur, without the victimization, would be *widely spread*. That is, the great danger in question is that each of very many people would suffer relatively little. In total, which is all that is important given the utilitarian prevention view, the distress would be such as to make the victimization, despite its severity, economical.

Here it is not an arguable proposition that the victimization would be morally tolerable. We do not think that an extreme imposition of distress on one individual is tolerable if the alternative distress for others, however great in total, is for any particular individual bearable. This is the absolute centre of a justified resistance to utilitarianism. We are governed in this, it seems, by what has been mentioned before, some commitment or principle of fairness or humanity or the like. It is part of this attitude that given that distress is inevitable, and that all the individuals in question are equally vulnerable or in general on an equal footing, we have to choose that distribution that most closely approximates to an equal one. In our present case, that distribution is the one that involves no distress for the single individual in question, the defendant, and not a great deal for anyone else.

We now do have a case of economical victimization, it seems, which would not be regarded as morally justified. There can be no doubt that it is justified by the utilitarian prevention theory. We must then conclude that punishment if it is justified is not justified by the utilitarian theory that it prevents offences economically. The theory is a logical consequence of the morality of utilitarianism. In rejecting it we reject that morality as well, the principle that an action or whatever is right or justified if it is likely to produce the best total consequences – a balance of more satisfaction or at least less distress than any other action that might be performed instead.

There is another morality, sometimes supposed to have been intended by John Stuart Mill,[26] sometimes regarded as a form of utilitarianism. We need to look at it, if quickly. It is labelled rule utilitarianism and we are told that it issues in a theory of punishment that does not justify the unacceptable victimizations.

Rule utilitarianism may be simply expressed as a certain principle.

A particular action is right or justified if it is according to a rule that itself has a utilitarian justification, even if the action is likely to produce less satisfaction or more distress than some other action that is possible.[27]

The principle was a result, in part, of reflection on exactly punishment. Traditional utilitarianism, as we have seen, was thought to issue via its prevention theory of punishment in the justification of victimizations, infractions of the rules of punishment. Victimizations were assumed always to be morally mistaken, and utilitarianism thus to be in question. Rule utilitarianism was regarded as a satisfactory alternative by those of the opinion that the rightness of conduct has to do only with the maximization of satisfactions and the minimization of distress. The rules of punishment were taken to have utilitarian justifications and therefore, given the new doctrine, to be inviolable.

I trust two things can shown quickly about this. Rule utilitarianism is not a utilitarianism at all if one regards utilitarian moralities as those that have to do solely with satisfaction and distress, their maximization and minimization. Secondly, the theories of punishment in which rule utilitarianism can issue do not include the theory of utilitarian prevention.

Rule utilitarianism is expressed, very vaguely, as the view that an action or practice or whatever is right if it is according to a rule that itself has a utilitarian justification. What does this mean? What is it that justifies us in taking up a particular rule as something to follow even if doing so on a particular occasion will result in less satisfaction or more distress than is necessary? Let us have in mind a rule that is infringed in the extreme case of victimization where the victim's distress would be far greater than any distress to any particular individual if there were no victimization.

Can it be that we are to accept this rule because *usually* or *almost always* following it has the effect of producing more satisfaction or less distress? We can assume this to be true. But this clearly does not provide a sufficient reason for accepting that we should never break the rule. Given this reason, it seems that we should not keep the rule on those occasions when breaking it would have the best welfare consequences. Can it then be that we are to accept the rule because following it *always* has the best consequences? We know this isn't true. Indeed, the belief that certain victimizations would have the best welfare consequences was precisely a reason for taking up rule utilitarianism.

These are the only possible grounds, in terms of best consequences alone, for adopting the rule in question. Neither is satisfactory.

Whatever the ground for taking up the rule as always binding, it must involve more than a commitment to maximizing satisfaction or minimizing distress. It may involve, obviously, some idea of desert or whatever. Also, of course, if the ensuing theory of punishment does involve an embargo on breaking the rule in question, it is not the prevention theory. Rather, it is an attempt to justify punishment by reference to several values taken together. It is a compromise theory, to be considered in due course.

RETROSPECT AND CONCLUSION

Let us look back over our progress from the beginning of this inquiry into backward-looking and then preventive theories of punishment.

We began by contemplating 14 backward-looking reasons for the conclusion that punishment is right. These backward-looking reasons included the literally useless reason for the rightness of punishment that the punishment is right, and the supposed proposition of literal fact that the distress of the punishment equals the culpability of the offence. We also looked at understandings of the desert claim having to do with a penalty system and rights. There were also the backward-looking reasons having to do with contract and consent. None of these 14 traditional backward-looking theories provided an actual reason for the rightness of punishment.

We took the view, however, that the retribution tradition had to have in it some actual reason for punishment, however good. What we found was (15) the reason that punishment satisfies grievance desires caused by offences. Penalties can be equivalent to offences in satisfying such desires and doing no more or less than that. To this reason for punishment we tentatively added or contemplated adding that a penalty can be according to a system connecting offences and penalties and thus at least a matter of consistency. We concluded that retribution theories in their reality could not possibly justify punishment.

About prevention theories, we first judged that much of punishment can be taken to reduce offences by certain means, including one means usually overlooked, having to do with unreflective obedience to law. As for the utilitarian prevention theory, however, we drew the conclusion that it is mistaken because it justifies not merely victimizations but wrongful victimizations. There was the possibility of the same conclusion with doctrines of public good and the like. The reasons mentioned for the victimizations being wrong was that they would be unfair, unjust, inhuman, and so on. It was conjectured in particular that such victimizations would violate some principle or rule of equality.

Traditionally, however, the victimization objection has been taken to rest exactly on reasons of desert or other backward-looking reasons. Reflections on victimizations have thus proceeded from and been taken as vindicating some backward-looking theory or other. Must we now revert to what seemed to be 14 hopeless reasons for punishment and attempt to reinstate one more of them to explain our own resistance to certain victimizations?

There surely is no hope in that. Circular retributivism does not become of any more use when it takes the form of the proposition that it is because a certain victimization would be wrong that it would be wrong. We shall not get anywhere either by way of the proposition of intrinsic retributivism that certain victimizations are intrinsically bad, or the propositions of culpability–distress retributivism or rights retributivism or jurisprudential retributivism or any other propositions in our survey or sampling of traditional backward-looking theories. Try the exercise if you want. Make your way through all of them. But you cannot have much hope. It cannot be likely that a supposed reason *for* punishing the guilty, in fact a terrible or weak reason, can become a good or strong reason *against* doing the opposite, victimizing the innocent?

This leads to another question. Do we find good or strong reasons against wrongful victimization in what we took to be the *reality* of retribution theories? Do we find such reasons in terms of something involving or analogous to or related to the satisfaction of grievance desires? And, let us add in, a penalty system?

The first thing to be contemplated is that the retribution theory as we ourselves have understood it cannot be a reason against victimizations. This is so for the reason that a victimization of the kind we imagined, and indeed other victimizations, could indeed satisfy grievance desires. The desires would not be satisfied by the distress of the actual offender, of course. That is not to say, given the deception involved, that the grievance desires owed to the offence in question could not be satisfied, of course exactly satisfied. It seems that a retribution theorist who gives up the traditional lumber, the various desert propositions and the like, and embraces the sense in retribution, cannot condemn certain wrongful victimizations. Or rather, he will have at least as much difficulty in avoiding that disaster as does the utilitarian.

Are you now tempted to the reaction that this upshot in effect disproves the principal conclusion we have drawn about the tradition and theories of retribution? Do you say that there is *one* impulse, commitment, reason or principle in retribution, and that it enters into both support for punishment and resistance to victimization? Do you conclude that since grievance satisfaction cannot explain resistance to victimization, it cannot either be the story of the support for punishment?

Tempted you may be, but in my judgement you have no choice but to resist the temptation. Nothing is going to make effective the doctrines of legal, circular, intrinsic, and such-like retributivism. Nothing is going to make them effective with the rightness of punishment or the wrongness of some victimizations.

Of course there is something else to be considered. We found more in retributivism about punishment than grievance satisfactions. Retributivism, we can conclude, can rely on justification by a penalty system as another effective part of itself. Retributivism speaks of such a system as *justice* and *law*, greatly dignifying it. We can allow that this consistency, which is what it comes down to, is important to retributivism. It does of course issue in opposition to victimization and condemnation of at least some victimization.

You may well feel, however, that all of us have more reason to condemn what we may indeed speak of as vicious victimizations. You may feel this is as true of those of us who assert retribution theories. We have more reason to condemn vicious victimizations than the reason of a consistent system that itself lacks a founding moral principle more impressive than the principle of exactly satisfying grievance desires. What is this other reason or ground that all of us may have?

We shall in due course come to a certain principle, the Principle of Humanity, and shall thus complete our rejection of the utilitarian theory of punishment and of course similar maximizing outlooks. We may also come to an explanation of why those who are retributivists about punishment are more condemning of certain victimizations than is explained either by their official theories or our realistic understanding of those theories. They may share a commitment with the rest of us, whether or not consistently with the rest of what they maintain. We shall also see more of how prevention theories rest on ideas of the freedom of offenders and of how they can be held responsible.

5
Reform, Rehabilitation, Treatment

PUNISHMENT AS REFORMATIVE

There have been a number of views recommending punishment or some other practice for dealing with crime on the ground that it will reform, correct, rehabilitate, treat, improve or cure offenders – and thereby reduce the number of offences. Often these doctrines have been ill-defined, and sometimes they have been presented as group orthodoxies beyond the need for critical examination. They differ very considerably in character and assumptions. The traditional ones, but not their successors, can be described as recommending the teaching or inculcation of moral principles. Some of them appear to be about as much concerned with the state of the offender than the prevention of offences. All of them, for related but different reasons, reject retribution theories of punishment, the theory of utilitarian prevention, and any prevention theory not resting on reform, rehabilitation, treatment or the like.

These theories are certainly not in any ascendancy now at the beginning of the twenty-first century, even among the high-minded. That is, there is little or no support for the idea that punishment or an institution of treatment replacing it can or might be justified solely by reform or treatment and its effects, without any recourse to ideas of retribution or of the prevention of crime by means other than reform, rehabilitation and treatment – the means surveyed in the last chapter. That is not to say, however, that compromise or mixed theories of justification, now to the fore, leave out reform or something akin to it.

Indeed, contemporary theories – say those of Antony Duff or Robert Nozick (pp. 176–94) – rest on such an idea or at least give it a large place. For this reason alone, it is a good idea to look at the pure reform and treatment theories of the past. They will throw a light on and serve to distinguish their successors. What also needs to be kept in mind is that what is new is not actually identical with what is right – and in particular that the newly or recently rejected is or was not necessarily rightly rejected. We should leave fashion to the designers of clothes and cars and to the majority of our politicians who engage in it.

Of the pure or single-reason reform theories to be mentioned here the first two kinds recommend the practice of punishment. The other kinds, which conceive of criminality as something like personal disorder or disability, recommend some practice of treatment (p. 8). Relatively little will be said of any of them, of any kind, partly for the reason that they are in a certain respect similar to the utilitarian prevention theory and so open to an objection familiar to you. The following chapter, however, will be given over to consideration of the doctrines of freedom, responsibility and determinism – and some kind of determinism enters into conceptions of criminality as disorder or disability requiring treatment. Further, to consider determinism will be to consider something like the assumption of all treatment theories – an assumption that individuals are at least in some way not responsible for things.

Might punishment be justified not by its intrinsic nature as defined but because it provides an opportunity for us to take steps to reform offenders and so to reduce offences? It seems unlikely that anyone has ever believed imprisonment to be justified *solely* by the supposed fact that it gives an opportunity to make men morally better and thus law-abiding by means of solitude, solitary confinement, time to think, counselling, therapy, medication, occupational training, learning to read, other education, religious services, exhortatory chats, some work, no drink, no drugs, regimens designed to build character, or pressure to confess their crimes? There has been a certain amount of faith in such things, but those who have had it have also been inclined to defend punishment by the belief that it is somehow deserved.

If one takes this first possible reformative doctrine by itself, it is open to easy dismissal. For a start, it is impossible to have anything like conviction about truth of the factual supposition that men are reformed by traditional ministrations and so become upright and law-abiding. Furthermore, the conclusion that is drawn requires an additional premise, which is as mistaken.

What we are told is that certain steps may be taken that reform men and make them law-abiding, and the conclusion is drawn that punishment is justified because it enables us to take these steps. What also needs to be established, of course, is the additional premise that *only* punishment would give us the opportunity, or the best opportunity. This cannot be true. It may be admitted that some form of control or restraint would be necessary if we were to attempt reformation in the suggested ways. This is not to say that we would have to punish. Punishment, you will remember, is a practice that aims to cause distress. A practice that does not have this feature is not punishment.

This second difficulty was officially avoided by the second sort of doctrine we shall consider, which was as familiar.[1] Here, it was punishment itself which was claimed to have a reformative effect. It was said to have this effect in three indirect ways.

It deters men from breaking the law, and thus they are inclined to become habitually law-abiding. At this stage, they do obey the law, but not from 'moral motives'. However, they are said to be more likely to advance from here than from elsewhere to a state in which they do obey the law from moral motives. This is the first way in which punishment reforms. Second, and more important, punishment may have the effect of emphasizing to a man his immorality.

> It is not only pain that is characteristic of punishment, it is pain inflicted because of wrong done and after a judicial decision involving a moral condemnation by an organ representing society. It is not only that the man suffers pain, but that he suffers as a consequence and sign of the condemnation of his act by society as immoral and pernicious. Now this surely is a striking way of bringing home to him, so far as external symbols can, the wickedness of his conduct. It is generally admitted that recognition of one's sin in some form or other is a necessary condition of real moral regeneration, and the formal and impressive condemnation by society involved in punishment is an important means toward bringing about this recognition on the part of the offender.[2]

Third, punishment has a moral effect on individuals other than those who actually experience it.

> If it may help the offender to realise the badness of his action, may it not help others to realise the badness before they have committed the kind of action in question at all? This must not be confused with a purely deterrent effect. A man who abstains from crime just because he is deterred abstains through fear of suffering and not because he thinks it wicked; a man who abstains because the condemnation of the crime by society and the State has brought its wickedness home to him

abstains from moral motives and not merely from fear of unpleasant consequences to himself.[3]

The second and third propositions do not rest precisely on the mistake that members of a society could not or would not regard offences as wrongful without the demonstration of punishment. They do rest on some such assumptions as this one, that if an action is not one that is punished by the state, individuals may not realize the extent of its wrongfulness. We are said to be inclined to allocate wrongful actions to two classes – those that may sometimes be excused and those that are absolutely prohibited. When an action is made a crime, and those who commit it are punished, the effect is to locate it firmly in the second class.

Punishment, then, to sum up, is both a deterrent and an effective condemnation, and as each it has reformative consequences. It contributes to a change in the beliefs of offenders and also others as to the wrongfulness of certain actions. It thereby contributes to a change for the better in behaviour.

A good many things may be said about and against these claims – after the necessary announcement of a general scepticism as to their factual truth. What is advanced is certainly a considerably simplified conception of the relationships between morality and the practice of punishment. It seems fairly evident that an effective creation of criminal law, in the societies with which we are familiar, usually depends upon an already existing consensus as to the wrongfulness or undesirability of certain behaviour. It cannot in general be the case that the making of an action into an offence results in a moral reallocation of the kind suggested. In certain cases, no doubt, making an action into an offence serves to increase and fortify beliefs as to its wrongfulness. But let me avoid a difficult and inessential discussion of the relations between punishment and accepted morality.

Let us suppose the existence of a society, very different from ours, where punishment does contribute very greatly indeed to law abidance by influencing beliefs and attitudes as to the immorality of offences. The suggestion we are considering is that punishment would here be justified solely by these effects. This can be shown to be mistaken in the way in which the utilitarian prevention theory has been shown to be mistaken. To accept a principle to the effect that punishment would be justified solely in virtue of its influence on moral beliefs and the further consequences in behaviour would be to commit oneself to unacceptable victimizations. No doubt it would be difficult to conceive of a victimization in which the victim was led to morality and lawfulness. His victimization might be justified, none the less, by its effects on others. Given the unacceptability of this victimization, the conclusion would follow that even in the imagined society punishment could not be justified by the suggested principle of reformation alone.

The utilitarian prevention theory, according to our argument, fails because it places insufficient limitation on what may be done to individuals in order to secure certain behaviour. It fails to take into account a limitation having somehow to do with humanity, fairness, justice, equality or the like. The doctrine we are presently considering fails because it places insufficient limitation on what may be done in order to secure changes in belief and attitude and consequent behaviour. It does not take into account a feature of punishment that surely is essential to any justification it may have. What would have to be true in order for the present doctrine to escape the objection? It would have to be true that in any conceivable situation we would prefer (1) a course of action which would result in certain moral beliefs and lawfulness to (2) a course of action having other results. This, I take it, can be shown to be mistaken. To do so would require both a detailed development of the doctrine and also a repetition of essentially the sequence of argument of the last chapter.[4]

There is also a special objection to the reformative doctrine we are considering and to others like it. If we attempt to prevent offences in the way contemplated with the utilitarian prevention theory, where only prevention is in question and not also reformation, our intention is to affect behaviour, but not by changing certain general beliefs and attitudes. If we attempt to reform by punishment, the changing of general beliefs and attitudes is an end in itself as well as a means to fewer offences. What will the consequences be if we succeed? What will the consequences be if we change the beliefs and attitudes of members of society with respect to certain actions? Those who are quick to suppose that a great deal will be gained usually make the assumption, so evident in the quoted passages above, that whatever is punished at present is certainly wrong. They assume, that is, that punishment will always create or reinforce attitudes that certainly are right.

This conventionality must be simple error. The history of the law has in it too many moral barbarities. At any time, indeed, the law includes elements that are open to question and in fact much questioned. What is required, with respect to these elements, is not that members of society should be influenced into belief in them by the practice of punishment. What is desirable, possibly, is both that the law as it stands be obeyed to some large extent, and that there be unrestrained discussion of the issues in dispute. Such discussion, after all, gives us the best assurance we can have of human and rational decisions and moral progress. Discussion should not be impeded, with respect to the issues in question, by a practice of punishment that coerces judgement in one direction. One might then maintain that given a choice between punishment of a reformative kind and punishment of only what we have called a preventive kind, where the preventive effect would be the same, the preventive punishment would be preferable.

You may object at this point that there cannot be any doubt about the moral correctness or indeed the moral necessity of some core of the law. Would it not be an indubitably good thing if at least certain offences were regarded by yet more people as wholly wrong? We are here in the neighbourhood of a number of considerable difficulties to which we will be returning (Chapter 8). There are large questions here. Let me, for the moment, mention only an ancient problem of the moral agent.

Out of what grounds does the good man act? What is suggested to us by the theory of punishment we are considering is that one takes an important step on the way to becoming such a man by being affected by condemnations issued by others. It is not that one is impressed by their reasons or their arguments – those could be provided in several ways – but rather by certain special declarations in which they issue. These declarations are punishments. But surely this is not a way to becoming a good man or a decent human being. Surely I am most admirable as a moral agent if I obey the law out of a sympathetic and impartial awareness of the effects on others of its being broken. My first major step toward this state will involve an awareness of the victims of offences rather than the condemnation of offenders.

One other remark already about punishment as reformative needs emphasizing. It has come to seem at least unrealistic to suppose that punishment itself as we have it has much reformative effect. It is possible to suppose that this was at least on the way to being a kind of illusion, nearly a fantasy, maybe an illusion and fantasy that served a purpose. This could have been the purpose of concealing from ourselves the true nature of punishment and its value for us, some of us more than others.

The idea that aiming and intending to cause suffering, distress or deprivation in a practice, and to be known as aiming to, is likely to have great, considerable or significant reformative effects – that, on reflection, is a remarkable idea. Another remarkable idea is that we can punish individuals into a moral acceptance of a society that most people take to be open to some doubt and many take to be open to more than doubt. Could imprisonment conceivably lead a man into acceptance as fair of an unfair society?

ILLNESS AND TREATMENT

Those who break the law, we have often been told, in one way or another, do so as a consequence of illness, disorder, disability or the like and so we should treat them rather than punish them. These judgements have been expressed or implied in books and articles but not, I think, satisfactorily explained or defended.[5] Cogency, I think, has generally been in short supply. The inherent assumptions are that the mental illness or disability, although widely conceived, is as much a matter of discovery and description as physical illness, and that it explains criminal actions. Above all, it is not something for which those suffering it are to be held responsible or at any rate held fully responsible. Punishment, almost invariably regarded by advocates of treatment as necessarily retributive in character, is thought to be out of the question. All of this, while orthodoxy to some, was questioned or denied by other psychiatrists, psychologists and others concerned with the law.

It seems an obvious truth, and one worth remembering, that the influence on the law of the social studies, medicine, psychiatry, psychology, and also certain theories of personal development, has been humanizing and beneficial – more so, certainly, than the influence of their traditional critics, who have been of retributivist inclinations and also conservative in politics.[6] That at least for a time, around the middle of the twentieth century, we tried a little less punishing and a little more of other things was in accord with findings in the social studies and the like and the recommendations associated with them. None of the traditional theories of punishment, or at least none of the associated beliefs about the numbers of people who rightly may be punished, can avoid serious emendation at the hands of psychiatrists, sociologists, and others.

There is a yet larger truth that must be kept in mind in connection with the general theories that all criminality is disorder, illness or something of the sort, not at all a matter of offences freely committed. This large truth involves no wide or extended idea at all of disorder, illness or the like. It has to do only with disorder, illness or the like that is now accepted to be such by ordinary and conventional medical judgement. The larger truth is that a majority of prisoners, up to 70 per cent, have mental health disorders. The British figures have counterparts elsewhere.

> Every prison in the country now warehouses the mentally disordered: the numbers have been spiralling upwards since the closure of the old asylums. This has reached a point which beggars the imagination: figures from the Office of National Statistics (ONS) show that, if we diverted to treatment all those prisoners who are mentally disordered and/or addicted to alcohol or drugs, 90% of inmates would no longer be held in jail.
>
> There are now 75,000 men and women behind bars in this country. The findings of the ONS suggest that nearly 50,200 of them have personality disorders; 6,175 are psychotic; and more than 35,000 of them have neurotic disorders. Several tens of thousands of them suffer a combination of disorders. More than 75% of them are intellectually impaired, with IQ's below the national average. And these are not figures that the government denies.[7]

It follows indubitably, whatever is said about all criminality being illness or disorder in a wider sense, that such contemporary societies as that of Britain are open to condemnation for their policies with respect to most or many imprisoned offenders. This is so since the actual provision of treatment for those who are indisputably unwell or disabled is insufficient, minimal or derisory. Nothing to be said of general theories of reform and treatment in what follows will take away from this condemnation of current policy. It is terrible that those somehow unable not to offend are treated like or too close to like those who somehow are able not to offend. This fact must hang over the rest of our reflections. It might have hung over our earlier reflections.

To consider the general theories, however, should we give up punishment entirely and substitute treatment? Certainly that thing has been supposed, or anyway said. Are all offenders ill? Whether or not one thinks so, of course, depends on one's conception of illness.

In English law, from 1843 until 1957, the McNaghten rules in unamended form provided a specification of mental abnormality – the abnormality required as a defence against a criminal charge. For a man to have been mentally abnormal in this sense, with respect to a particular act, he must at the time have suffered as a consequence of disease of the mind from a defect of reason such that he did not know the nature of his act or that it was wrong. The 'diseases of the mind' in question are traditional madnesses or incapabilities, or some of them. Not to know the nature of one's act, in this context, is for example not to know that what one is attacking is a human body. A wrong act is taken to be an illegal act.

Clearly enough, given a conception of mental illness based on the McNaghten rules, one would be a long way indeed from the generalization that all offenders are mentally ill. The rules, certainly, were persistently criticized as too narrow. In the main, this narrowness consists in regarding a man as sane who knows what he is doing, and that it is wrong, but lacks the emotional capacity even to begin to act in any other way. Such men, it is said, are often obviously and classically mad and it is absurd that they should be held responsible for actions which are the consequence of their illness. In other countries there have long been much wider conceptions.

One might try at this point to arrive at a more inclusive idea of illness by putting aside consideration of the law and its history and turning directly to the doctors or other practitioners, or to some of them. Abnormal mental life, we used to be told, although endlessly various, can be divided into forms of illness that are dependent on some distinct bodily disorder and forms of illness that are identified at the psychological rather than the physical level and for which organic causes have not yet been isolated.

In the first group are to be found dementia and also the various forms of mental defectiveness. The confusion, delirium, and loss of intellectual capability that is typical of states of dementia may result from physical sickness, injury, kinds of intoxication, or inheritance. The forms of mental defectiveness, including idiocy, imbecility, and feeble-mindedness, are also of known physical basis. As for the second group of conditions, it can be broken down into a number of sub-groups, the first of which takes in disorders of emotion. Central here are states of anxiety, of depression, and of mania. A second sub-group includes schizophrenic states, marked by disordered thinking, emotional excesses and incongruities, hallucinations, odd or bizarre conduct. A third sub-group includes states of obsession and compulsion, various forms of hysterical illness, and also psychopathic states. Among psychopaths one finds a significant number of offenders, recidivists in particular.

None the less, given even a determination to make the fullest possible use of the notions of this schema, it seems fairly clear that not all offenders can be regarded as falling under it. If this is the extent of sickness, not all offenders are sick. Not all are unable not to offend. This, of course, is the attitude of many medical authorities. If a man is to be regarded as mentally ill or incapacitated, he must exhibit some established syndrome, where 'established' means something like 'included in standard textbooks of psychiatry'.

There remain other ways in which one can attempt to show that all offenders are disabled or the like. Several of these are more promising. One can begin with one of the related but competing theories of personal development and arrive at a host of disorders. I have in mind those theories of which Freud's was the exemplar. His theory probably remains neither better nor worse than others, despite what is now known of his own loose way with truth, which does indeed bear on his theory. It encompassed, among its fundamental concepts, those of the unconscious mind, basic instinctual drives, such early sexual phases as the anal-sadistic, sublimation and repression, the Oedipus conflict and its resolution, the pleasure principle and the reality principle, the formation of the superego. It would be pointless to attempt any encapsulation of the theory. Given it, one can display the actions of offenders as consequences of emotional states which are themselves the results of deviations from a normal course of development.[8] There are many possibilities.

Offenders, it may be said, are individuals suffering from character disorders, and these consist in faulty relationships between id, ego, and superego. Mainly because of unsatisfactory emotional environments or simply inconsistent treatment in early life, no adequate superego or conscience has been developed. Offenders are like children whose instinctual drives for immediate gratification have not come under control. Or, it may be said of some individuals that their experience of the Oedipus conflict was not satisfactorily resolved and they have been left with an ungovernable reaction to figures of authority and indeed authority in any form. Alternatively, some men may offend because they desire punishment. The feeling of guilt which issues in this desire may have its origin in early sexual experience. Or, a man's behaviour may be explained by the fact that there was no successful emergence from the stage of anal sadism, or by the fact that through a certain experience he has regressed to that stage. Or again, it may be said that an individual has become fixated in that common illusion of children, the family romance, and steals in order to try to maintain it.

Whatever else may be said of the enterprise, the notions of the theory seemed to be such as to allow it to be put to very wide use. It is not obvious that it cannot be applied to all offenders. Rather, it is a matter of argument whether all offenders suffer from personality or character disabilities resulting from abnormal emotional development. There are also related doctrines which offer similar possibilities of general application. Some of them are found attractive for their relatively commonsensical air. It is supposed by a good many people that there is a causal connection between antisocial conduct and separation from one's mother in infancy, rejection by her, or a loss of affection.[9] One or more of these experiences gives rise to a personality disorder and it in turn produces criminal behaviour.

There used to be another less familiar alternative in a strictly physical account of personal development of a kind elaborated by the proselytizing Professor Eysenck, doyen of English psychologists.[10] Here too, our attention was drawn to inherent dangers of disorder and its consequences. In this account we were reminded, for example, that when an external stimulus excites a sensory surface of the body, excitation is passed on through synapses to the brain and then to other parts of the body. There is also inhibition, which is a kind of resistance to excitation. These two processes enter into another one which is of fundamental importance to the individual's development. This is conditioning, the process of establishing responses to stimuli. If a puff of air is directed at the cornea of a man's eye, he blinks. If he hears a particular sound each time he feels a puff, then, after sound and puff have occurred together a number of times, a conditioned reflex is established. That is, some percentage of times when he hears the sound and there is no puff, he blinks. The extent to which the reflex is established may be said to be determined by the degree of inhibition of his nervous system and the number of times he has experienced sound and puff together.

As with the development of the blink response, so with human behaviour in general. A child misbehaves in a particular way and is then punished in some way. His response to the punishment is fear and pain. By a process of conditioning exactly parallel to that one which produced the blink response, he comes to respond with something like fear and pain to misbehaving itself, and indeed to the thought of it. As a result the child comes to avoid the behaviour in question to some particular extent. This is a matter of conditioning, not a making of conscious choices.

It was not supposed by Professor Eysenck that all individuals who have nervous systems of such kinds that they condition badly do in fact become offenders. Two other requirements had to be satisfied before it was taken as a probability or better that a particular child would come to break the law. It was noted that it is a consequence of inheritance that an individual be of a certain degree of emotionality or neuroticism. He has a place on a personality scale. Persons at one extreme of the scale, who are very high in emotionality, have such qualities as aggressiveness, restlessness, moodiness. Persons at the other extreme are likely to be calm, reliable, carefree. A high degree of emotionality in the suggested sense is the second condition of criminality. The third requirement was environment and in particular childhood punishments and disapprovals.

Criminality, then, was reducible to conditionability, emotionality and 'input'. If the possibility of certain other factors was sometimes mentioned by behavioural psychologists, it was not seriously considered. Certainly there was no room for free decisions as usually conceived.

The deduction which may be made from our general theory is relatively uncompromising. We would regard behaviour from a completely deterministic point of view; that is to say, the individual's behaviour is determined completely by his heredity and by the environmental influences which have been brought to bear on him.[11]

There are still other ways in which criminality has been described and claimed to be explained in terms of disorder or incapability. Criminality itself is now regarded as based in physical conditions open to treatment or control by drugs, some of which have been very effective. Very differently, deviant syndromes were explained by sociologists as primarily a consequence of environment rather than individual development. Offenders, on one view, have simply acquired the common pattern of behaviour of the neighbourhood or of some peer group. 'When persons become criminal, they do so because of contacts with criminal patterns and also because of isolation from anti-criminal patterns.'[12] They, like everyone else, have norms imposed upon them. The norms in question happen not to call for obedience to the law, or to all laws. Indeed, they sometimes call for infractions.

With respect to both this and the other kinds of explanation of criminality, incidentally, it was not always true that the supposed sickness or disorder or disability was thought to give rise to criminal behaviour. Rather, there was an evident tendency to regard the behaviour itself as the sickness, disorder, or disability. To be mentally healthy was to behave in certain ways – to be unhealthy was to break the law or to act in other antisocial ways.[13] Given this point of view, it was pointless to attempt to explain the behaviour by the disability, but not pointless to try to explain the behaviour, whether or not conceived as a disability, by some independent factor or factors, perhaps the social environment.

Finally, of course, there have been some combinations of these several doctrines. Offenders are what they are, it has been said, as a consequence of both personal and social factors. We can try to explain a man's becoming a criminal in terms of both Freudian categories and the sociologist's notion of anomy. We can add in, certainly, abnormal brain function. Perhaps something like a spirit of compromise has grown up among psychologists, sociologists, and others concerned with the theory of criminality. It has not grown so far, to my knowledge, as to produce large fruits. There has also been more emphasis on particular kinds of offenders and an increasing unwillingness to regard criminal behaviour as homogeneous stuff. Full-time thieves are indeed very different from rapists and both of them are quite unlike husband killers or the man who assaults his neighbour on account of his race or colour.[14]

Several of the general doctrines, of course, have been conjoined with quite specific recommendations as to treatment. If offenders are suffering from disabilities which are to be explained in a Freudian way, then it seems that psychoanalysis or psychotherapy is needed. For overwhelming reasons, there has been a reluctance to propose such a treatment system. Still, it has been difficult to see an alternative for Freudians and the like, given their condemnations of punishment as barbarous or useless, a dismissal of the utility of other kinds of treatment, and the acceptance that we should try to prevent offences.

On the other hand, if offences are importantly the result of unsuccessful conditioning, or successful conditioning of an antisocial kind, then behaviour therapy is presumably the answer or a major part of it. A shoe fetishist may be so conditioned that the sight of a shoe in certain circumstances, far from exciting him, produces nausea or terror. The same procedure could be attempted with all antisocial behaviour. We might also take steps to alter the conditionability of individuals. Something of this kind, involving the use of drugs, was attempted with delinquent boys. Finally, whatever steps we take later in their lives, we might consider the desirability of testing the conditionability of schoolchildren. 'Once this particular aspect of the child's nature was known, we could . . . pick out those who, by virtue of their poor conditionability, are predestined to become criminals and delinquents, and recommend to their parents a kind of upbringing that would minimise that possibility.'[15]

There were, needless to say, other recommendations as to treatment attached to other diagnoses. Those who were impressed by the argument that offenders are the products of maternal deprivation sometimes advocated particular kinds of institutions, unlike prisons, where individuals can come to a kind of maturation earlier denied them. Finally, there were the less doctrinaire proposals to the effect that we should establish a treatment system comprising within it approaches of various kinds.

OBJECTIONS

A lot of questions are raised by these doctrines. Consider, for a start, these four propositions, each of which has been asserted or at least implied. (1) All offenders, perhaps save some of the traditionally mad, are suffering from personality or character disorders resulting from a certain abnormal emotional development, and these disorders are the main causes of their behaviour. This can be called the Freudian position. (2) All offenders, perhaps save some of the traditionally mad, are the products of certain processes of conditioning, and their behaviour is to be mainly explained in this way. This is the view of some experimental psychologists. (3) All offenders, again excluding some of the traditionally mad, offend mainly because they have been formed by a certain social environment – a sociological view. (4) All offenders are to be explained in terms of of some sort of brain malfunction.

One might attempt to trim, amend, or interpret these propositions in various ways in order to make them consistent. If they are taken as they often have been intended, however, at least three of them must be false.

It is difficult to resist certain familiar suspicions about the Freudian one, either if offenders were presented as the consequences of unsatisfactory relations between id, ego, and superego or if they are explained in terms of more particular hypotheses of a Freudian kind. General questions about psychoanalytic theory raise themselves. One can easily question the nature and the extent of the evidence for the propositions put forward. One can as easily question the precision of the concepts at the base of the system. One can discard a number of defensive strategies, including the simple and simple-minded rejoinder that each criticism of psychoanalytic theory can be regarded as no more than resistance to the truth.

As for the second proposition, the one based on the notion of conditioning, it seems best taken as a simplification of a hypothesis not yet clarified and tested. Here again, for good reasons, there was controversy even among those who were engaged in the relevant disciplines. One good reason was that the theory flattens out what seem to be striking differences. At least certain human decisions, whatever phenomena they are, appear to be very different from blink responses.

Finally, with respect to the possibly more testable assertions of the sociologists, let us notice only that again there was extensive disagreement among those most qualified to judge, and that the explanatory power of a number of familiar sociological claims was in doubt. It was difficult to accept, as a complete account of why some individuals offend, that they were members of a certain group, class, or society. Indeed it was impossible.

We can pass by brain malfunction and drugs, and come to a conclusion. It cannot be supposed that any of the four propositions, or more discriminating versions of them, has been shown to be true. It seems likely that each of them, to say the least, represents human behaviour by way of a too simple and distorting model. Nor can the efficacy of different modes of treatment be regarded as established. Should we think about a less doctrinaire theory, some compromise made from the various elements? Let me simply notice some difficulties that will have to be faced by any such wide theory drawing on various sources, and its attendant recommendations as to treatment. I take these difficulties as likely to be insuperable.

The doctrine we are anticipating will be distinguished, first, by some denial of free choice and responsibility on the part of offenders. This is what is common to the views of criminality as sickness or disability at which we have glanced. The practice recommended in place of punishment, secondly, will be one of treatment, a practice in which characters, personalities, views and attitudes are changed as a means to changing behaviour. These changes will not be brought about by what I shall call *argument*, or not wholly so. What will be the claimed justification? It will be that the practice recommended in place of punishment will in some way improve offenders and in that way prevent offences. It will serve a utilitarian end or some end of a related kind, maybe spoken of in terms of the public good. The claim will be, in so far as the doctrine is of the single-principle kind we are discussing, that this in itself is sufficient to justify the practice.

One difficulty in accepting such a doctrine, as in the case of the reform theory of punishment, will be that one would again be committed to what we may persist in calling victimization. Hitherto, we have understood victimizations to be departures from rules which govern our practice of punishment. Victimizations of the sort hitherto considered are or would be the work of judges. Let us extend the notion of victimization far enough to cover any impositions of distress not in accord with convictions of justice, humanity, or the like.

Someone may still object that one cannot have victimization as a consequence of treatment rather than punishment. The ground of the objection may be the supposition that treatment cannot be against the will of the patient. But this is certainly not a necessary truth, obviously, and in many circumstances unlikely to be a truth at all. It is mere utopianism to suppose that if punishment were replaced by treatment, of whatever effective kind, offenders would cheerfully present themselves for their remedies. The only realistic alternative to punishment, of the kind in question, would be a somehow coercive system of treatment.

This fact, incidentally, provides an answer to one quite different objection that might be made against a treatment system of the kind at which we were glancing. It is objected, familiarly, that such a system would perhaps help offenders but would not sufficiently prevent offences. That is, it might change known offenders by treatment but it would not influence others against offending. The supposition is that the prospect of being treated would not be deterrent. For several reasons having to do with the fact that treatment would be imposed on individuals, enforced, this seems a mistake.

To return to the main point, however, it seems obvious that a medical authority might impose too much distress on an individual either in the interest of curing him or improving his condition, or in the interest of that and of preventing offences. That, at any rate, would be a possible consequence if the practice in question was governed only by some principle to the effect that treatment was justified if successful in securing such ends. It is such a practice and principle that we are at present discussing. If a practice of treatment was established, and it did exclude victimizations, one would have to accept that any justification it had was not simply that offenders were treated and offences prevented.

A second difficulty with this treatment theory, also one faced by the reform theory of punishment, would have to do with the changing of beliefs or attitudes mainly by means other than argument, a giving of reasons. The general case against other means is that there are values of the first importance in maintaining the place or rather the places in society of rational discussion. The effects of what may be called indoctrination are likely to be felt far beyond the area in which it is used. It is entirely mistaken to say[16] that our present practice of punishment succeeds in indoctrination or attempts to indoctrinate. What it primarily attempts to do is to change behaviour.

It might reasonably be pointed out, on the other hand, that we certainly do influence children by other than rational means. This is so, and to some extent defensible. It might also be admitted that in certain cases behaviour therapy for adults is justifiable, even against the wishes of the individuals in question. These would be cases in which there was a danger of very great harm to particular individuals and no other more tolerable way of avoiding it. It certainly does not follow that society could justifiably treat all lawbreakers or potential lawbreakers in this way.

A third difficulty is in fact larger, has in effect been touched on already, and can be stated quickly. What we are contemplating is in fact something like the imposition of a morality on individuals. Whatever else is to be said about that, it had better be a decent morality. What will that be? Does somebody have the idea, by any chance, that it is to include some retribution theory of punishment? The larger question of the nature of a decent society arises here. So does the question of whether we are living in such a thing. We will be coming to that question by another route.

There is also a fourth difficulty, one having to do with the allocation of a society's resources. One sometimes had the feeling that for reformists no expenditure might be too great if it reduced crime significantly. It is as if there was no question but that an army of therapists would be best engaged in dealing with those who committed criminal offences, about half of which were motoring offences. Surely the claims of other sectors and institutions in society must be considered. Should we have so many therapists or practitioners of whatever kind? If so, what numbers of them should be concerned with, say, the education of children rather than with criminality? Our practice of punishment is often said to be inefficient and wasteful. If we are far indeed from having one, there remains a possibility that a radically different system would be inefficient and wasteful in various ways. One can certainly conceive of two societies such that one with a higher incidence of criminality would be far preferable.

There must of course also be the very large question of whether the practice associated with a wide theory of treatment will work. To say the least, as already remarked, our experience of past theories and practices has not been reassuring.

Finally, with respect to difficulties in the doctrine we are anticipating, there is the fact you will remember that it will involve a denial that any offenders are free in their offences and to be held responsible for them. That will take explaining and working out. This is not the main reason for now turning to the general question of determinism, freedom and responsibility, but it is one.

The large and grim truth passed by earlier, that most or many of the individuals in our prisons have serious mental disorders as standardly defined independently of theories of punishment and treatment, and thus have been less than free and responsible in what they have done, and will also be so in what they do in the future, is relevant to determinism but will not play a part in our consideration of it. The large and grim truth will play a part later on.

6
Determinism

Backward-looking theories of the moral justification of punishment certainly presuppose that all offenders were in some way and in some degree free in committing their offences, and also in some way and degree are to be held morally responsible for them. The latter proposition is of course not that offenders and others are found *legally* responsible for offences, found to have committed an offence, to be guilty in terms of the law – however legal responsibility is related to moral responsibility. The proposition presupposed by backward-looking theories, rather, whatever it comes to, is that all offenders were morally responsible for the offence. That is much of what somehow makes the punishment right as distinct from merely legal.

In particular the freedom and the responsibility of offenders is presupposed by retribution or desert theories and also contract, consent and related theories, as well as by the retribution theories so understood as to make sense of them, in terms of the satisfaction of grievance desires. In looking at those theories, however, we did not pause to consider which of different conceptions of freedom and responsibility are depended on by the theories. Nor did we look into the question of the truth of the presupposed propositions about freedom and responsibility. Are these theories as vulnerable on factual grounds having to do with freedom and responsibility as prevention theories are in connection with prevention? More vulnerable?

The utilitarian prevention theory and its relatives also presuppose that offenders were somehow and to some extent free and morally responsible in breaking the law. If they were not so, if for example their actions were wholly unintentional or greatly provoked, there would not be the same kind of prospect of more offences in the future by the same offender – offences in need of being prevented. It is true that punishments resting on strict and vicarious liability are an exception, since the offenders are not necessarily morally responsible for offences. Backward-looking theories must also accommodate or contemplate strict and vicarious liability, of course.

Reform and perhaps rehabilitation theories of punishment – as against treatment – also rest on suppositions about freedom and responsibility. That a man can be held responsible for a certain offence is why he needs to be reformed. Theories advocating treatment in place of punishment are different, indeed different from all the theories of punishment just mentioned. They presume that all offenders in their offences lacked some or other freedom and responsibility, or sufficient degrees of these. It is for this reason that treatment is called for in place of punishment. As you will anticipate, there will also be presuppositions of freedom and responsibility with the mixed or compromise theories of punishment to which we shall come in the next stage of this inquiry.

It is clear, then, that no inquiry into the justification of punishment can be complete without a consideration of freedom or rather freedoms and of holding people responsible. No inquiry can be complete, that is, without an inquiry into *determinism*, the family of theories taken by some philosophers and indeed ordinarily taken to deny that we are free in our choices or decisions and our ensuing actions and thus to be held responsible for them or credited with responsibility for them. Do you remark to yourself that it follows that there has been no shortage of incomplete inquiries into the justification of punishment? That is true. Is this a scandal? Yes, if not the only scandal in philosophy, or the only scandal in the philosophy of punishment. You yourself may save a final judgement on this first scandal until hearing more about the large subject of determinism and its consequences.[1] You may in particular delay a final judgement on the idea that determinism is something of perennial interest but not something that really has to be taken seriously.

Determinism is indeed not one thing. Quite a few kinds of it can be distinguished, theories with different subject matters. They take different classes of events, larger or smaller classes, to be effects of certain sequences of causal circumstances. Or, if they are concerned with the same class of events, they may give some priority to different sorts of causes, for whatever reason or out of whatever idea, motivation or fascination.

Universal determinism had an inchoate existence in ancient Greek philosophy, and came into greater clarity with the rise of modern philosophy and science in the seventeenth century. It asserts that all events without exception, of whatever sort, are standard effects. That is to say, of course, that all the predecessors of any effect are also such effects. A second determinism, physical determinism, asserts that all physical events without exception are standard effects. It may understand physical events in terms of things taking up space and time, or as whatever events that are countenanced by science at a time. It may include the further claim that all causes and conditions of physical events are themselves physical events.

Determinism as most commonly understood in philosophy generally – as distinct from the philosophy of science – is human determinism. It is what is immediately relevant to punishment. It is the theory, entailed by universal determinism but open to separate consideration and support, that *our lives consist in effects*. More particularly, all of the antecedents of our actions, say contemplating possible alternatives, coming to have a forward-looking intention, choosing how to go ahead, actively intending or willing the action and then supervising it, are just effects, things subject to the rule of cause and effect, and so are the actions themselves.

There are also many lesser determinisms, incidentally. Almost all of them have a special concern with special classes of causes as against effects. One of these is Freud's, associated with psychoanalysis, which, as remarked earlier, concentrates on childhood sexual episodes and related matters later. Putting aside other more or less therapeutic enterprises, there are the other lesser determinisms that assign special causal powers to economic and social circumstances, religious or other upbringings of children, sides or aspects of evolution rather than evolution and heredity generally, genes, items in neurobiology, sorts of personalities, fate half-conceived as something other than causality, and the stars. The lesser determinisms, including the therapeutic ones, have not had any significant attention from philosophers.

It is mainly human determinism that has been a large, persistent and troubled subject in the history of philosophy. It has for the most part been considered in a schematic or general way. That is, it has been understood as not much more than the proposition that actions are effects, effects of such causal chains as to raise a question about their freedom and about responsibility for them. This proposition has had the attention of most of the greatest of philosophers, and very many others. Has its inexplicitness also contributed to the disregard of the problem of determinism and freedom by other philosophers? And by theorists of punishment?

In any case, it is clear that there are three problems about human determinism. The first is its formulation, the large problem of getting to a conceptually adequate theory of it, one that is clear, consistent and complete. As has become plain, or plain to some, this must now be an endeavour within, or at least fully informed by, that main and flourishing part of philosophy that is the philosophy of mind. The next problem is that of the truth of the theory. That is not settled, either way, in the sense of being generally and firmly agreed or maybe any other sense.

Thirdly, there is the problem that remains if or when a theory of determinism is taken to be conceptually respectable and also true. Determinism for good reason is best taken in the way that it has already been stated, as not in itself the view that we are not free. Nor does determinism as best understood include that proposition. Rather, it does no more than prompt or raise the question of whether we are free and responsible, the question of what follows from it, its consequences for us. There is disagreement about the answer, and so there is reason not to write a denial of freedom into a definition of determinism.

It should not be a matter of disagreement, and probably no longer is, that human determinism would or does affect a great deal in our lives, much more than punishment and theories of it. It affects a range of things involving our own choices and actions as well as those of others. It affects our life hopes, personal relations, claims to knowledge, holding people responsible and crediting them with responsibility where state punishment is not in question, the right-ness of actions, the moral standing of people over periods of time or their whole lives, and practices of punishment and reward other than those by the state.[2] There is more than one good reason to attend to those other areas of consequence, in a general inquiry into determinism. One reason is that findings with respect to conse-quences of determinism in one area, say our life hopes or claims or knowledge, fortify findings in another area, say moral responsibility. But we shall have to restrict ourselves to the business of holding people morally responsible for choices or decisions and actions, and perhaps crediting people with moral responsibility for them.

A SKETCH OF DETERMINISM

If there are determinisms of quite a few kinds, one being human determinism, there are also somewhat different kinds of human determinism. What follows here is a sketch of one theory of it, the kind of thing most considered by philosophers. Like any decent human determinism, it does indeed present our human actions and their antecedents as merely effects. It presents our human actions as effects of certain causal sequences or chains. In these sequences there occur the antecedents of the actions – choices, intentions and the like and also the neural or brain events that go with them – all of which conscious or mental events and neural events are themselves effects of yet earlier parts of the causal sequence. Some of these yet earlier parts are environmental, and others are bodily and conscious events in the life of the individual.

This would not be a determinism in an interesting or traditional sense if it involved a loose idea of an effect. There have been a number of such ideas, the most recent being of an event made *probable* by antecedents, no more than probable. Here what causes something else does no more than make it probable. An effect of this kind, however probable it was, was in the end a chance event, an inexplicable event. It is inexplicable because given the world exactly as it was, the event might as well not have happened, as in fact you have just heard. We do not here have our standard idea of an effect. Whether or not there are mysteries, standard effects are not mysteries. A standard effect is something that had to happen, the only thing that was possible.

Such an effect, of course, is not made necessary by a cause as usually understood. What caused the match to light, we say, was that it was struck. But it might have been struck and not lit. It would not have lit if it was wet, or if there was no oxygen present. What makes an effect happen, rather, is a whole set of conditions, one of them being the one we may call the cause. It is the set of conditions together, which can be called the causal circumstance, that guarantees the effect, leaves it alone as possible. As for a more explicit account of the relation of necessitation, what it comes to in my view is roughly as follows. The fact that A necessitated B is the fact that since A happened, whatever else had been happening, B would still have happened.[3]

This deterministic philosophy of mind we are considering consists of three hypotheses. It is best to look at what is temporally the middle one. This hypothesis concerns all conscious or mental events – I use the two terms synonymously – and in particular, choices, decisions and intentions, the antecedents of actions. The hypothesis proceeds by way of a fairly ordinary view of the nature of mental events, or such mental events as choices or decisions. The governing aim of these views is to give an account of an individual's decisions such that he or she can in a certain strong way be held morally responsible for them. Thus it is said of an individual's decision at a time, for one thing, that he could have decided and done otherwise than he did, given all things as they then were, and given all of the past as it was.

It is no longer the case that these traditional views can ignore the brain and neuroscience, but they take account of it in a particular way. Some may accept the psychoneural correlation hypothesis, the proposition that neural events necessitate simultaneous mental events. But they somehow deny that mental events and actions are merely effects. They may make use of a certain common interpretation of part of physics, quantum theory, thereby drawing the conclusion that the mentioned mental or conscious events are merely made probable and not necessitated by antecedent events.

These views cannot stop with an indeterminist account of these events, of course. If they did, such events would be chance events or too near to chance events. These by their nature, when you think of it, are events for which an individual could be in *no* sense responsible. They have no explanation. Thus the traditional views conflicting with the hypothesis on the causation of psychoneural pairs have at their centre another kind of explanation of decisions.

Decisions are *originated* by the individual or some faculty or capability or part of the individual – say *the will* or the *self*, maybe the *creative self*. Or decisions are originated by a strange event within an individual, maybe a funny causal circumstance that may or may not work, or, as you might say, not go off. What this comes to, looked at in what is perhaps the best way, is that a decision is not a standard effect, not necessitated, but nonetheless has such a source in the individual or something within him so that he is responsible for it in the mentioned strong sense – of which more will be said in due course. An alternative idea, that the decision is an ordinary effect, but that its cause is not itself such an effect but is originated, faces the same and perhaps more difficulties.

One hope and indeed obligation of such traditional views must be to give a respectable positive account of the fundamental relation of origination or free will. This would go beyond what has so far been reported, that the views take it that I stand to my choice in such a way that I could have made a different choice given things as they are and have been, and that I am in a strong way responsible for it.

This clearly is not to define or characterize the relation as fully as can be wished. However, it is not necessary to agree with a philosopher or two who condemns these views as actually nonsensical or actually contentless at this crucial point.[5]

The third hypothesis of the theory of determinism is as simple as the hypothesis on the causation of psychoneural pairs. The *hypothesis on the causation of actions* involves a general definition of our actions, of course including speech acts. Actions in general are bodily movements or stillnesses somehow owed to active intentions – which active intentions also somehow represent or perhaps picture the movements and state of affairs that follow on them. The hypothesis on the causation of actions is in part as follows.

> Each action is an effect of a causal sequence one of whose initial elements is a psychoneural pair which includes the active intention that represents the action.

This is the least controversial of the three hypotheses of this determinism, or, as it seems to me, most uncontroversial.

So much for a sketch of a determinism that may be true of those who break the law and all the rest of us.

DETERMINISM DESPITE QUANTUM THEORY

Many philosophers have discussed such a determinism without committing themselves to its truth. There has generally been discussion of the consequences of such a determinism for morality. The question asked has been this: *if* such a determinism is true, what follows for morality? We shall be considering this question, but let me first explain why some or many are indeed inclined to take the antecedent as true – that is, to take determinism as true. As is clear, a judgement or assumption on that is of course needed in connection with punishment. In particular, a judgement is needed on the tendency to take determinism as less than serious, just a question for some philosophers, not a question that actually intrudes on the lives of ordinary theorizers about punishment, a question that may have an answer that qualifies, weakens or destroys their theories.

One reason for believing determinism, already implied, is that a determinism allows for an explicit and articulated account of ourselves and our existence, an explicit and articulated philosophy of mind. We have a sketch of it on the table. That is no small thing.

is that there is no experimental evidence in a plain sense that there are any. There is no such evidence within physics. There is no such evidence three-quarters of a century after Heisenberg and Schrödinger developed quantum theory. In that very long time in science, including the recent decades of concern with a certain hopeful theorem, there has been *no direct and univocal experimental evidence* of the existence of quantum events. There have been newspaper articles announcing that the evidence or proof was about to be found next month but no articles that it has been. It has not happened that science has been left no room for real doubt by something, let alone science and philosophy. Philosophy is entirely relevant to the matter, by the way. As has been remarked before now and will be illustrated in a minute, the interpretation of quantum theory, its application to reality, as distinct from the body of mathematics in which it actually consists, is something of a clearly philosophical character.

A second thing to be noted of the items called quantum events has to do with a prior issue of which you have had a hint from my sceptical usages. What are these items if they do somehow or other exist? How are they to be conceived? How are these items offered to us in the interpretation of the mathematics or formalism of quantum theory actually to be understood? How are we to think of these things that are supposed to turn up in our brains and, as some say, leave room for traditional free will?

Well, standard accounts by physicists of these items do agree about something. The accounts bravely say the items are baffling, weird and wonderful, self-contradictory, inexplicable, etc. These events so-called, we have long been told, do *not* involve particles as ordinarily understood and defined, and the special use of the term 'particle' within interpretations of the mathematics cannot be satisfactorily defined. So with uses of 'position' or 'location' and so on. The items are not located anywhere in the usual sense.

The situation can be indicated quickly by noting a collection of physicists' own speculations and conjectures as to what quantum events in general are, what this supposed bottom level of all reality comes to. It is now not brand new, but it has not been replaced by anything very different. Quantum events so-called are observer-dependent facts, or subjective ideas, or contents of our consciousness of reality, or epistemological concepts, or ideal concepts. Or they are propositions, probabilities, possibilities, features of a calculation, mathematical objects or devices, statistical phenomena, measures and measurements, abstract particles, probability waves, waves in abstract mathematical space, waves of no real physical existence, abstract constructs of the imagination, theoretical entities without empirical reality, or objects to which ordinary logic does not apply. What most of those things are is unclear, but that is not the main point.

It was remarked above that physics has not provided any direct and univocal experimental evidence of the existence of events that lack standard explanations, events that are not effects. The noted collection of speculations about the nature of quantum events shows more that that. It remains a clear possibility, indeed a probability, that physics has not started on the job, after 75 years, of showing that there are events that lack explanations. This is so, simply, because it remains a probability that quantum events, so-called, are not events. They are not events in the ordinary sense gestured at above or according to any of the finer conceptions. In brief, it is probable that they are *not* things that occur or happen, but are of the nature of numbers and propositions, out of space and time. They are theoretical entities in a special sense of that term.

The nub of this is simple, and not at all technical. Consider a plain determinist who says in a bar or pub that everything is an effect. He is set upon by a word-minding adversary who says triumphantly that the number 5, as distinct from any actual inscription or representation of it in writing or whatever, is not an effect, and therefore determinism is false. The simple determinist's proper reply is that he never did suppose, and has no need of supposing, that 5 is an effect. What he supposes is that everything that *happens* is an effect.

Someone inclined to determinism, and a little tired of a kind of hegemony of physics in a part of philosophy – the part having to do with determinism and freedom – may be capable of saying still more in defence of determinism. They may even remain capable after considering relevant and admirable contributions by leading philosophers of science.[8] As the above collection of speculations and conjectures by physicists indicates, even without the addition of some wholly inconsistent and 'realist' speculations, the interpretation of the mathematics of quantum theory is not merely baffling, weird and wonderful, etc. It is *a mess*. That is what would be said of any such enterprise of inquiry that did not enjoy a general hegemony, in more than the mentioned part of philosophy. If science did not *work* – which working or success, by the way, is perfectly consistent with the common interpretation of quantum theory being false or indeed worse – that interpretation of reality would long since have been put aside as a theoretical disaster.

What we have, then, to sum up so far, is that the proposition that all events have explanations has unique inductive and empirical support in our experience, that there is no experimental evidence in a standard sense for quantum events as interpreted, that the failure to provide experimental evidence for them may be the result of a confused concern with theoretical items other than events, and that the sum of what is said of quantum theory is not conceptually adquate.

A final thing to be contemplated about the supposed quantum events goes flatly against all of this objection – but, as it turns out, not necessarily against determinism as we have quite ordinarily conceived it. Let us assume that quantum events so-called, despite the collection of speculations by physicists noted, *are* to be conceived as events. That is how they are to be understood, as things happening. Let it also be assumed, against the premise of the macro-events of our experience, that they *do* exist. They are right there among other micro-events, at atomic and subatomic levels. They are events that lack explanations, events of true chance.[9]

Now understand by determinism the theory sketched earlier or any other decent articulation of the idea that human choices and actions are effects of certain causal sequences or chains – sequences such as to raise the further and separate question of whether the choices and actions are free and responsible. Determinism so conceived is in fact a matter of only macro-events. It remains so if it is further developed into explicit philosophies of mind that say more of the relation of choices and actions to the brain, to neural events. The latter, the stuff of neuroscience, as already remarked, are as much macro-events as choices and actions themselves.

It is clear that anyone inclined both to the existence of the true chance or quantum events and to determinism as defined is not at all forced to choose between them, but can have both. She is not stuck with levitating spoons. Micro-indeterminism is not necessarily in conflict with ordinary determinism. Her essential idea will be that quantum events in our heads do not translate upwards or amplify into macro-events that also lack explanations. The quantum events in this respect may cancel out one another – or something of the sort. It is a familiar kind of idea. Given the entire absence of events of real chance within standard neuroscience, this is perhaps the easiest theoretical position for those who want their philosophy to be in accord with a leading or majority opinion in science as it is now rather than as it will be, the paradigm now rather than some paradigm to come. I refer, of course, to the indeterminist interpretation of quantum theory.

The conclusion of these thoughts is clear. The macro-determinism in question raises exactly the traditional problem of freedom despite being married to micro-indeterminism. Nothing changes with respect to any of the matters we are considering. Macro-determinism with micro-indeterminism leaves exactly where it was the problem about determinism most attended to by philosophers and others, that of its consequences for our lives – our freedom and responsibility in choosing and acting. Nothing changes with punishment.

This is not the place to take further the issue of the truth of determinism, or to defend further what may seem to be a philosopher's audacity in having a view of the import of quantum theory. Let us turn to the issue of what follows with respect to morality since or if determinism is true.

COMPATIBILISM AND INCOMPATIBILISM

There is a venerable tradition in philosophy known as compatibilism, which flows from Thomas Hobbes in the seventeenth century and David Hume in the eighteenth.[10] It is dedicated to the idea, still surprising to undergraduates, that if determinism is true, each of us *can* nevertheless act freely and be held morally responsible for actions or be credited with responsibility for actions. Moral responsibility for an action does indeed presuppose that the action was freely chosen, but freedom and determinism can exist together. They are logically compatible.

This is so, we are told, since freedom consists in what you have already heard of as *voluntariness* (p. 26). Many definitions have been given of voluntariness. Their central idea is that a voluntary choice or decision is one that is according to the desires and the nature of the individual. It is his or hers in that sense. It is a choice or decision not forced upon him or her by something external, or usually external, notably other persons or a constraining environment. Again, a voluntary choice may be regarded as a matter of embraced desires as distinct from reluctant desires – say the reluctant desire to give up your wallet to the man with the gun.

Indubitably, to come to a further and fundamental point, freedom of this kind is perfectly consistent with determinism. Evidently this freedom can amount to choices being owed to a certain sort of causation rather than no causation. What makes a man in jail unfree is the jail, his not being able to do what he really wants to do. What conflicts with freedom as voluntariness is not determinism but compulsion or constraint, being made to go against your desires and nature, maybe being subject to or a victim of your own internal compulsion.

There is another venerable tradition in philosophy known as incompatibilism. Some of Immanuel Kant's reflections on freedom are within it, but a less complicated and more single-minded exponent of the view in question was Hobbes's great adversary, Bishop Bramhall.[11] Incompatibilism is dedicated to the opposite idea that if determinism is true, none of us can be held morally responsible for our actions or credited with responsibility for them.

That is because moral responsibility for an action presupposes that the action was freely chosen not only in the sense of being voluntary. A free choice, we are told, is also one of free will, one that was originated. It was owed, we may be told, to an uncaused event that none the less was in the control of the chooser. The philosophers of this tradition, as remarked earlier, have succeeded in giving only a thin account of origination. One clear thing, however, is that origination is logically incompatible with determinism. An originated choice is precisely not just an effect. Rather, it is something disconnected from antecedents – or, to speak more carefully, not connected with them in the way that is the case with an effect.

It has long been supposed that either compatibilism or incompatibilism must give us the truth about the consequences of determinism for moral responsibility. Indeed this has seemed to be a logically necessary truth. Freedom, it has seemed, either is consistent or is not consistent with determinism. One or the other has to be true. It has been my own view, which now has more support, that the logically necessary truth, to put the matter one way, has a false presupposition. The real facts about the relation of determinism to freedom are not at all conveyed by the necessary truth. They are not conveyed by either compatibilism or incompatibilism, but rather by something else.

ATTITUDINISM

We can approach the subject by getting clearer about the matter of holding people morally responsible for actions or crediting them with responsibility for actions. There is an advantage to be had from not peering further at the word 'free' in order to see if freedom is consistent with determinism, as philosophers have done, and not attempting to devise still more proofs of the content of the word, but instead looking directly at what might be called the human reality of the problem of determinism and freedom, or rather one part of that reality. What does holding people morally responsible for actions and crediting them with moral responsibility for actions come to?

This ascribing of responsibility is not to be identified with judging actions to be wrong or right. That what I did was wrong is indeed presupposed by my properly being held responsible for it, but it is not the same fact. So with my being credited with responsibility and my being judged to have acted rightly. They are not to be identified. I can do wrong without being held responsible for the action, do right without being credited with responsibility. Nor, more obviously, is holding someone responsible for a particular action the same as judging her to be a bad or inhuman person, where that is to make a judgement that pertains to much more than one action, but to character or a pattern of life or indeed all of a life. So with crediting someone with responsibility for an action and judging her to be a good or human person.

Quite as clearly, holding someone morally responsible for something is not just believing that an action was somehow a free one. Certainly a belief or idea of freedom is contained in or bound up with holding someone responsible for something. But it is quite as much bound up with the opposite thing – giving someone moral credit for an action. Also, you can think of some action as having been a free one without getting around to the question of holding the person responsible at all – or crediting the action to him. So there is more to ascriptions of responsibility than a belief or idea about freedom. There is a usage such that 'a responsible action' is somehow a free one, but this does not affect the main distinction.

It seems evident that to hold someone morally responsible for an action is to *disapprove of them morally with respect to that action*. It is to have an attitude to them. To credit someone with moral responsibility is to *approve of them morally with respect to an action*. Something else, one last distinction, is worth adding. If holding someone responsible is not the same as judging an action to be wrong, or assessing a person over time, perhaps a lifetime, or having a belief as to freedom, it is also distinct from what may *follow* on holding the person responsible, which is an action of blaming or punishing her. The latter is clearly distinct from the former. So with crediting with responsibility and a subsequent action of praising or rewarding.

Let us put the subject of punishment or anyway punishment by the state aside for a while and try to arrive, by way of an example or two, at some general conclusions about ascriptions of responsibility and thus compatibilism, incompatibilism and attitudinism. Suppose a man, foreseeing his coming divorce, contrives to divert a large part of the couple's joint money and property to his children. He does so in order to deprive their mother of her share of them and to win away the affection and loyalty of the children. Unless the situation is extraordinary, we shall certainly hold him responsible. What does this particular fact come to?

It is clear, to repeat, that your holding him responsible, your disapproving of him morally with respect to the action, does not come to just a belief, something true or false, about what can be called the initiation of the action, how the action came about in terms of a decision or the like. More than just a proposition of this kind is in question. You do indeed have an attitude to him with respect to the action. If this attitude has such a belief within it, it also involves much more.

It is no easy thing, by the way, to give a general definition of an attitude – a definition covering, to take some relevant examples, moral approval and disapproval, large hopes for your life, non-moral attitudes to persons, confidence that beliefs are knowledge, judgements as to the rightness of actions, and feelings about the general moral standing of people. It will have to suffice to say that an attitude is an evaluative thought of something, feelingful, and bound up with desire, the mentioned feeling being feeling in a narrow sense, somehow similar to or even bound up with sensation. Different attitudes, say resentment as against hope, call for different particular descriptions.

In the case in question, what does your attitude of holding the man responsible come to? It is of absolutely fundamental importance to the question of the consequences of determinism, in my view, that it may on different occasions come to different things. To hold him responsible is to be engaged in or subject to one or another of *two* different attitudes. Each of us engages in or is capable of both these attitudes. We do or can move back and forth between them. We are not as simple as compatibilists or incompatibilists suppose us to be.

One attitude partly involves certain feelings in a broad sense. These are feelings of repugnance for the man with respect to his vicious or dishonourable desires to deprive his wife and to win away the loyalty of the children. It is our tendency to withdraw from him and from his desires. These feelings are distantly related to aesthetic ones. But this first attitude also involves other feelings, of more importance. We may say that the situation is to be laid at his door, or that he should not get away with it scot-free, or that he should be exposed, or indeed that the wife should get satisfaction. This second set of feelings in this attitude, in a general sense, consists in desires – at bottom the desire somehow to act against the husband or have others act against him. He should have, at the least, the discomfiture of knowing that others disapprove of him. These desires are in a large category of desires, with much more in it than what you will remember, the grievance desires that enter into retributive punishment by the state, and retributive theories of it.

To stick to the example, on what do your retributive feelings about the man rest? Or, as we can as well say, what belief do they incorporate about the initiation of his action? Well, they will very likely or almost certainly diminish or collapse under certain conditions. They will collapse in the unlikely case where you come to believe that determinism was true of the husband, absolutely true of his first desire to take the step in question, and his forming of the intention, and his carrying it through – everything involved. This has to be a speculation, since it is a fact that most of us do not often, if ever, succeed in believing determinism in the sense of such an explicit theory as was sketched above. Our culture is against it. Still, the speculation about a collapse of feelings seems to me very persuasive indeed, near to irresistible. It is supported by, among other things, our resistance in actual cases to pleas of inexplicit or commonsensical determinism or half-determinism on behalf of those of whom we are morally disapproving, particularly those of whom we want to go on disapproving. Nothing is more common than resisting excuses for terrible behaviour that have to do with unhappy childhoods, social backgrounds, etc.

If your retributive feelings about the husband would collapse if you came really to believe that determinism was true of this episode in his life, it seems clear what they rest on when they persist. It is a certain conception of the initiation of the decision and the action. You take a particular thing to be true, or more ordinarily have images that tend in a certain direction. You somehow take it that the decision was *originated*, a matter of *free will*. You take it that the occurrence of the husband's decision was not fixed by the state of the world when he took the decision, or preceding states of the world. He could have decided otherwise given things as they were and as they had been. If our resting retributive desires on an assumption of origination in this way is a contingent fact about human nature, or even a fact that will not be with us to the end of time, it remains a fact.

So – we can hold another person morally responsible for an action, holding him or her responsible in a strong sense, and doing this is inconsistent with determinism. The same is true of holding oneself responsible for things. I have not done greatly more here than display this fact of inconsistency, but certainly much more can be said to show it to be a clear and strong fact.[12] Part of the story is its going together with other facts having to do with life hopes, knowledge claims, and so on.

Suppose we think of this particular way of holding others and ourselves responsible, this particular attitude, and, perhaps more importantly, think of the analogous way of *crediting* ourselves with responsibility, morally approving of ourselves. Suppose we think of these things, and we also contemplate that determinism is true. Suppose determinism gets a hold on us. That is unlikely, but it can happen. What is our response likely to be? It is likely to be dismay or an anticipation of dismay. In short, our response is likely to be that determinism wrecks what might be called our satisfactory practice of assigning moral responsibility, something that enters into a lot of life. Above all determinism wrecks an image we have of ourselves as estimable agents of a certain kind.

However, if it is possible that in holding the husband responsible you take this particular attitude to him, with the given upshot in connection with the contemplation of determinism, it is just as possible that on another occasion you take another attitude, with a different upshot. None of us is immured in the first attitude.

On another occasion you have, again, feelings of repugnance for him. But your attitude, in its second and more important part, has more to do with your perception of the harm done to the wife and very likely also the children. Your attitude in its second part may be said to consist mainly in a desire to affect the husband in such a way that matters are rectified, or, if that is not possible, to affect him in such a way as to reduce the likelihood of such actions or related actions in the future. Your desires, in a phrase or two, are desires to affect his motivations and perhaps those of others in order to prevent harm. If your attitude to the man is importantly directed to the future in this way, what conception does or may it involve of his initiation of his action?

Well, you would not have the given attitude to him if, as must be unlikely in this case, he succeeded in acting in ignorance of what he was doing, in entirely successful self-deception. If that really was true, you would or might have no rationale for trying to change anything but his state of knowledge. Nor would you have your desire to affect him if, as again must be unlikely, he was compelled by someone else to act as he did. There would be no need to change *him*. Nor would you have your desire, at any rate exactly as you do, if he had had a real but finally unsuccessful desire not to have the low desire that did issue in the diverting of the monies. Nor of course would you have your attitude if you took him to be insane or radically immature or suffering from some other incapacitating disorder. In these latter cases, he would not, so to speak, be a suitable object of intentions of the kind in question.

Your holding him responsible or morally disapproving of him, in this second way, does indeed involve a conception of the initiation of his action. But evidently it need not be a conception of the decision as originated, but only of the decision as *voluntary*. In brief, to revert to something like the too general description of voluntariness mentioned earlier, you may take it only that the decision flowed from his own unconflicted desires and nature. That does not follow automatically from the mentioned facts about giving up an attitude – it might also rest on something else – but they point in that direction. The simplest and perhaps strongest evidence for the existence of the attitude is our remembering our own experience.

Suppose we think of this second way of holding people responsible, and again contemplate that determinism is true. The fact of the matter is that the attitude in question, including its belief component, is perfectly consistent with determinism. We may thus make a different response in the matter of moral responsibility and determinism, a response different from dismay. It can be spoken of as intransigence. It is to the effect that if determinism does affect an attitude with an idea of origination in it, the previous attitude, we can try to resolve not to be troubled by this. We can persist in the second attitude. Determinism does not wreck the assigning of moral responsibility. It does not conflict with all of it.

This story of two attitudes – attitudinism – has been told in a very schematic way. What has been provided are stark models, not any nuanced or complete pictures of our feelings. But perhaps you have been persuaded at least of the possibility that there are two different things that fall under the description 'holding someone morally responsible for an action'. Both of them support responsive actions on our own part, although not necessarily the same actions. What is important is that the first attitude, which of course has variants, involves conceiving of the initiation of an action in terms of origination as well as voluntariness, and the second attitude, along with variants, involves only voluntariness. To speak differently, one attitude involves one conception of freedom as a reason or part of a reason for action on our part and the other attitude involves another conception.

Let me put these claims into a nutshell, or a smaller nutshell, by way of another example. Suppose it happens that your son, for no good reason, perhaps the colour of his skin, or a bit of independent style on his part, is attacked in the street and injured. You may have a vengeful attitude that centres on the thought that his assailants, whatever their histories, and with things just as they were, could have acted differently there and then. They could then have stopped themselves. If you meet them you may be tempted to more than words. But you may also have an attitude that has to do with preventing more such things from happening, improving the future, and focuses on the desires and intentions of his assailants. Clearly you do not have to suppose that your son's assailants had free will, the power of giving rise to uncaused decisions. You may move between these attitudes, both of them ways of holding someone responsible. You may as a result make different responses to determinism.

The theory of attitudinism, as against compatibilism and incompatibilism, is surely persuasive. But there are things said against it. We had better consider a sample of them.

ARGUMENTS FOR COMPATIBILISM
AND INCOMPATIBILISM

In the last couple of decades, a good deal of diligence has gone into a certain incompatibilist line of thought. Plainly stated, it is that if determinism is true then an action of mine today, let us say the action of complying or going along again with my unjust society, is the effect of a causal circumstance in the remote past, before I was born. That circumstance, clearly, was not *up to me*. So its necessary consequence, my action of compliance or complicity today with my hierarchic democracy, is not up to me. Hence my action today is not free and I am not responsible for it.[13] That is just obvious.

This line of thought is dignified by having the name of the *consequence argument* for incompatibilism. It is worth noting that in its essential content, its logic, the argument has nothing to do with our being unable to change the past. It is that the past had in it no act of origination, and in particular no relevant act of origination. It had in it no act of origination that had the later action of compliance with my unjust society as content or object, so to speak, and as effect. Instead it had in it that remote causal circumstance and a causal sequence from it leading up to the action of compliance. If the past *did* have such a relevant act of origination in it, although I still couldn't change it and the rest of the past, things would be OK. My action of compliance could be up to me.

It is also worth noting that the argument has nothing essential to do with a causal circumstance in the *remote* past. To repeat, what the incompatibilist supposes would make my action today up to me, make me free and responsible, is an act of origination relevant to today's action of compliance. Suppose that the act of origination for the action of social compliance would have had to be in the last five minutes – originations wear out, so to speak, if they do not issue in actions within five minutes. If they are to work, they have to be renewed. We do indeed believe something like this. If so, for the incompatibilist, my action's having been the effect of a causal circumstance just over five minutes ago would make the action not up to me.

Suppose on the other hand, absurdly, that a previous embodiment of me *did* perform a relevant act of origination. That might cheer up the incompatibilist, even if it was so remotely in the past as to be just after the Big Bang, and even if that event was immediately followed by a causal circumstance, certainly remote, for my later action of compliance.

Thus what is crucial for this line of thought is a relevant act of origination. And hence, to mention one thing in passing, the argument has as much need of giving a decent account of origination as any other argument of its ilk – any incompatibilism. What in fact has happened in connection with the line of argument, however, is a lot of reflection on something else, aided by modal logic, the formal logic about necessity and possibility. We could transform it into reflection that makes the essential content or logic of the argument explicit, talk about a causal circumstance just over five minutes ago, but there is no need to do so.

The modal reflection has been on whether it does really follow, from the fact that a remote causal circumstance was not up to me, that its necessary consequence, my action today in going along with my society, is not up to me. The reflection has included technical variations on the plain version of the line of thought, and also technical objections to and supposed refutations of both the plain line of thought and the variations.

It is not easy for me to see that this has been philosophical time well spent. Does it not seem clear that in an ordinary sense of the words, it does indeed follow that if the remote causal circumstance was not up to me, neither was what was connected with it by an unbroken causal sequence – my action today? Will anyone say that there is *no* sense of the words in which it follows that if the remote circumstance was not up to me, neither was its necessary consequence? No fundamental or important sense in which lack of control is transitive? Might you join me in saying that if modal logic were to prove that there is no such sense of the words, or no important sense of the words, so much the worse for modal logic?

Now consider some very different argument on the other side in the traditional dispute between incompatibilists and compatibilists – some compatibilist struggle in the last couple of decades, or rather two such struggles. Both are attempts to defend this tradition's fundamental conception of our freedom, at its most simple the conception of a choice or action that is not against the desire of the person in question. An unfree choice or action by contrast is one made as a result of the bars of the prison cell, or the threat to one's life, or the compulsion of kleptomania.

Against this idea as to our freedom, it may be objected that we could be free in this way and yet not be in control of our lives. This voluntariness is not *control*. Exactly this was a complaint of incompatibilists. It gave rise to a struggle in response by compatibilists. It is plainly a mistake, we heard from them and still do, to suppose that if I was free in this sense today in my action of social deference, I was *subject to control*. What *control* would come to would be my being subject to the desires of another person, or something akin to another person, maybe within me. Given this proposition, evidently, it is not the case that determinism, which is indeed consistent with the compatibilist idea to our freedom, deprives us of control of our lives.[14]

So far so good, you may say. But clearly a question remains. Could what has been said by the compatibilists be taken as coming near to establishing that there is but *one* way in which we can conceive of *not* being in control of our lives, the way where we are subject to someone or something else's desires? To put the question differently, and more pointedly, does this come near to establishing that there is but *one* way, the compatibilist way, in which we can *be* in control of our lives, which is to say one way in which we conceive of being free? That all we think of or can care about is voluntariness?

There are rather plain difficulties in the way of this. There evidently is something very like another idea of self-control or freedom, having to do with origination or free will. Is it not against the odds, to say the least, that this dispute into which our compatibilist is seriously entering is between his own conceptually respectable party and a party that has *no different idea at all*, nothing properly called an idea or anyway no idea worth attention, of what our freedom does or may consist in? There *is* what has been said of origination.

Let me mention yet more quickly the effort by some compatibilists to make more explicit their idea of freedom. It is at bottom the effort to show why the kleptomaniac and other such unfortunates, on the compatibilist account of freedom, are in fact unfree. Certainly it could be thought there was a problem for the account here, since the kleptomaniac in walking out of the department store yet again without paying for the blouses presumably *is* somehow doing what she wants to do, presumably is *not* acting against desire.

Our compatibilist is indeed on the way to a solution if he supposes, a little bravely, that all kleptomaniacs not only desire to make off with the blouses, but also desire not to have that desire. By means of this idea of a *hierarchy* of desires, that is, the compatibilist is indeed improving his conception of a free action – it is, at least in the first part of the conception, an action such that we desire to desire to perform it.[15] Suppose more than that – that the whole philosophical enterprise, this hierarchical theory of freedom, works like a dream, with no difficulties about a regress or about identifying a self with a particular level of desires or about anything else.

Will that have come near to establishing that there is no other conception of a free action? Will it come close to establishing that we have operating in our lives only the hierarchic conception of voluntariness? Will it come close to establishing the lesser thing that this conception is fundamental or dominant or most salient or in any other way ahead of another one? Come to think of it, *how* could it actually do that? Are we to suppose that from the premise that one conception of freedom has now been really perfected it follows that there is no other conception of freedom or none worth attention?

So that you do not suppose I have been partial, let us glance back at the incompatibilist struggle and complete our reflection on it. Think again of me today, acting again in compliance with my unjust society, and take the action to be the effect of a causal circumstance in the remote past, before I was born. It does indeed seem, as was maintained above, there must be *some* proposition to the effect that if the remote circumstance was not up to me, neither was the action of compliance with my society that was made necessary by the circumstance. But something else is surely quite as clear.

There *is*, isn't there, a clear sense in which my action, necessary consequence though it was, may well have been *up to me* – perfectly up to me. Suppose I was struck a month ago by an utterance of the philosopher F. H. Bradley. It was that to wish to be better than the world is to be already on the threshold of immorality. Suppose I had then consciously determined after a month's serious reflection that henceforth I would consistently *act on the side of my society*. Suppose it had come about that a great desire drew me only to this – and of course that I desired to have the desire, and so on. In fact my whole personality and character now supported my action of defer-ence. I could not have been more for it. This conjecture, or any more restrained and realistic one you like, comes close to establish-ing that it must be a *very* brave incompatibilist who maintains that there is no significant sense in which my action of compliance was up to me.

THE REAL CONSEQUENCES OF DETERMINISM

We are now in a position to draw the first of two general conclusions about the real consequences of determinism. It is that both of the long-running traditions, compatibilism and incompatibilism, are mistaken. The first, as remarked, comes down to the proposition that freedom is voluntariness, that this is what we know or can know it to be. The second is that freedom is voluntariness together with origination, as we know or can come to know. The two tradi-tions are in one way alike. They are alike in sharing the view that all of us have *a single, settled conception* of free choices and actions. But in fact we do not have one conception, but two.

Certainly, if freedom were one thing, it would be true that either it is or it is not consistent with determinism. That would be a logically necessary truth. But freedom is not one thing. Freedom, and in particular the freedom that enters into or is presupposed by our holding people responsible, is two things. In place of saying freedom is or is not consistent with determinism, which utterance has a false presupposition, we need to say that one freedom is consistent with determinism and one freedom is not.

Let me add one more reflection in favour of attitudinism. Those who agree with the compatibilists Hobbes and Hume in their simpler view of our lives must give some explanation of why their incompatibilist opponents over centuries have persisted in their different view, their supposed error. The explanation that repeatedly has been given, in short, is three or more centuries of confusion, linguistic and philosophical confusion, about a single shared idea. That is unlikely. The incompatibilist party of Bishop Bramhall must also provide what can be called an error theory – an explanation of why those who think like Hobbes and Hume have persisted in their view of a single thing that we are all supposed to know. Bramhall and his party talk of weak empiricism and wordplay. Karl Popper, the philosopher of science known not to have solved the problem of induction, speaks of *Hume* as muddled.[16]

These explanations seem to me nearly absurd. What explains four centuries of dispute is not that we all have a single shared conception of freedom – which one side or the other does not have the sense or wit or persistence to analyse clearly. What explains the dispute, or is a large part of the explanation, is that each of us, in place of having a single shared conception of freedom, has two sorts of attitude, containing different conception. With respect to disagreements generally, the absence of convergence or agreement is often hard to explain when what is at issue is only a matter of fact. It is not hard to explain with attitudes, let alone attitudes that in ways conflict in a single breast.[17]

My second conclusion about the consequences of determinism, which must be brief, has to do with what has seemed to me to be our right response to determinism. You have heard that if we have in mind the first way of holding people responsible and crediting people with responsibility, involving origination, and bring this together with determinism, our response is or may be dismay. We have been mistaken in an attitude – and also, of course, in acting on it. You have also heard that if we have in mind the second way of holding people responsible and giving credit to them, involving only voluntariness, and bring this together with determinism, our response is likely to be intransigence.

What we need to do is recognize that each of us has or is capable of the two sorts of responsibility attitudes, and see more clearly the proper effect of determinism on us. What it comes to is that determinism neither wrecks moral responsibility, thus being a rightful cause of just dismay, nor leaves it untouched, thereby rightly giving rise to only intransigence. We must give up something but we can also keep something. We can keep the attitude to others and ourselves that has within it a picture of actions as voluntary. Further, what we can keep is worth having. In particular I remain capable of moral credit for my actions. I can have a kind of moral credit which has to do with wholly human or exemplary desires and intentions. The thought can and should be put into a certain context, a context that gives it further support. This has already been mentioned.

The subject of our reflections, in so far as they have concerned the consequences of determinism, has been moral responsibility, and so, as remarked earlier, I have in a way been true to another tradition. It is a philosophical tradition that brings together consideration of both compatibilists and incompatibilists and supposes that determinism is important or most important with respect to its consequences for moral responsibility. Arguably this is mistaken.

Determinism is at least as important in human terms, surely, for its consequences for what can be called our life hopes. These are an individual's principal hopes for his or her future. As in the case of moral responsibility, we have or are capable of two attitudes here – one involving the conception of an unfixed future, one involving a future of voluntary actions. We have or are capable of having two kinds of life hopes. Determinism also has consequences for what can be called personal as distinct from moral feelings or attitudes. Resentment and gratitude are examples. It is possible to think that these consequences too are more humanly important than the consequences for moral responsibility – and, as can be added, related consequences in connection with attitudes having to do with right actions and good persons. Also, determinism has consequences with respect to our claims to knowledge, our confidence of laying hold on truth.

In all these areas of consequence, as it seems to me, the situation is the same. We have or are capable of two sorts of attitude having to do with freedoms, and thus we may respond to determinism with dismay or intransigence. Our attitudes having to do with origination, and our attitudes having to do only with voluntariness, can have much said of them. They are open to judgement of various kinds. They may be in different ways clear, confused, generous, selfish, reasonable, objectionable, wrong or right. They include attitudes of retribution, of which we know, but they also include fellow-feeling and love. They come together into the two groups as a result of their contained ideas or images of free choices and actions.

That is not the end of the story, however. We may indeed respond to determinism with dismay or intransigence as a result of a focus on the first or the second group of attitudes. But, on reflection, we can also attempt to respond in another way. We can attempt to change our feelings. We can see what we must give up, and see what we can keep, and see the value of what we can keep. This can be called the response of *affirmation*. It is a response to what now seems to be the real problem of determinism, a kind of practical problem. It is certainly not the problem of seeing or proving which of two ideas is our one and only idea of freedom – or our one important idea of freedom.

It is a problem of what to do when determinism becomes persuasive or seems to be true, and it gives rise to unsatisfactory and troubling responses in us, those of dismay and intransigence. What we need to do is see that while determinism takes something from us, it leaves us with something that gives great value to life, makes it possible to affirm life. As written in another place, it was the philosopher Schopenhauer's view, perhaps, that our existence is to be mourned, that we would decline the gift of life if we could anticipate its nature beforehand. The philosopher Nietzsche, in his way also a determinist, said different, that we may affirm life. It is Nietzsche with whom we can and must agree.[18]

PUNISHMENT

So much for a survey of a great problem and an attempt to resolve it. We can now return to punishment.

Retribution theories of punishment, beyond doubt, have almost always rested on beliefs that all of us, and offenders in particular, have the freedom to act or not to act that is the power of origination or free will. Almost all theorists of retribution assert the fact, however clearly. Those who take a deserved penalty to be one whose distress equals the culpability of the offender take the culpability to be a matter in part of the offender's free will in the offence. Do the backward-looking theories of consent and contract also presuppose origination? Some seem to, but let us not pursue the question.

The utilitarian prevention theory, as you may well have anticipated, certainly has no need of this belief or assumption of free will. In fact most or many utilitarians have followed Bentham and Mill in being at least inclined to determinism. What they assume is that offences can be free in the sense of being voluntary. The same is or may be true of other theories of punishment in terms of prevention.

As for reform theories, and theories advocating treatment in place of punishment, summary is less simple. Those who suppose that punishment itself reforms men, or gives an opportunity for reforming them, may have in mind that they broke the law of their own free will. But perhaps they can without difficulty proceed in terms of belief in voluntariness. To propose treatment in place of punishment is to take all offenders as sick or something of the sort, and hence subject to conditions that are unlikely to be owed to freedom of either kind, because not owed to decisions or choices at all.

What follows from these reflections on freedom is first that retributivism's particular way of holding offenders responsible for offenders has indeed almost always been the way that includes an assumption of origination. It is moral disapproval partly consisting in an idea of actions as originated. The attitude fits into the large group of various attitudes of which we know. The utilitarian prevention theory, whatever has been the case with it, can rest on no more than an attitude of moral disapproval itself resting on freedom as voluntariness. For the most part, advocates of the theory have indeed made no other assumption and have held men to be responsible only in the given way. The attitude in question fits into the other large group of attitudes.

Our earlier consideration of various retribution theories issued in their rejection on various grounds, some of them moral grounds. Certainly it was for a moral reason that we rejected retributivism understood as the justification of punishment by way of grievance satisfaction. It was remarked that retributivism has always seemed not so vulnerable as prevention theories to refutation on the basis of ordinary facts (p. 76). An inquiry into determinism surely changes that. Certainly it is my view that retribution in punishment and at least most retribution theories are also to be rejected or put seriously in question because they take something to be false that is in fact true. That thing is determinism. There is a factual objection to retributivism that is *stronger* than the factual objection to prevention theories that punishment in fact does not prevent offences. Retributivists have reason for dismay. They also have reason for affirmation, here the response of giving up retributivism and taking up and being satisfied by a prevention theory of punishment.

This is the point at which to make good on a promise (p. 73) to spend a little more time on the analysis of retribution theories into the proposition that punishment is right because it satisfies grievance desires and does no less and no more than satisfy them. When that conclusion was drawn, it was drawn on its own. It was about only punishment and was part of no wider reflection. We now take it that we have in our lives one way of holding people responsible, including ourselves, that is a kind of attitude that has in it a belief or idea as to originated action, and desirous feelings against the person in question. Such feelings may be no more than the inclination to have it brought to someone's awareness that he does not have our approval for what he has done. They may be much stronger. They may be desires for much more than his discomfiture.

As you will anticipate, what were called grievance desires for the distress of offenders are exactly strong instances of the range of desirous feelings now in view in connection with holding people in general morally responsible. Grievance desires are at the top of the scale of what we can call retributive feelings in general. So the proposition having to do with punishment and grievance desires is indeed buttressed by fitting together with a larger fact of our existence. The fact of grievance desires is no isolated item, not something made suspect by uniqueness.

Another thing needs a little attention. Is what has been said of origination and retributive desires generally somehow too simple? In particular, can it be the case that the voluntariness of an action, as against its being taken as having been originated, is also a source or ground of grievance desires and of retributive feelings in general? In short, can it be the case that someone's distasteful, bad, grim, appalling or horrific intentions and feelings, these being his and no one else's, can contribute to exactly our retributive feelings? Might it be the case that if determinism were to become a matter of ordinary belief, we would find ourselves as retributive as before in our ascriptions of moral responsibility, now basing them on the voluntariness of actions? That it would not matter that a decision to act was just an effect, that in that sense it could not have been otherwise?

Fortunately, for the purpose of the arguments we are considering, we do not need an answer to this question of what might be called the future resources of human nature. As we now are, it is beyond question that our holding people responsible in the retributive way *is* bound up with our ideas or images of free will – the idea that someone could have done otherwise in a situation as it was. It is indubitable, too, that the retributive theories of punishment, and what they come to, are bound up with this same illusion, as they do indeed seem to be.[19] That origination is an illusion, as can usefully be added, does not depend on exactly the theory of determinism that has been sketched. It could as well rest on any other decent formulation of determinism.[20]

One last matter to fill your philosophical cup to overflowing. You have heard that the truth of determinism deprives us of a way of holding others and ourselves morally responsible, and also deprives us by itself of the retributive theories of the justification of punishment. That is true, but it may be that a caveat is needed.

If you think about your own past life, and if my experience in thinking about mine is a guide, you can come to find yourself in an unexpected situation. It is that you can both be convinced of determinism and also subject at least to reservations of a certain kind about your past – reservations that have a similarity to just a previous holding yourself responsible for your past that went with an assumption of your free will. It can seem that these present feelings are not those that go with the idea of voluntariness, a picture of yourself as having acted in the past out of your own desires, desires good and bad, decent and indecent.

Here begins more philosophy. How is this sense of accountability to be explained? Might an explanation begin with an understanding of the yet more fundamental subject of the very nature of a person's consciousness? Might an understanding of the accountability begin with more inquiry into the fact that we take what we call a cause to be more explanatory than the other equally necessary conditions for an effect – and that a person, so to speak, is such a cause? You will have to look elsewhere for a little more along these tentative lines.[21]

The question that arises here, in this inquiry, is whether retributive theories of punishment, having been rejected on account of determinism, might be reformed by way of some proposition or propositions consistent with determinism, and thus whether they might escape the fatal weakness of depending on a denial of determinism. The question does arise. That is one fact. Another is that even if retributive theories could be saved from the objection having to do exactly with origination, they would be far from secure.

The moral objection to justifying punishment by the satisfaction of grievance remains overwhelming. The other objections to all the traditional retribution theories are as they were. It is intolerable, too, to suppose punishment might be justified, despite the truth of determinism, because a *question* arises about one possibility of another radically different ground for desires and their satisfaction. We are not allowed to imprison men and women for 20 years, or to kill them, because a question arises that might result in the preservation of theories of punishment with respect only to one objection, the objection from determinism.

7
Compromise Theories

RETROSPECT, SEPARATE QUESTIONS

There was a lot wrong with traditional backward-looking theories of the justification of punishment with which we began this inquiry, mainly the retribution theories to the effect that we are obliged rather than permitted to punish offenders because they deserve it. One such theory confused what was needed, a moral reason for punishing a man or woman, with a legal reason. Several theories begged the question by in effect taking the argument that punishment is right because it is deserved to be the argument that punishment is right because it is right. Another theory, about the intrinsic good of the suffering of the guilty, was open to the reply among others that different and opposed goods, and bads, can be postulated as easily.

No plain sense of the factual kind could be attached to the theory that a man's culpability in an offence has a commensurable penalty that it equals. There was no gain in talk of an offender's forfeited rights, or preference scales, and none in the elaboration of a system of offences and penalties without any explanation of the supposed justifying relation in it. For several reasons we did not get further forward with attempted justifications of punishment in terms of annulment of the offence and an offender's right of consistency to his punishment. Nor was there much gain in backward-looking theories of a non-retributive kind, those in terms of a hypothetical rational contract, the better idea of consent to loss of immunity to punishment, and satisfactions in putting down burdens.

To the various difficulties with these theories had to be added another objection, mentioned at several points. It comes to this, that surely if punishment is justified this must be because it does some good, indeed has some good effect or effects, where that is definitely not only the proposition that it is related in some way to a past offence. A goodly number of jurisprudents, lawyers, and indeed a philosopher or two, have not shown themselves fully aware of the

logical or conceptual failings and indeed the disasters of the traditional theories just recalled. But very many of them have been quick
to recognize and assert that not enough can be said for punishment
if all that can be said for it is that it is deserved, where that means
only that it stands in some seemingly factitious relation to a past
event, the offender's offence. It was indeed a recommendation of
the retribution theories that they prohibited the punishment of
those who did not deserve it, or rather the victimization of them.
But this fact of the theories being *against* victimization could not at
all make good their weak or worse reason *for* punishment.

We ourselves did find something justificatory to be said for
punishment in retribution theories by abandoning a kind of
respectability, indeed piety, not to mention tolerance for obscurity
and near-nonsense, and instead understanding the theories in terms
of grievance satisfaction. The retribution theories were reduced to
the proposition that punishment is justified because it can satisfy
the grievance desires brought into being by an offence, and do no
more and no less than that.

One thing to be said against this this uniquely clear reason for punishment, a reason resting on a real effect, an actual if all too human
good, was that it could not be a sufficient reason for punishment. It
could not be that the denial of great goods to offenders could be
justified by the smaller thing of affording grievance satisfactions to
others. That this could not be justified was not then explained in
terms of a moral principle or an articulated morality, which indeed
was not needed. As might have been remarked, grievance satisfactions
do not persist in the way of the distress or worse of 20 years in prison.

Something else to be said of the uniquely clear retributive reason
for punishment is that it did not convince respectable and decorous
philosophers and other theorists of punishment. They have not
been willing to suppose the tradition of retribution can be a matter
of no more than a lower part of human nature. They have been, to
my mind, a little too impressed, unreflectively impressed, by both
the pomp and real value of the law. Many have continued to be
convinced both that at long last there is a better retribution theory,
their own particular one, and that it has a certain role, of which
more in a moment, in combination with something else.

The utilitarian prevention theory, the original one among theories
seeking to justify punishment by actual good effects or consequences, has an uncertain but perhaps sufficient basis in a certain
proposition of fact. That is the proposition that it does somehow

prevent sufficient offences for it to be justified. The theory had the recommendation, obviously, of providing a substantial reason for punishment. However, it too had its weakness. Despite attempts of one kind and another to sustain it, it failed for a particular reason. This was not that it justified victimizations that already occur in the law, and are taken as defensible, but that it justified morally intolerable victimizations (p. 105). There was the same sort of difficulty with justifications of punishment in terms of reform and rehabilitation, whatever else could also be said against them. In short, the utilitarian and reform theories provided a reason *for* punishment but not a reason *against* victimization.

In such a circumstance, inevitably, something suggested itself to philosophers and others. This was that the general strength of retribution theories, a prohibition against doing something, could be combined with the general strength of some preventive theory – recommending punishment on the basis of some actual good to be realized. The combination, evidently, would not have the weaknesses when separate of the things conjoined. The good would not necessarily be the good of the utilitarian theory, the greatest possible total of satisfaction, which might not fit well with the prohibition on giving a man more or less than he deserved. The good might be the prevention of offences otherwise conceived. It might include the effect of the reformation of offenders. Thus were born the mixed or compromising theories of punishment, necessary or unnecessary, successful or not. What they come to in general, whatever is to be said of them, is that punishment is justified because it is or may be both deserved by the offender and also preventive of offences in the future.

Did the mixed theories owe their emergence to another idea or feeling, by the way? That would be the fact that they are different from traditional retribution theories in not being so vulnerable to the truth of determinism. Certainly there has long been a kind of apprehension, pretty independent of philosophy, that determinism is true. It has been on hand, if in the background rather than the foreground, to trouble the advocates of retribution. If the mixed theories cannot escape the worry, since they have to do partly with desert, their parts having to do with prevention are reassuring. If the worst comes to the worst, something will be left of them. But this is speculation, not very serious. There is another introductory matter seemingly of more importance.

Mixed theories have commonly been introduced in a certain way, favoured by the distinguished jurisprudent H. L. A. Hart and others before him, including the philosopher John Rawls.[1] It will be worth looking at this way briefly for several reasons. One is that it sometimes appears to be intended as an argument, or something like an argument, for the conclusion that punishment must be justified by several principles or reasons. Another is that it is at least regarded as a preferred or indeed essential mode of procedure. Our own procedure has been, and mostly will be, to consider the single and inclusive question, 'What, if anything, can morally justify the practice of punishment?' A number of philosophers and legal theorists still regard this as an error, one at least likely to have considerable consequences.

It was Hart's view, in some accord with the linguistic or analytic philosophy of his day in Oxford, that in our inherited ways of talking about punishment we persistently oversimplify separate issues. What we must notice, if we are to avoid confusion, is that there is more than one question to be considered.[2] There are separate questions. This is so because there is the institution or practice of punishment itself and then there are its several different features. Only certain persons are punished, and only certain penalties are imposed. The institution therefore raises several quite separate questions of justification.

There is the overall question, 'What justifies the general practice of punishment?' or, 'What is the good of maintaining this institution?' This can be named the question of the general justifying aim of the institution. Secondly, there is the question of liability. It is this: 'To whom may punishment be applied?' Finally, there is the question of amount. 'How severely may we punish?' We are invited to see that there are these three distinct questions – and thus also to see that different answers are in place with respect to them.

Surely, it is said, the general justifying aim of punishment must be the prevention of crime. Who can really disagree? As for the second question, the question of who may be punished, surely the answer is that only those who deserve it or are guilty may be. And, with respect to the third question, a partly retributivist answer is surely in place. A man should not be given a larger penalty than he deserves. In some such way as this we are led toward the view that punishment is justified only by several different considerations – in short that it serves some preventive end with respect to crime but is limited in doing so by considerations of retribution. What justifies punishment in part is what was earlier called negative rather than positive retribution. To see that there are separate questions about punishment is to see that there are separate and different answers.

Is this so? Consider the second question, 'To whom may punishment be applied?' It is a long step in the direction of irrelevance to see this as peculiarly a question for a judge.[3] If one answers as if one were a judge, of course, there is more than a temptation to give the answer that punishment may be applied only to those found to have broken the law. This may be to regard the question in a way which makes it irrelevant to our inquiry. A judge may indeed be said to be justified in singling out for punishment those found to have offended. This is to say, ordinarily, that his action is in accord with his powers and duties, as defined by law. But we are not inquiring into *legality*, into legal powers and obligations. We wish to know what can be said in moral justification of what is done by judges in accordance with their legal powers and obligations – and maybe personal moral obligations (p. 20).

We need to understand the question 'To whom may punishment be applied?' in another way – a way such that it might have the moral answer toward which we are being urged. It can indeed be taken as another question, a little more explicit. 'What, if anything, morally justifies our punishing only those found to have broken the law?' Does the fact that we can or should ask this separate question – that fact by itself – give us reason to answer it in terms of desert? This is the crux of the matter.

The answer is plain enough. Certainly it is the part or side of punishment, spoken of as liability, to which our attention has been directed, that has led many people to retributivism. But that the separate question can be asked does not guarantee or even make probable such an answer. It remains perfectly possible, given only the fact of the separate question, to side with Bentham and declare that the answer to the question about who is to be punished is simply that those are to be punished whose punishment will prevent future offences.

That is not all that comes to mind. We are contemplating the question, 'What, if anything, morally justifies our punishing only those found to have broken the law?' Could the fact that it is only these individuals who may be said to deserve punishment provide a *sufficient* answer to the question? Obviously not – although exactly that is what is suggested – since desert is not a sufficient justification for punishing any individual. We know it. That desert is a sufficient condition is the plain retribution theory, which has been rejected.

It is rejected, indeed, by the philosophers whose compromise views we are considering. This introduction to mixed theories is not encouraging.

Similar remarks need making in connection with similar results, about the third question, 'How severely may we punish?' The question does not commit us to an answer, or even need to incline us towards one.

As for the first question, about the general justifying aim of punishment, it is ambiguous in a way peculiar to itself. It may be taken to be about just the *aim* of punishment, which is certainly to be distinguished from its justification. It is sometimes true that to mention the aim of a particular line of action is to mention an accepted justification. On other occasions this is not so. Our aim in a war may be to occupy some land, but our justification may be some past fact or supposed past fact. It does seem true to say that one aim of punishment is prevention. A goal we want to achieve is a state of affairs where there are fewer offences committed. But it is clear that if the question about the practice or institution of punishment is to specify a part of our present inquiry, which is a moral one, it clearly cannot be taken to be about only the aim or goal of the practice.

If we are asking what adequate moral justification can be given of the practice, it is perhaps natural to think first of the prevention of offences. But that we can ask the separate question goes no way towards establishing that answer. That fact, rightly, would not have delayed Kant for a moment in giving his retribution theory of punishment. The situation is the same as with the first two separate questions.

In any case, it is on reflection quite mistaken to think that an answer can be given to the question of the moral justification of the practice in terms of, say, the utilitarian prevention of offences alone. This is exactly what has been established by the argument about victimization. Some such argument is accepted by exactly those who espouse compromise theories – those now espousing them to us right now. How then can they suppose that the moral justification of the practice can be prevention alone when rightly or wrongly they also require another different reason, in terms of desert? That this second reason may be related to particular features of the practice, the convicting and sentencing procedures, is immaterial. That a reason is necessary for a part of something entails that it is necessary for that thing. Something the same may be said, not that it matters much, for the reason having to do with prevention. Prevention has to do with the particular fact or side of punishment that it is public. It certainly does not follow that it is not necessary to mention it in defending the institutition.

It is not at all clear, then, why anyone who feels that a compromise or two-value justification is necessary should also think the practice as a whole justified by only one of them. There is some explanation, no doubt, in the confusion of aim with justification. This confusion may be made easier, incidentally, by an assumption similar to one noticed above. That is, it is sometimes supposed that the question about the justification of the practice is peculiarly one for legislators. Legislators are concerned with a society's larger intentions, including the prevention of offences, although not exclusively so concerned. Even if they were concerned solely with aims, nothing would follow about the answer to our question.

Does it need to be added that we can of course express a moral question, in some sense about the institution or practice, whose answer will be in terms of prevention alone? It is: What is to be said for the practice of punishment other than that it is governed in certain ways by limitations on who is to be punished? That the answer to *that* question may be prevention alone of course does not give us the proposition that the practice is justified by prevention alone. There is the same uselessness in similar questions that can be formed about who is to be punished and how much.

So, the mere fact that we can ask separate questions about punishment is consistent with *all* the answers being solely in terms of desert, or solely in terms of utilitarian prevention – or, as is obvious, and as we shall be contemplating, solely in terms of a certain kind of consequences of punishment. There is no reason for thinking that some separate-questions procedure inevitably or logically leads one to a compromise theory. The existence of separate questions does not constitute any argument for the conclusion that punishment must be justified by several principles.

Is it nevertheless true that we are likely to fall into confusion if we do not ask these questions, or some other set of separate questions? Must this be the best procedure? This seems to be partly the claim that philosophers who have given single-reason answers about punishment, inadequate ones, would have done otherwise if they had asked separate questions. This too is unconvincing. In fact we here have a further and yet simpler objection to what is urged upon us. Utilitarians did not ignore the fact that there are prohibitions with respect to who can be punished and to what extent. In effect they isolated the questions about the basis of these prohibitions and gave answers to them. Hart discusses Bentham's answers.[4] One can say of the traditional retributivists, similarly, that they were not unaware of the claim that the practice of punishment does have certain preventive effects. Following Kant, they commonly introduced this fact into discussion in order to deny its moral relevance (pp. 17–18).

Are *we* likely to fall into confusion if we do not ask separate questions? We shall not fall into the confusion of thinking that a single-reason answer in terms of retribution or utilitarian prevention to the single and inclusive moral question about punishment will do. Why should we? Nor does it seem likely that we will risk other confusions. Certainly we must keep in mind the different features of the practice of punishment – and not only those having to do with certain prohibitions. We must indeed consider what contribution may be made to the justification of the practice by particular features. But this we can do without a mechanical separation of questions. One question will do.

Our fundamental and final concern, obviously, must be with what justification can be given for the practice of punishment taken as a whole. This is a satisfactory formulation of the question which all theories of punishment try to answer. It is precisely the question, of course, which any theory must end by trying to answer. Needless to say, once you think of the matter, it is also precisely the question finally answered by all compromise theorists without exception, however mixed or compromising their answer. Hart, for example, was not giving a partial or incomplete answer to the question of what justifies punishment or answers to questions that do not come together into a summation. He was not failing to provide what every relevant theorist of punishment provides, a summary verdict on that thing.

PREVENTION AND RETRIBUTION

There are a lot of mixed or compromising theories of punishment. There are too many for surveying in this book. Is there another reason why we need not exhaust ourselves making our way through them? Whether or not that is so, let us look at three of them. If they are indeed mixed theories, all have or claim to have a mainly or importantly retributive character, which fact is reflected in their names. Each of them, further, at least attempts to add to the

15 understandings of desert-claims that we have, in fact 15 retribution theories.

The first, the work of Hart, follows on from the assumptions and arguments about separate questions that we have been considering. Those assumptions and arguments, however, are not actually premises for the theory. It does not depend on them. They do not determine whether it stands or falls. It may be the right answer. Certainly it has been an influential theory, not only among jurisprudents and lawyers, and it remains so. It serves as our example of the most expected and obvious compromise theories, those that somehow justify and limit punishment to what is both preventive and deserved.

The practice of punishment, we hear again, involves a prohibition on punishing most individuals. We hear in effect that in general or for the most part we punish only those individuals who have intentionally or negligently broken the law. Admittedly, as you will remember from what was said in connection with the utilitarian theory of punishment, there are already within the law many cases of what are generally regarded, or regarded by many, as being justified victimizations. There are convictions under statutes of strict and vicarious liability. Impositions of what were spoken of as exemplary penalties, which go beyond what may be said to be deserved, are also defended.

Still, the practice of punishment does involve a wide prohibition against penalizing most individuals. In general, we in effect hear first from Hart, we punish only those who could have kept to the law when in fact they broke it. Also, he remarks, this belief that men could have done otherwise than they did is no less than the keystone of retributive theories of punishment.[5] Subsequently we hear that for the most part, the far greater part, our punishments are of persons who are 'morally guilty'. And further, they are 'those who have broken the law – and voluntarily broken it'.[6]

There is more to be said, however, than that punishment in general is imposed on those who could have done otherwise, are morally guilty, and have voluntarily broken the law. This has to do with the side of punishment that earlier was called liability. There is also the matter of how much they are to be punished, the matter of amount. Here there are rules of justice of various kinds.

(1) Penalties must not cause more distress than would occur if they were not imposed. (2) A penalty must not be imposed if a man's action falls under a special rule of justification, such as the rule

having to do with injuring in self-defence. (3) A man is to be excused a penalty if his act, although of a kind the law seeks to prevent, was unintentional, involuntary, or something of the sort. (4) A man is to receive a mitigated penalty if he faced a special difficulty in keeping the law, perhaps because of provocation. (5) Finally, a man is to be treated as others in his situation are treated. Similar offenders are to be treated similarly.

As you will be aware, some of these various considerations give us some ways in which punishment can be taken to be justified, in part, by its having a preventive effect. Exactly what effect Hart has in mind is not clear. He speaks of Bentham and utilitarianism, indeed at length, but we need not conclude that what he contemplates as the effect of punishment is exactly the the greatest total of satisfaction when compared with alternatives to punishment. Let us leave this unsettled.

More particularly, to return to the wide or general limitation of punishment to those who have intentionally or negligently broken the law, and so on, we are to understand that a part of the justification is that this serves prevention. It is those who have broken the law in the given way who are more likely to do it again. The same sort of principle plays a part with respect to (1) the rule against penalties that cause more distress than would occur if they were not imposed. So with (2) the rule about justification in offending, such as the one about self-defence. It is remarked that one of the aims of punishment is the protection of individuals from attack. It would be inconsistent, then, to punish a man for defending himself from attack, whatever else is to be said about it.

But of course this is not the end of the story of justification. What is called retribution is also part of the story. It is part of what justifies the wide or general fact of punishment that it is for the most part done to offenders. Retribution is also part of the justification of (3) excusing a man if his action was unintentional or involuntary or something of the sort. So too is retribution a justifying consideration with (4) a mitigated penalty because of, say, provocation. The same can be said of (5) similar offenders being treated similarly – you will remember that such a consideration entered into our own final analysis of traditional retribution theories.

We now come to the crux. What actually is the reason of retribution for the parts or features of punishment just noticed? The answer, if it may be surprising, is clear. In general, punishment is to be imposed only on *those who could have kept the law when in fact they broke it* for the reason that *they could have kept the law when in fact they broke it.* That fact, you will remember, is given as the keystone of retribution theories and retribution. The same sort of reason is given when what is in question is why *those who are morally guilty* or *have voluntarily broken the law* are punished. The reasons, more particularly, are that *they are morally guilty* or they *have voluntarily broken the law.* Is 'voluntarily' here used in the special way in which we have been using it?

To come on to the rules, and in particular the rule (3) that a man is to be excused a penalty if his action was unintentional, involuntary or something of the sort, the justification of this feature of punishment is that his action *was* unintentional, involuntary or something of the sort. As for (4) the reason for a mitigated penalty on account of provocation, it is that the offender *was* provoked – that he acted in something less than perfect freedom. And as for (5), I take it that there is to be equal treatment because it *is* equal treatment.

What all this comes to is an answer, good, bad or indifferent, to what is meant when a punishment is justified as a retribution. What it comes to, presumably, is a further answer to the question – we have had a lot of answers – of what it is for a punishment to be deserved. To revert to our previous style, the claim that a penalty is deserved for an offence is understood roughly as follows.

(16) The offence was freely and responsibly committed.

To look back over our inquiry, we have at various points taken a proposition about a punishment's being deserved for an offence to *depend* on or *presuppose*, roughly, that the offence was freely and responsibly committed. That indeed was a main point of our inquiry into determinism. At the end of that inquiry, further, it was concluded that retribution theories have rested on an assumption of that particular kind of freedom that is free will or origination as against what was called voluntariness.

What we have now, in the theory of punishment we are considering, is that the retribution reason for punishment does not assume or presuppose a proposition about freedom and responsibility, but *is* that very proposition. If the theory is not explicit about the kind of freedom and moral responsibility it propounds or asserts, is there an indication that it is indeed free will? Certainly it is origination, not voluntariness, that goes most naturally with talk of moral guilt.

It has to be said, however, that another paper than the one we have been considering gives reason to think that the freedom and responsibility taken to be the essential content of the talk of retribution may be no more than voluntariness. This is surely atypical of thinkers about retribution, and is such as to raise a question about the stability or durability of the theory.

So much for a quick exposition of a supposed justification, or rather part-justification, of punishment. We come to this question: Why is it the case that a man's having broken the law when he could have kept it is itself a reason for punishing him? Why is it that his having somehow broken the law is itself a reason for punishing him, and for punishing him to a certain extent? And so on. All of this needs to be kept separate from something else.

It needs to be kept in mind that in the theory we are considering, to look at the other side of it, full attention is given to the voluntariness of actions or the lack of it because voluntariness is necessary with respect to the other justification of punishment, that it is preventive. The central proposition here is that it is those who freely and responsibly offend who are most likely to commit more offences unless deterred or the like. More is said by Hart along the same lines.

Our requiring a free and responsible action has the recommendation that members of society are thus able to determine by their choices, at least to a considerable extent, what their futures will be. They are able, that is, to opt for law abidance and its consequences or disobedience to law and its possible consequences. Thus there are considerable satisfactions to be gained – individuals can enjoy a particular security, one that would be denied them under some system which did not make their own choices the determinants of their futures. The satisfactions of security are, essentially, satisfactions which accrue from confidence in prediction. I can rule out the possibility of at least certain unpleasant surprises if I feel capable of keeping the law. There are also gains of another kind. That I choose what will happen to me, to some considerable extent, is itself a source of satisfaction. In order to see this clearly, one need simply compare the experience of choosing with the experience of, say, being coerced.

This sort of thing, the worth of a free and responsible action in arguing in a preventive way for punishment, is pretty plain. But, to revert to our questions, it is far from plain why the fact of voluntariness in an offence by itself is a justification or part-justification of punishment. As the advocates of forward-looking theories say, what is the worth of this dead fact of the past? To say better than that, all of us value such great goods as not being in pain and being free. Is this not our shared nature? These great goods do indeed give us reasons and justifications for things. If the elusive importance of a past voluntary act considered independently of anything else exists at all, must it not by comparison be near to insigificant?

Perhaps in anticipation of just such a response, Hart writes elsewhere of what he speak of an important general principle.

> Human society is a society of persons; and persons do not view themselves or each other merely as so many bodies moving in ways which are sometimes harmful and have to be prevented or altered. Instead persons interpret each other's movements as manifestations of intentions and choices, and these subjective factors are often more important to their social relations than the movements by which they are manifested or their effects. If one person hits another, the person struck does not think of the other as just a cause of pain to him; for it is of crucial importance to him whether the blow was deliberate or involuntary. . . . If you strike me, the judgement that the blow was deliberate will elicit fear, indignation, anger, resentment: these are not voluntary responses; but the same judgement will enter into deliberations about my future voluntary conduct towards you and will colour all my social relations with you. Shall I be your friend or enemy? Offer soothing words? Or return the blow? All this will be different if the blow is not voluntary. This is how human nature in human society actually is and as yet we have no power to alter it. The bearing of this fundamental fact on the law is this. If as our legal moralists maintain it is important for the law to reflect common judgement of morality, it is surely even more important that it should in general reflect in its judgements on human conduct distinctions which not only underlie morality, but pervade the whole of our social life. This it would fail to do if it treated men merely as alterable, predictable, curable, or manipulable things.[7]

We certainly do distinguish between those who injure us deliberately, those who injure us involuntarily, and, one may add, those who do not injure us at all. We act differently in response. In so far as we are *justified* in so doing, however, this may have to be explained by something other than the mere fact by itself that some injuries are the consequences of voluntary actions. We are certainly not justified in responding in the same way to all those who injure us voluntarily, including policemen and our victims who are acting in self-defence. What can be said for acts of blaming may be what can be said for certain punishments. The fact taken by itself that an act was voluntary may not in itself be morally important in either case.

Let us grant that in ordinary life we do react differently, and quite spontaneously, simply and solely because an act was voluntary. That is, let us admit that we have distinctive emotional responses. Is it suggested, on the basis of these facts, that the bare consideration that a man has freely offended gives us a moral reason for punishment? Such an argument, in my view, would certainly be mistaken. We may be able to give a partial *explanation* of a feature of our practice of punishment by reference to these facts. Nothing is more likely than that there will be a connection between that practice and our ordinary attitudes and behaviour. To concede that is not to concede the point at issue. It is not to concede that the fact, taken by itself, that a man has freely and responsibly acted in a certain way is itself a moral reason for our further action. As many more say, if our action will do no good, if no good will come of it, what is the point of it – indeed what is the good of it?

The theory of punishment we have been considering has the recommendation of being well-informed with respect to the working institution of punishment. It has the recommendation too that it does not indulge in speculative thinking about retribution and desert. It is a long way from earlier pieces of retributive thinking we have considered. It has in it no flights of fancy.

As it seems to me, however, the theory very clearly pays the price of its restraint. It produces no substantial or significant reason for punishment in terms of retribution. It invites replacement by the argument, such as it is, based on the satisfaction of grievance desires. Let us leave the result of such a replacement unconsidered for a time. The theory does of course have the recommendation of seeing that more than a reason of punishment in terms of desert is needed. It does not have another recommendation that we have not so far considered, or not much considered. Except for suggestions of utilitarianism, it does not contemplate what it is that a justified theory of punishment is to prevent – what its consequences are to be. We shall be giving that question more attention.

CORRECT-VALUES RETRIBUTIVISM

The conservative and libertarian philosopher Robert Nozick's explanation of the justification of punishment is such that beginning with a summary of it is a good idea. It begins with a familiar idea of a *deserved punishment*, technically expressed, and contemplates in passing that such a punishment may be self-justifying – justified because deserved in this sense. However, Nozick then seeks a separate rationale for such a punishment, first by distinguishing it from revenge. He goes on to find that a deserved punishment is an *act of communication* involving several intentions and the like on the part of the communicator. This act, perhaps imprisoning a man for 20 years or killing him, tells or shows the man how wrong his offence was. It *reconnects him with the correct values* from which he disconnected himself by his offence, correct values he flouted – and still flouted if he was subject to determinism. By his imprisonment, these values have *a significant effect on his life*. Nothing but the punishment could bring about the significant effect of reconnection with them. It *may* happen that such a punishment also does something different. It may *morally improve* the offender. But this if it happens will be a bonus. It is enough for a justified punishment that an offender is reconnected with correct values.

To these principal propositions are added various others. An offender is not only to be reconnected to correct values by his deserved punishment. We are to try to force him to compensate victims of his offence. Further, in addition to the deserved punishment, we may consider what is called matching punishment or the original *lex talionis*, which is acting against the wrongdoer in the very way he acted against his victim, so far as this is feasible. In punishing retributively, we not only have the reason of connecting the offender with correct values, but also others. One is that we connect ourselves with value. And, with such great evil-doers as Hitler, we may also have to respond to wrong as wrong, by killing him even if he could be reformed. Finally, to come to an objection contemplated by Nozick, there is the idea that we might be obliged by this thinking to punish people who are disconnected from correct values but have not committed any offence. The reply given is that this would be a violation of their rights.

All of which is not to say that any current punishment is well designed and functions well in terms of retributive punishment as now explained. That choice of words indicates, I take it, that current punishment as it is can none the less have a significant justification in terms of desert, communication, connection with correct values, the possible but unnecessary bonus of moral improvement of those punished, and so on.

So much for the summary. Let us now make our way through some of these propositions and think a little bit about them, the first having to do with a familiar idea of a deserved punishment, technically expressed.

> The punishment deserved depends on the magnitude H of the wrongness of the act, and the person's degree of responsibility r for the act, and is equal in magnitude to their product, $r \times H$. The degree of responsibility r varies between one (full responsibility) and zero (no responsibility) and make take intermediate numerical values corresponding to partial responsibility.[8]

The idea expressed in this manner is best and most kindly taken as the familiar one that a deserved punishment is one that is equivalent to the culpability of the offence – where that is ordinary talk and not the idea of a hopeless calculator who supposes that there do exist measurements that do not exist. That is, we need to remember, of course, that Nozick's sentences expressing the idea are not literally true. There are no units for the counting or measurement of wrongness, there are no units for the counting of responsibility, there is no multiplication of harm times responsibility, there are no units for the counting of punishment, and there is no equality or inequality in magnitude between $r \times H$ and a punishment. Taking the words literally, none of those things exist.

That is not to say, of course, that we cannot *put* numbers on the things in question and then operate with those numbers. We can put numbers on them in the way that we put numbers – examination marks – on particular answers to examination questions. Or the way that we put numbers – grades – on apples or other fruit that we assign to different categories or qualities. Or the way we put numbers – points – on an ice-dancer's performance. Or numbers – demerits – on a pupil's contribution to the school community.

Is the point that we cannot count or measure wrongness, responsibility and so on a trivial or small one since it is to be granted that we can put numbers – in terms of dollars or years, say – on wrongnesses of acts and punishments? I doubt it. To talk in terms of magnitudes, products, numerical values and so on is to invite someone to think that what is in question is a single and clear argument for a punishment. That is less likely to happen when we speak more accurately, say in terms of putting numbers on things. Also, the untrue way of speaking leads us away from *our* role in responding to offences and as punishers in these so-called magnitudes, etc.

That is not what is most important, of course. It is not the main objection to the assertion of an equivalence between the offence and the punishment. What is most important can be put in terms of things that *can* literally be measured and *are* literally equal. Take a morning's activity that produces a table four feet long and a stool two feet wide. Take an afternoon's activity that produces a bench six feet long. Is the morning's activity an argument for the afternoon's activity in virtue of the equality by itself? Obviously not. There may some other reason why the equality in question is a good thing, or a reason why it is a bad thing, or a reason why the equality has no value at all, positive or negative.

So with an equality between or rather an equality put on $r \times H$ and a punishment. It is only the dulling force of convention, and conventional thinking in whatever form, including a form that trivially mimics mathematics or physics, that may conceal the absurdity from us. To add an example, a war does not become right for the sole and only reason that it will equal another war in deaths and destruction. Add your own further examples.

As against this, Nozick does contemplate in passing that an assigned equality or equivalence between $r \times H$ and a punishment may indeed be self-justifying and need no further explanation – that is, the equality may in itself be a justification for imposing the punishment.

> Is it necessary, though, to offer an explanation at all of retributive punishment? Perhaps its appropriateness is just a fundamental fact, with nothing further underlying it: people who commit wrongs simply deserve to be punished.[9]

At best, this is or amounts to a particular theory noticed in our earlier inquiry into traditional retribution theories, earlier, intrinsic retributivism, where the suffering of the guilty is taken as an intrinsic good (p. 24). What we have is the proposition that there is intrinsic good produced by adding the punishment to $r \times H$. The fatuity of this argument is made evident by a possible response of the same force in argument – or lack of force. It is that there is intrinsic goodness in forgiveness or whatever, and hence that there is intrinsic good in *not* adding the punishment to $r \times H$.

Very rightly, despite his moment of contemplation, Nozick does suppose that a better answer, an actual answer, is needed to the question of why it is right to impose a punishment that can be talked of as equal to the $r \times H$ of the offence. This better answer is what he calls a rationale of retributive punishment, indeed the rationale. It is a long way from the clear sense that we make punishment in some sense or way equal to $r \times H$ in order to prevent offences and do so at no greater cost of suffering than is needed.

The way to Nozick's chosen rationale of punishment is cleared by getting rid of the obstacle of suspicion that retributive punishment is revenge, that making a punishment equal an offence is taking the correct revenge. The various points made about punishment and revenge, some of interest and many contentious, reflect the general fact accepted by almost all of us that punishment however justified is the work of an authority, most notably a national state, according to law. It is not the work of an individual who has himself been harmed by his victim or has another personal link to him.

One contentious point is that revenge unlike retribution is done for a harm and not necessarily a wrong. This at least overlooks the fact that both are done for supposed wrongs, however personally judged. I have to persuade myself of some defect in the neighbour whose windows I break or even the child I shoot as a soldier in the course of my state terrorism. Another contentious point, in this case one that likens revenge to retributive punishment as it will be conceived, is that revenge is always done with the intention that the victim should know why it is occurring and know that he was intended to know. That seems untrue. On the contrary, I may take revenge in so careful and self-preserving a way that the finger does not point at me at all.

None of this is of importance, first of all because it seems very hard or impossible to suppose that punishment, certainly punishment by the state, *is* revenge. No clearing of an obstacle of suspicion is needed. And, most relevantly, that some of us suppose it is *like* revenge is perfectly consistent with the differences adduced between punishment and revenge, including the contentious ones. Further, as Nozick admits, it does not follow, from the fact that retributive punishment is not revenge, that the former is justified. As he might also have thought, the upright ways of doing philosophy do not include clearing non-obstacles in order to clear the way to something else.[10]

Near the centre of the view we are considering are intriguing thoughts of the philosopher of language Paul Grice. They have to do with what it is to mean something by some sounds or marks.

The thoughts, arrived at by means of contemplating examples and counter-examples, include such intricacies as that my communicating with you in an ordinary way includes not only my intending that you come by way of my sounds or marks to have a belief or whatever, but also that you know I intended my sounds or marks to have the effect.[11] There is no great difficulty in arriving by way of this account of the conditions of communication at the proposition that punishing someone, and in particular punishing someone so that the penalty can be said to equal the responsibility r multiplied by the wrong H, is a kind of act of communication. If we may be helped to forget that punishing is also other things, this proposition is made clear to us.

> Retributive punishment is an act of communicative behaviour. . . . The (Gricean) message is: This is how wrong what you did was. . . . We might see punishment as an attempt to demonstrate to the wrongdoer that his act was wrong, not only to mean the act is wrong but to *show* him its wrongness.[12]

There is no great problem about taking punishment to be communication. As Nozick might have remarked, there are innumerable examples elsewhere of such non-linguistic communication. Holding out water to a thirsty man is, among other things, a kind of communication, something like the speech-act of saying, 'Here is water for you.' So is pointing a gun at someone's head, or marrying them, or leaving them, or going to war. Punishing someone, among other things, is indeed a kind of act of communication.[13] But suppress any question you may have with respect to that, or, more likely, the use to be made of the fact, and consider instead what this act of communication is also said to be or achieve.

> The wrongdoer has become disconnected from correct values, and the purpose of punishment is to (re)connect him. It is not that this connection is a desired further effect of punishment: the act of retributive punishment itself effects this connection.[14]

Or, as can be added,

> Correct values are themselves without causal power, and the wrongdoer chooses not to give them effect in his life. So others must give them some effect in his life, in a secondary way. When he undergoes

punishment these correct values are not totally without effect in his life (even though he does not follow them), because we hit him over the head with them.[15]

Let us not linger over these thoughts either, but press on to something else that throws a strange light on them. The reconnection about which we are hearing is *not* something else. Reconnecting an offender with correct values is *not* getting him to realize that his offence was wrong.[16] That is not what happens as a result of the penalty that is said to equal his past wrong and responsibility. Reconnecting, in a word, is not *reforming* the offender, not the moral improvement of the offender.

Reformation is something that *may* happen, but is not necessary for the justification of punishment that is being claimed.[17] It is a bonus, not something to be counted on or needed. Nozick must take this view, as in effect he admits, because it requires at least optimism to suppose that retributive punishment, indeed any punishment, however communicative, does in fact make men conventionally moral.[18]

A question now arises. Indeed, it cannot be avoided. If we allow that imprisoning a man for 20 years in a sense means something, in a sense communicates something to him, what is the *further fact* that it reconnects him with correct values – if that does *not* mean he is made to realize that what he did was wrong, that he is somehow made morally better?

Reader, I am getting tired of this stuff, and will not persist much longer with it. Speculate, if you want, about what reconnection with correct values comes to. Follow Nozick's habit elsewhere and bring bits of philosophical imagination to bear on the question, maybe a joke. My own conclusion at this point can be brief. This obscurity, which is indubitable, and thus this weakness or absence of argument, this mere performance, suggests very strongly that retributivism, and the doctrine we have been contemplating, has in it or underneath it something it does not express.

Another question may have arisen in your mind before now, one raised by any theory of punishment as communication. If your aim is to *tell somebody something*, is it necessary to do so by putting him in jail for 20 years? If you do not even have the aim of changing his mind about correct values, why is it necessary to put him in jail for 20 years? Nozick's answer, it seems, is in the following lines, some of which you have heard already.

Correct values are themselves without causal power, and the wrongdoer chooses not to give them effect in his life. So others must give them some effect in his life, in a secondary way. . . . we hit him over the head with them. Through punishment, we give the correct values, qua correct values, some significant effect in his life. . . . The complicated (Gricean) intentions enable us to act as a vehicle. . . . Only those complicated conditions enable the correct values to act upon him. . . . There is now no puzzle about why we do not simply speak or telegram the (Gricean) message, without adding a punishment.[19]

What that says, perhaps, is that values are such things as to need a realization in conditions of communication in order to have a certain effect on someone. The conditions are achieved in punishment. Therefore there is no puzzle as to why we punish. That appears to be a non sequitur, one that forgets about the conditions of communication realized in *language* and a good deal else, a non sequitur that also hits you over the head and which I leave for your consideration.

Whatever point is intended about the necessity of punishment to the wholly obscure effect, the point is itself sufficiently obscure as to be unlikely to be forceful. To which can be added the thought that it is dishonourable to present the alternative method of communication as 'seeing films, reading novels, and hearing explanations of the causes of his behaviour and the tales of his victims'.[20] What a serious communication theorist opposed to punishment could perfectly reasonably propose is an institution of something like the size of punishment, no doubt a little less expensive. What *we* can instance, in objection to Nozick's proposition of necessity, is such an institution.

What you have heard so far, properly reduced, seems to me as follows. A deserved punishment, as nothing else can, communicates to the offender that an offence was wrong to some particular extent. Since this is unlikely to reform him, a proposition is needed in explanation of why we go in for this communication. It is that the punishment reconnects him with correct values.

This piece of mystery-mongering raises a further question so far unasked. What are these values? If everything else were as clear as glass, this question would still need answering. Presumably there are values of a good society or indeed the perfectly just society. These can be the values, that is, of the society that is morally ideal. Nozick wrote another book specifying this society.[21] The morally ideal society is the one where all the goods, say food, are where they are, in the ownership of particular people or entities, as a result of a certain history. They are where they are because the owning people mixed their labour with them or with something related to them, and so came to own them, or they are where they are as a result of sales and gifts, maybe a long sequence of these tracing back to the labour-mixing. Or, thirdly, the goods are where they are as a result of acts of rectification that put right departures from a history of sales and gifts, say robbery, maybe by governments in the form of taxes.

There are brief and unquestionable summaries of this society of unquestionably correct values. It is the one where no person and no group or entity has any outstanding moral obligation and no person has a moral right to anything they do not already own. The only moral rights people have are to the things to which they have legal property rights. This is a society in which a family starving to death may have no moral right to food. It is a society in which no person and no entity may have any moral obligation to save the family, maybe with a father who is psychotic, paranoid, phobic or dim, from starving to death.[22]

What I mean to do by this reminder of our instructor's correct values is mainly one thing. It is to note again that if we are told that a system of punishment has to do with values in whatever way, we will need to know something of what those values are. They may be such as to raise a question, to say no more than that, with respect to the moral decency of the system of punishment.

So much for Nozick's principal propositions in justification of punishment. I leave his other propositions to your own consideration, to your reading of his book. You may also wish to consider the question of the consequencs of determinism for his propositions.

LIBERAL-COMMUNITY RETRIBUTIVISM

There is another communication theory, said also to be a kind of retribution theory but not a pure retribution theory. If a metaphor helps, it takes punishment, anyway in part, to be *the voice of the law* and what is hoped to be *the voice of the community*. It is the work of Antony Duff, a philosopher who adds to his logic the politics of what is called communitarianism as well as the more traditional politics of liberalism. The theory, in its first full statement in the book *Punishment, Communication and Community*,[23] is that punishment

> should communicate to offenders the censure they deserve for their crimes and should aim through that communicative process to persuade them to repent those crimes, to try to reform themselves, and thus to reconcile themselves with those whom they wronged.[24]

When this is true of punishment, it is justified. It is justified when it is this 'species of secular penance'.[25] This is not at all or not mainly penance in a usual sense – a voluntary self-punishment inflicted as an expression of repentance for having done something wrong. Rather, what we have is the kind of penance that is imposed by somebody on somebody else with a certain aim.

Certainly an idea of desert is fundamental or at least integral to this theory. We have it, further, that desert is in a necessary rather than a contingent connection with a forward-looking idea of reform or whatever, and so the theory is not what we have been calling a mixed theory. Punishment is justified as

> a communicative enterprise focussed on the past crime, as that for which the censure that punishment communicates is deserved; but also looking to a future aim to which it is related, not merely contingently as an instrumental technique, but internally as an intrinsically appropriate means. . . . Punishment will now look both back (as retributivists insist it must) to a past crime as that which merits this response, and forward (as consequentialists insist it must) to some future good that it aims to achieve.[26]

Whatever is to be said about the supposed mistake of taking this as a mixed theory, of which a word more will be said, you may, reader, have fallen into another mistake. It has to do with the necessity or otherwise of reform in the theory. You may be confirmed in the mistake by understanding that the theory is not the commoner idea just that punishment *expresses* to the offender a deserved condemnation.[27] It is not just that punishment is the voice of the law and maybe the community, but rather that the voice is really heard by the offender. Expression of something, as we are reminded, requires only somebody to express something. On the other hand, 'communication involves, as expression need not, a reciprocal and rational engagement'.[28] In communciation, at any rate, we try to engage with someone else, get a response mediated by the other's grasp of what we say.

Despite this fact about communication, it does seem to be a mistake to suppose that on this theory punishments are justified only when they are likely to result in the repentance, reform and reconciliation of an offender with respect to his wrongdoing.

> . . . the law should aim to bring him to recognize and repent that wrongdoing: not just because that is a method of persuading him not to repeat it, but because that is owed to him and to his victim. To take wrongs seriously as wrongs involves responding to them with criticism and censure; and the aim internal to censure is that of persuading the wrongdoer to recognize and repent his wrongdoing. This is not to say that we should censure a wrongdoer only when we believe that there is some chance of thus persuading him. We may think that we owe it to his victim, to the values he has flouted, and even to him, to censure his wrongdoing even if we are sure that he will be unmoved and unpersuaded by the censure. But our censure still takes the form of an attempt (albeit what we believe is a futile attempt) to persuade him.[29]

Whether or not in perfect consistency with what is said elsewhere,[30] that is pretty definite. A punishment on this view does not have to have even a chance of reforming in order to be justified. It is not that we are to go ahead with it because we cannot be sure it won't work. What the view comes to, we can take it, is that punishment is right when it tells an offender something, and in some way he understand it, even if it and his understanding have no reformative effect on him. The thought may incline us to suppose this is more of a retribution theory than so far supposed, purer retribution than supposed.

The quoted passage, incidentally, also indicates the sense in which the theory is not a mixed one. What this comes to, anyway in part, is that taking something as having been wrong involves or even *is* responding to it with censure. You logically cannot do the first thing without doing something like the second. So to take a penalty as deserved, anyway in a certain sense, or to make a judgement involved in taking a penalty as deserved, is to do something that carries censure with it, rather than something that may have censure added to it. The point does not preclude us from thinking, however rightly, that in the theory punishment is being justified by more than one thing.

This is a good moment to ask what general understanding of the relation of desert between an offence and a penalty informs the view, however and wherever it informs it. How are we to understand the repeated statement that a penalty may be deserved for an offence, owed for an offence, however and wherever such a proposition functions in the theory? The question actually comes up in a somewhat puzzling way. It is not presented, so to speak, as a fundamental or first-order question to which the theory needs an answer in order to exist, an answer that is indeed fundamental to the theory. Rather, the question comes up in a kind of addendum to the theory or the main theory, an addendum on what is called its sentencing policy – the offences-and-penalties system that goes with the recommended justification of punishment.[31] Still, it seems clear to our instructor, more enlightened than many predecessors, that his many previous references to desert have to have an understanding supplied for them, that such a thing is needed for them, indeed that it is intrinsic to any version of retribution.[32]

The general answer to the question of what the talk of desert comes to is given in terms of *proportionality*, a penalty's being proportionate to an offence, and proportionality is explained in terms of the offences-and-penalty system.[33] In short, we have something that was considered in our look at traditional retribution theories, an attempt to explain propositions of the form 'Penalty P is deserved for offence O' as the penalty's being according to a system of penalties and offences. In the course of our guide's exposition of the penalty system, the ordinary one of which we all have an idea, we learn interesting things about kinds of proportionality, relative and absolute and positive or negative. We are reminded that we do indeed have what are called intuitions or anchoring points – such as that five years in prison would be grossly disproportionate for a parking offence, and a fine of $10 a grossly disproportionate sentence for a brutal murder. But it is admitted that this leaves us with a lot of questions. We cannot make determinate judgements. Perhaps it is is admitted that we cannot make an initial and general judgement that will guide us in thinking about or defending or amending or reconstructing the system.

> We must recognize, I think, that any attempt to to work out a penalty scale (either its anchoring points or its content) from scratch is doomed to failure. There is no archimedean point, independent of all existing penal practice, from which we could embark on such an enterprise. We can only begin from where we are now, with a penalty scale whose content and upper and lower limits have been determined by a host of historical contingencies.[34]

That recognition is indeed not very clear. Is it the recognition that there is no general principle or proposition of proportionality or desert that informs the making or altering of a penalty system? Certainly none is supplied. It is not said, for example, that we are guided by actual facts of equivalence between culpability and distress, something like facts of actual weight or length. Does the retributive communication theory of punishment then lack content of a fundamental and essential kind? Before we answer that question and others that arise from what we have before us, there is another matter that needs attention. The communication theory has a recommendation so far unnoticed, however well it fits together with what we have on the table already. It is a recommendation lacked by all of the traditional retribution theories of punishment considered earlier.

The central theme of retribution, as we know, is that a punishment is deserved for an offence. Whatever else that comes to, it includes a reference not merely to what is against the law, but to what is wrong. As remarked before now, no reflective retributivist maintains that an offender deserves punishment no matter the moral worth of the law in question, no matter the moral standing of the offence or crime. No serious retributivist would suppose, for example, that someone deserved punishment in his sense for the crime of not going to the authorities about the whereabouts of a person who would end up in a gas chamber if located.

So it is very clear indeed, and should long have been clear despite many oversights, that any retribution theory of punishment depends on a conception of what things a society ought to make into crimes. Whether or not the answer to the question is partly obvious – rape and torture presumably cannot be left out – the question must have a full answer. Seeing and saying so is a recommendation of Duff's thinking.

> A normative theory of punishment must include a conception of crime as that which is to be punished. Such a conception of crime presupposes a conception of the criminal law – of its proper aims and content, of its claims on the citizen. Such a conception of the criminal law presupposes a conception of the state – of its proper role and functions, of its relation to its citizens. Such a conception of the state must also include a conception of society and of the relation between state and society.[35]

In short, a justification of punishment rests on a justification of a society. It is of considerable interest that the problem of the justification of punishment was so often for so long considered entirely independently of the question of what actions are wrong, what actions are to be punished, indeed what a decent society is. Justifications of punishment in terms of retribution were advanced as good almost always without specifying the category of things for which punishment was said to be deserved. It was very unlike the utilitarian prevention theory, which explicitly rested on the idea that the laws of a society should serve the end of the greatest total of satisfaction or well-being.

The communication theory we are considering does not leave out a kind of account of the society for which it offers a justification of the punishment in it. It is a society such that both of two political philosophies are realized in it, or on the way to being realized in it, these being liberalism and the more recent and conceivably transient doctrine of communitarianism. In this way the theory takes forward earlier work in the defence of punishment by way of the several ideologies, notably the work of Nicola Lacey.[36]

The political philosophy of liberalism, in fact a general prescription, is often summed up as being to the effect that a society to some considerable extent should not impose a general theory of how life ought to be on its members. Rather, the society should be pluralistic or tolerant – within certain limits it should leave its members to pursue their own ideas of what is called the good. It should leave individuals to themselves except when they cause harm somehow conceived to others. What is fundamental to this enterprise, as is often said, is individuals and their rights – they are to have freedom or autonomy, privacy, and the protection of a neutral state more engaged in protecting their contracts than in any larger endeavour.[37]

The second political philosophy, communitarianism, is said to be even harder to define than liberalism.[38] However, we hear that a state and society have an obligation to forward some theory of the good and perhaps that they cannot help but do this. It is said to be essential to this view that it gives some greater value and role to a community, say a country, than does liberalism. This prescription goes with a certain conception of persons as somehow less individual, as in fact somehow owing their natures to their communities. It is not easy to be confident whether the basic ideas of communitarianism, on balance, locate it to the right or the left of liberalism in the political spectrum.[39]

That is not the end of the matter of punishment and society. The society that enters into the justification of punishment provided by the communication theory is in fact to be taken as one that is true to *both* liberalism and communitarianism. The society we are to think about has the name of being *a liberal political community*.

> A liberal political community will recognize individual freedom and autonomy as crucial values: as human goods to be fostered and encouraged and as rights that must be respected by other citizens and by the state. . . . Although it will insist upon autonomy, freedom and privacy as central goods, it will not seek to enforce any simple all-embracing or comprehensive conception of human good.[40]

However, for a start, it is also true that the members of a liberal political community will

> constitute a community insofar as they aspire, and know that they aspire, to share the community-defining values of autonomy, freedom and privacy . . . and insofar as they aspire, and know that they aspire, to an appropriate mutual concern for one another in the light of those values. That mutual concern will involve a readiness to assist one another in pursuing and preserving the community's distinctive goods – though such assistance will often be organized and directly provided by the state – and, more crucially for present purposes, a respect for one another as fellow members of the community that precludes simply exploiting others for one's own ends or treating them in ways that are inconsistent with the community's defining values.[41]

So much for an exposition of a ramified, qualified and distinctive theory of the justification of punishment. We have accumulated elements of it that give rise to more questions than have been partly answered. Let us proceed through them, following something like the order of the quoted passages.

As already granted in connection with a different kettle of fish, there does seem to be sense in saying that punishment *is* among other things a communication, censure or condemnation. It can indeed be said to *tell* offenders a certain thing, and to promote their understanding of it. That thing is that a society or rather a state takes their offences to have been wrong. Of several responses we might make to this fact, the main one is surely that this is not enough to justify punishment. If this is all that is to be said for it, not enough can be said. The addition of this good to some fact of punishment's being deserved is not enough to justify it.

That punishment is the voice of the law is not enough to make right imprisoning a man for 20 years, quite likely a man who has never quite known what he was doing in the world, or killing him by putting him in an electric chair or injecting him with something loathesome. It is essential to keep in mind here, of course, that the communication in or by punishment is distinct from and is not at all recommended as having any effect in reforming offenders, any effect in preventing offences. On the theory we have, as you have heard, we are to punish when we believe there is no chance at all of the punishment's having a reformative effect. Despite the quoted passage (p. 186) there may be some uncertainty about the point. But I take it that punishment would have the given value of being a communication if it never had a reformative effect.

It must be, if that is so, that the justification of punishment on offer depends on some other thing than communication and penance. Indeed it does. What goes with the insufficient fact of communication is that somehow punishment is deserved. It is curious that that additional thing, despite familiar lines in the book to the effect that retribution theories fail in not finding some other real good in punishment, is not a good consequence or effect of punishment. What is added to the seemingly insufficient fact of communication is indeed that somehow punishment is deserved. A first question here has to do with the first passage quoted above and what might be called the role or part played by some or other relation of desert in the theory. Punishment when justified, you heard, will 'communicate to offenders the censure they deserve for their crimes'. What does that mean? Certainly it is not clear and unambiguous. Let us disambiguate.

Remember, first, that the communication or censure *is* the punishment. The communication is not additional from or different from the 20 years in prison, maybe the judge's words on the offender's character and like things, or the accusing attitudes of the guards. If we concentrate on this proposition, surely indubitable, what we have in references to a deserved communication, censure or penance is at bottom a traditional retribution theory, most likely about culpability and distress in some way, onto which some thoughts on communication are imposed. What goes together with the proposition that punishment is communication is just that punishment is deserved. This understanding of the theory goes together nicely with what is regularly mentioned in passing but not officially declared as a main proposition, that punishments are 'owed' to the offender or his victim.

We can remember or suppose something else, however. It can be supposed that the theory is not that punishment as an imposition of distress is deserved, but only that punishment as a communication is so. The punishing of the man has several sides or properties, and it is its being a communication, which we have supposed it can be, that is deserved. But what does it mean to say that a communication is deserved? What is a deserved *communication*? It is not easy to say. If we keep firmly in mind that it is not the distress of the punishment that we are contemplating, but exactly and only the communication or censure, is its being deserved perhaps its being true, merited, or well based? Is it that the message fits the facts?

If that new idea is not the right one, here is another. What is deserved is exactly the distress of being censured or condemned for wrongdoing, as against the more ordinary distress of punishment, say being kept in prison for 20 years. It is to be noted that both of these new ideas can be supposed to make for what we have heard about, an intrinsic connection between the past wrongful offence and what is now deserved. If what is deserved is a true condemnation, that is one with or is logically entailed by taking the offence to have been wrong.

These three answers issue in judgements that can be expected. The first of them makes the communication theory into a traditional retribution theory with the addition of a not very substantial proposition about communication. This is surely not enough to justify the 20 years in prison. The second one, about a true communication, might be thought to go even less far towards a justification. The third, whether or not separated from the first, calls for the same response. That is not all.

These answers issue in more of what you have noticed often enough before now, a conviction that what is said of retribution and desert by justifiers of punishment is obscure. It does indeed invite some sort of reductive analysis, if not diagnosis. The second and third answers also issue in something else. It is a question with which our theorist of punishment seeks to deal. If our aim is only to engage in a true or well-founded condemnation, or to cause to someone only the hurt or the like of just that condemnation, why are we putting him in jail for 20 years? But leave that.

Another question about the theory's reliance on desert or retribution can be dealt with more quickly. Put aside the first new idea – a deserved condemnation is merely a true or well-based one. The other two ideas raise the question asked so often in the course of our inquiry. *What* is the relation of desert between an offence and a penalty, the relation that makes the penalty right and justified? Well, what is said of that was reported in the exposition of the communication theory. But no account of the relation of desert can possibly be given by taking up the mere synonym that the deserved penalty is the proportionate one, of course. Nor is a general account given by way of citing a penalty system. You cannot convey what is supposed to be the justifying principle of a penalty system by pointing at it. The communication theory therefore *does* lack content of a fundamental and essential kind. A preventive theory of punishment also points at such a penalty system, a very similar one, but that theory gives its rationale in terms of rational prevention (p. 98).

The obscurity about the relation of desert, and about what it is suppose to relate, certainly bears on another matter, a practical one. The obscurity is not just a failing in a theory but may also at least contribute to a practical problem. Penalty systems are not settled once and for all, but come up for revision. As new proposals come up, how are we to decide on them if we have no general guide? It is no good saying you look at the rest of the system and do something new that fits in with the rest of it, is it? We have to have a general understanding of the rest of it that guides us in the change, indicates why one thing would be inconsistent with another.

What of communitarianism and liberalism? You have heard something of them, in the words of their expositor, and of their synthesis in the doctrine of the liberal political community. You have had the words delivered to you in order to make less unfair a question or two that might be better answered after a lot more reading. What does communitarianism come to? What does liberalism come to? What does the liberal political community come to?

We need answers to the questions because we need to know what the wrongful acts are that this retributive communication theory will take to be rightly punished. Let me say plainly that in my opinion the given exposition of communitarianism and liberalism shares the character of all other expositions of which I know. It is at least elusive. This is partly a matter of indeterminate ideas – say freedom and indeed community – and the piling on of qualifications. I hope to speak for you, reader, in saying that we do not have much useful distinction between communitarianism, liberalism and the doctrine of the liberal political community. We do not have plainness in the account of any of them. What we have, it might be said, is a report of good intentions not carried forward into determinateness.[42]

Do you say in reply that we *do* know what is in question, or know well enough? Do you say, despite the fact of political conservatism in our societies, that what is in question with liberalism etc. is in fact societies that are more or less like ours – societies with more of this or that kind of provision or institution? Well, that does not accord with Antony Duff's reservations.[43] But suppose we *can* get an idea of the subject matter of the communication theory, in so far as it concerns a society, by thinking of the things that are crimes in Britain and America at the start of the twenty-first century.

That does indeed give some content to the communication theory. We know more of what we are talking about. But there remains a large problem. We now do know in a sense what the basic aim of the communication theory is, but this is not to know very much, not enough. The aim is to defend our societies as they are, or to defend societies to which we can extrapolate from our societies. But we do not know, in any enlightening way, what is supposed to make these societies worth defending. That leaves the communication theory incomplete in the most important way. If it has the distinction over almost all of its predecessors of seeing a need, it does not satisfy that need.

Return for a moment to the utilitarian prevention theory of punishment. As already remarked, we know exactly what it is that recommends a certain system of law, criminalizing of behaviour, prevention of offences. It is that the system is the one that is taken to maximize satisfaction or well-being. What is the comparably enlightening generalization with respect to the liberal political community? It has certainly not been produced.

We shall be coming back to this crux of theories of punishment. But, to end the present discussion, what is to be said of the communication theory is that it shares the failure of traditional retribution theories of punishment by having a hole at its centre, a hole where there ought to be clarity about desert. It adds that hole to what needs a great deal more to recommend it, which is punishment as communication. The theory invites being rewritten into something else.

Would further study make it clearer to me? Would it help with other problems you may have, say about communicating with the many offenders who are mentally ill? Well, further study might be worth it, and I commend some study to you.

8
Non-Problem, Other Conclusions

THE END OF ALL RETRIBUTIVISM

It is now clear enough to me, and maybe to you, that theories of the justification of punishment wholly or partly in terms of retribution or desert are not conceptually adequate. If conceptual adequacy consists in clarity, consistency and validity, and completeness, almost all traditional retribution theories fail the first requirement, that of clarity. Those that struggle through that requirement fail the others. There is nothing weaker in place of an argument than the circularity of failing to see that what is really being offered as a proof of something's being right is that it is right. There is not much more than hope and pomposity in talk of moral rights.[1] There is an absurdity in leaving out part of a subject matter, above all leaving out a greater distress when considering a smaller satisfaction. And so on.

It is true that we have not considered all retribution theories. It is conceivable that somewhere in a lesser or even greater journal of philosophy, or a book about to come out, a conceptually decent retribution theory exists. It was conceivable, too, as I think the philosopher of science Ernest Nagel remarked, that a certain story in the *New York Times* was true. It was to the effect that in upper New York state a grave had been opened and a beard was still growing five years after burial. Nagel said that there was no need to go and see if a possibility was realized. There is also a kind of inductive evidence against the existence of a conceptually adequate retribution theory.

Such theories, certainly including the more recent ones we have just been considering, also fail in a second way, a way in which conceptually adequate thinking can also fail. The theories seem to assemble propositions but offer no reason for punishment that can strike plain men or women as not only a reason but as *substantial*, or strike them that way when they are actually thinking. There is minimal sense, but no ring of truth. In the end, you can suppose, this plain jury is the one that matters, a reasonably suspicious one not given to speculation. As you have heard a few times, the infliction of punishment if it is justified must do some actual good, serve some purpose, where the latter sort of thing is something that does not leave you in any doubt.

This second problem with retribution theories, their factitiousness and other weaknesses, is connected with the first one, is it not? That is, you can suppose that the obscurity etc. of the theories is part of the explanation of their failing to offer a substantial reason for punishment. You can also suppose, no doubt, exactly oppositely, that the lack of a real reason for punishment is part of the explanation of the obscurity. You can indeed be suspicious of the obscurity. You can wonder about a cover-up, whether or not a self-aware or deliberate one. You can think of a connection between the amoral selfishness of the conservative tradition in politics and the obscurity – the absence of a general moral principle defending self-interest and the obscurity.[2] No doubt, too, those two suppositions running in opposite directions can be brought into consistency.

All of those remarks, of course, are about retribution theories as conventionally or literally understood, as presented by their makers. We took the view early on, however, that they must have something significant in them – something worth calling a reason. It was not to be conjectured, really, that a large tradition of thought and feeling in human life, let alone a dominant practice over centuries, had in it no more than kinds of obscurity, gesturing, irrelevance and nonsense.

Does a last objection come to your mind about the idea that there must have been some gain to be had, some satisfying consequence, in the practice of retribution? Is there an objection, more exactly, to the idea that that good has been just grievance satisfaction? Since it is not easy to escape convention, you *can* wonder if this reductive analysis or diagnosis is in error. It can occur to you, for example, despite agreement with the objections to traditional retributive theories, that you do not have to say that it is the consequence of satisfaction to victims of offences and others that is really being offered to justify punishment, but rather a different consequence. That different consequence is just the distress itself caused to the offenders, *that* consequence of punishment. What is offered in justification is something real, the distress, which thing is in a certain relation to the past offence.

That may sound all right for a minute, and we can give it a name – *distress retributivism*. But on reflection, it doesn't work. It cannot conceivably be a reason for punishment, indeed a reason for anything, *just* that it causes distress, causes distress without any further effect. Reasons simply cannot be no more than propositions whose content is only that doing something will make things somehow worse – *only* that. Nor is the situation improved in the slightest by the addition that doing the thing will make things worse according to a certain effectless way of looking at them, i.e. in terms of a relation to a past event.[3] It remains the case that the supposed reasons cannot be such, since they remain propositions about increasing distress or the like with no comprehensible or at any rate significant or effective addition.

In that case, to go back, there cannot be a reason for punishment that is simply its consequence of distress for the offender. There must be something somehow desirable about it. And, to come to the end of a minute of wondering or doubt, I trust forever, there is only one thing that this can be. It is the satisfactoriness of the distress, necessarily to someone or to people other than the person suffering it. There seems to be no possibility of avoiding the understanding of retribution theories in terms of the satisfaction of grievance. At least at bottom. This rewriting of the theories very likely should have more added to it about who mainly or primarily has grievance desires in many cases, how they come about, how they are supported, and so on.

We can add, for example, that grievance satisfaction is likely to be bound up with certain related feelings about convictions and punishments – strong or firm feelings that what is happening is in accordance with the general way that things ought to be or have to be in a society, that the society's system of governance or control is working as it should be, that things are in order. We can also add that grievance satisfaction is strongest and most persistent in those members of a society who have most of the goods in it, the beneficiaries of the society, those most desirous of its continuing as it is. These fortunate persons are also the most effective in bringing about and maintaining the attitudes of a society. They include, as is worth remarking, most of the judges and politicians, not to mention the writers of books on the justification of punishment, and also the owners and executives of our media. This sort of thing enlarges or buttresses the proposition of grievance satisfaction. If the proposition becomes less simple it does not become less strong.

That buttress or maybe more integral part of the proposition of grievance desires needs to have added to it what can indeed be distinguished from it, and was mentioned in passing a minute ago. That is the political tradition of conservatism in our societies, the strongest such tradition in them. It is notable that there is a striking likeness between the retributive tradition of punishment and the conservative tradition in politics. It is as good as established, to my mind, that the political tradition cannot conceivably be identified and characterized in the ways it supposes. It is not identified and characterized, for example, by opposition to change or to change as against reform, by support for a non-theoretical kind of political thinking, or by a unique view of human nature as low. It is not identified by support for freedom in general or, most relevantly, by support for a principle of desert.[4]

What is more important, however, is that this tradition of pure self-interest is indeed bound up with the grievance satisfaction that is the reality of retributive theories of punishment. You may wonder, indeed, even at this late stage of our inquiry, whether at least a mistake of emphasis has been made. Have we been too much constrained by a certain intellectual convention? Should we have escaped the ruling idea that retributivism is to be explained non-politically? Should we have escaped the idea that its nature is to be found in terms of moral rather than political thinking and philosophy? It is certainly possible to resist the embarrassing answer that we have been wasting our time. It is not possible to resist the truth that a proper analysis of the tradition of conservatism shows the fact of its support for or more central role in the tradition of retributivism.[5]

Another very different kind of attention also needs to be paid to the proposition of grievance desires. It first came up when we were looking at retributive justifications of punishment, as distinct from retributive prohibitions on victimization. Certainly the consequence of satisfaction is *a* reason for punishment, however readily defeated by a reason against having to do with the offender's distress and also effects on a family and so on. Grievance satisfaction, that is, was an effective understanding of *positive* retributivism. Can something like it be used, however successfully, as an understanding of *negative* retributivism, that prohibition on intolerable victimizing of the innocent and intolerable over-punishing of the guilty?

There is a clear assymetry here. The satisfaction justification of punishment is the result of being able to find no real good being recommended in conventional understandings of retributivism with punishment. What we find in retributivism is only distress, and of course obscurity and the like. But in the case of retributivism's objection to victimization, on the other hand, there is already something real and substantial on hand to be gained by not victimizing – the satisfaction in place of extreme dissatisfaction on the part of the contemplated innocent victim. We are not constrained to find *another* reason against victimization. We do not need and are not going to be persuaded by the proposition that retributive resistance to victimization has to do with only the counterpart of a grievance satisfaction – a satisfaction taken by other people in the satisfaction of a person not victimized.

So an analytic account of negative retributivism must be different from the analytic account of positive retributivism. What is that account to be? Shall we return to our traditional understandings of desert claims in connection with positive retributivism, (1) to (14) and then the contributions of Hart, Nozick and Duff, and see if anything can be put to work with negative retributivism? You may be as sure as I of the result. We are not going to get a reason against a possible victimization, for example, by way of the supposition that there are measurable, commensurable and unequal facts in the innocence of a person and that person's being put in prison. There are no such facts. We are not going to get a reason for the victimization's being wrong either if the supposed reason is the mouthful that the victimization is not an annulment. And so on with the other candidates, and also the thoughts of Hart, Nozick and Duff. In short, the conceptual inadequacy of retribution theories, to call it no more than that, surely precludes our finding an adequate reason against victimizations in them.

That is not to say that there is no actual reason against victimizations in the tradition of retributivism. Here too a kind of realism must lead us to resist thinking that a large tradition has no significant content. Could it be that the significant content of negative retributivism is simply recoil from distress that is somehow unfair or the like? Let me leave that question hanging for a while, except for one comment. If retributivism was more theoretically respectable, if it was something like conceptually adequate on the subject of desert, we would be rather too brave to insist on a different analytic understanding of negative as against positive retributivism. The facts are otherwise. It is not too much to say that the tradition of retributivism, both positive and negative, taken as it presents itself, is a mess. Of a mess, it may well be reasonable that the sense made of one part of it is not the sense to be made of another part.

If conventional retributivism of neither the positive nor the negative kind can be sustained, and if positive retributivism as properly analysed cannot be sustained either, and if the situation with negative retributivism as analysed is at least unclear, it is also true that there is objection to the utilitarian prevention theory and outlooks like it, objection that is as indubitable and fatal. The victimization objection is perhaps the foremost instance of the general objection to utilitarianism in terms of unfairness, injustice or the like, so superior to objections in terms of smaller ideas in moral philosophy.[6] Further, the marriage of the utilitarian or some other prevention theory to retributivism is hopeless if the latter is taken conventionally. The marriage will at least be uncertain, as we might have taken time to see, if negative retributivism is understood in some analytical way.

Some may think, or think for a moment, that all this makes our situation dire, in fact hopeless. This pessimism may arise from a certain confusion. In one form, it is the confusion of thinking that the only consequentialism is the utilitarian one or something rather like it – that if we take up consequentialism we necessarily go for the greatest total of satisfaction, or at any rate we necessarily are maximizers of something that excludes considerations of importance, maybe about innocence and the rights of the innocent. This attitude is more common than it should be, and seems to have entered into the thinking of Duff.[7] But plainly it is mistaken in terms of the ordinary definition of consequentialisms given above.

In this ordinary sense, there are innumerable consequentialisms. One is that we should act so as to produce fairness somehow conceived or defined, maybe as an equality. Another is that we should act so as to benefit our own nation or people, or a group or class within it. Another is that we should act so that some specified set of rights is respected. Another can aim at a mixture of things, including rights. It is natural to take it that any consequentialism will be maximizing, that it will be for the greatest total of something, perhaps respectings of rights, but not even this is necessary.

The result of these reflections is that there is no need whatever, if we are to justify punishment by consequences and yet avoid unacceptable victimizations, to attempt to do so by adding a non-consequential or backward-looking consideration to utilitarianism or any like thing. Rather, we can seek to justify punishment and exclude victimizations exactly by proposing that whatever we do by way of punishment and victimization must have certain consequences pertaining to both of these – fair or human consequences or whatever.

In short, then, with respect to the matter of mixed theories, there never was a need to justify punishment by adding something different in kind to a recommendation in terms of consequences. There was the clear and open alternative of turning from that utilitarian recommendation in terms of consequences to a non-utilitarian one in terms of consequences. To put the matter differently, there was the alternative of turning to a consequentialism of some kind of justice or decency.

That brings to an end this whole inquiry into wholly retributive and partly retributive theories of punishment, positive or negative, whether taken conventionally at their face value or in their reality when properly analysed. Let us sum up.

First, retribution theories are at least in general conceptually inadequate, and, second, if there are exceptions that are conceptually adequate, they fail to give an adequate or real reason for punishment. Third, all or most retribution theories, positive and negative, at least as they have been and probably are, presuppose that offenders had the power of origination or free will, and therefore could have done otherwise than they did at a particular moment given the past and present as they were. It is in fact a wonderful supposition, close to unbelievable when seen clearly. It is a mistake to take determinism as unclear, maybe not definitely either true or false, or just a kind of *opinion*, maybe an outdated opinion. It is a mistake to take it as anything that cannot really be effective as an objection to a theory of punishment. It may be a mistake owed in part to a commitment to a kind of society. There is usually desire in half-belief.

Fourth, a properly analysed as against a conventional retributivism gives an actual reason for punishment, but patently an insufficient one. Fifth, there is no need whatever for negative retributivism itself, stuff about factual equivalence or whatever, whatever recoil from distress may be in it. It has been an illusion to think so, certainly not a conclusion based on argument. A prohibition on kinds of victimization can be a large part of the content of a theory of what consequences the practice of punishment must have – as will be demonstrated shortly.

But there are larger conclusions to be drawn from our inquiry into all the theories of punishment.

THE DECENT SOCIETY

What, if anything, justifies the practice of punishment? That was the question with which we began, a question raised first by the fact that punishment is an intentional causing of suffering, distress or deprivation. It is the question to which the philosophy of punishment has always been directed. How does that question stand to another larger one? How does it stand to the question of what kind of society is right? That is what is sometimes called the question of the just or the good or the decent society, or the question of justice or the like in society. It has to do with the distribution of things, or at any rate the possession of things, and of course the means to getting or keeping those things, and is the fundamental question of political philosophy. It leads to the question of what ought to be the relations between societies, say rich societies and impoverished societies, say the United States or the United Kingdom and Malawi, Mozambique, Sierra Leone and Zambia.[8] Since it is indeed a question of what is right, incidentally, there is the obvious consequence that political philosophy is most importantly a part of moral philosophy.

Retribution theories of the justification of punishment have always been discussed independently of the question of the decent society. That is to say that it has been supposed that it is possible and reasonable to say what, if anything, justifies punishment, without attending to the other larger question. It has been tacitly assumed that punishment is being considered in connection with a great, decent, justifiable, defensible or perhaps somehow necessary society. Something like this was Kant's confident assumption when he said, among other things, that punishment must in all cases be imposed only because an individual has committed a crime (p. 17). Questions have always come up about this sort of thing.

But do you not actually need to think of what things rightly are crimes? Completeness in your inquiry requires that, doesn't it, even if nothing else does? It will not be enough, of course, to think of what things *are* crimes in some particular society at some time. No consistent retribution theorist now takes or can take the view that punishments are justified with respect to *all* the things that have been crimes, say helping someone to escape slavery in the United States or resisting genocide in Germany or Palestine later. But is the question of what things are to be crimes, including what is to be prohibited with respect to what we call *property*, not rather close to the question of how a society ought to be?

It has been easier for retributivists than others to put aside the question of the decent society. What has helped them to do so, attitudinally speaking, has been concentration on the past rather than the future. That it, whether or not they have been reasonable to do so, whether or not they have been required by principles of inquiry to do otherwise, they have found it easy not to pay attention to the consequences of punishment in exactly the making, maintaining and defence of a society. They have, as they have said, looked to the past. But, still, that leaves entirely open the question of what the actions actually are for which punishments are deserved, and of course what future actions are to be punished. They must have had a little more help in their oversight, maybe the help of self-interest.

We are now contemplating that traditional propositions of desert and the like are no part whatever of the justification of punishment, that they are useless and unnecessary. Rather, retribution is in fact a matter of certain of the consequences of punishment, consequences of satisfaction in the distress of a punishment. These must bring other consequences to mind – the distress itself and possible consequences of the distress, maybe good consequences. So to take such a view is naturally to escape the past and to escape the illusion of traditional retribution theories that the question of the decent society is not on the agenda and does not need to be.

The situation of holders of the utilitarian prevention theory of punishment and its common informal forms has of course been different. It has been different, at any rate, in that their gaze has been on the future. Furthermore, the utilitarian theory of punishment in question is indeed an application or product of a general principle, the utilitarian principle, which does indeed apply to societies. In fact it was first formulated in connection with societies and their law, the general question of how we ought to organize our lives together and indeed what laws there are to be.

That is true enough, but it brings something else to mind – in addition to the fact that the general principle fails because it justifies certain victimizations. Utilitarians and like-minded persons have indeed paid a kind of official attention to the question of the decent society, and given the official answer that it is the utilitarian society or something like it. It must be their position that punishment is justified when it prevents things that are or would be offences in such a society. That leaves open a certain question. It leaves open the question about actual punishments in our actual societies, societies that certainly are *not* governed by the principle of pursuing in all things the greatest total balance of all kinds of satisfaction (p. 86). So there is at least a question, a question of importance, to which utilitarians have not given the amount of attention that might have been expected.

To come round to mixed theories, there evidently is as much reason for them to give some time to the larger question of the decent society – with respect both to their element of retributivism, for the reasons you know, and yet more obviously with their element having to do with prevention. Still, to glance back at our samples of such theories, no such thing was explicit in Hart's doctrine. Despite his attention to utilitarianism and his partial rejection of it, he did not really consider the question of what things should be against the law, which of course is also to say what things should be in accordance with or permitted by the law. This, to say the least, made for incompleteness. Did this have something to do with the inclination of many lawyers and jurisprudents to think too well of the institution in which they live their lives?

In the case of Nozick, there was the same incompleteness in the discussion of punishment. But given his political and moral philosophy generally, his libertarian conservatism, it was possible to fill in his conception of crime. It was to the credit of Duff that he did indicate a conception, in terms of the liberal political community, the child of liberalism and communitarianism. Still, his concern was to justify a possible system of punishment, a system in a possible society, not in our actual societies as they are. He did not give much attention, anyway verdictive attention, to that question hard to avoid.

What we have, then, is that the theoreticians of punishment, very nearly all of them, and all of them until recently, have considered the question of the justification of punishment without attending to the general question of the decent society. As for the further question, of the justification of our actual punishment in our actual societies, it is safe to say that hardly any thought has been given to the matter. Some philosophers of punishment, such as Kant, have assumed without reflection that their justifications apply to their society. Other philosophers have put aside the question of the justification of our actual punishments. They have offered only a justification of punishment for an 'ideal' society, only an 'ideal theory'. All of this, to say the least, is open to question, indeed objection. It is another embarrassment for philosophy.

Do you think otherwise? Do you still have the idea that it is reasonable enough to look into the justification of punishment without looking into the question of the decent society? Do you say that we can, if we want, think of societies *in general* and ask about the justification of an authority's infliction of a penalty on an offender or someone else found to have committed an offence, an action of a kind prohibited by law? That we can do this without attending to differences between the communist society of the Soviet Union and the immeasurably different fascist society of Germany's Third Reich? Between South Africa before or after apartheid? Between America, Britain, Cuba, North Korea, Saudi Arabia, Israel, Palestine, Iraq as it was before the attack on it and now is, and societies different from all of these?

In fact we do not have the choice of looking into the question of the justification of punishment by any state without looking into the question of the decent society. We cannot give any answer at all to the first question without giving an answer to the larger one. This can be argued for in several strong ways, already noticed in passing. And, as already implied, it can be established in another way, as good as demonstrated.

The argued dismissal of retribution theories of punishment as traditionally understood is fundamental to this demonstration. It simply follows from this that in considering the justification of punishment we must consider its conseqences, as indeed we all do, and consider no more than that. In fact, you can speculate, it is not theoretically possible that there is anything else to consider. What are the bad and what are the good effects of punishment by the state? The possible good effects cannot be other than progress towards, achievement of, maintenance of, defence of, or entrenchment of a particular kind of society. Not all societies, as we well know, are the same.

To speak a little differently, punishment enforces the law of a society. New punishment makes new law. Not punishing brings a law into a nullity. Actual law is more the child of punishment than the father. And law along with convention in thought and feeling, you can almost say, *forms* a society. To make law and convention, you can almost say, is to make society. There is no more possibility of justifying punishment without justifying a society than there is of justifying a war without justifying its ends or results. There is no more possibility of justifying punishment than of justifying any other large institution or practice of a society, say its distribution of income, or its system of education, without justifying the society to which that distribution contributes so greatly.[9]

Just to think of this, I hope, is to know it is true. It is to know what overcomes the oversight, mistake, self-deception or deception of much philosophy. Punishment is to be considered, therefore, in terms of what it specifically seeks to and does to some considerable extent prevent or reduce. Punishment is to be as much considered in terms of what it does *not* seek to prevent or reduce. It may leave alone those omissions that create and maintain societies that have in them members or classes of members who are wretched. Punishment is to be considered, too, as an institution that creates, strengthens or fortifies that other determinant of a society, convention. What is enforced as law is a guide, what some take as the only guide, to what is to be thought, felt and done where the law gives a choice. Punishment gives to a society, more than does anything else, a sense of what is tolerable in what we do and fail to do where action and practices are not prohibited by law.

There is another question about which we do not have a choice if we have embarked on the question of the justification of punishment. To say what justifies punishment, necessarily by way of a judgement as to the nature of a decent society, is to be committed to a judgement on our own actual societies and our own actual punishments. The inclination of utilitarians who do not look closely is in fact not an option. You cannot choose what seems to be logically entailed by your answer to the question of a decent society. It is worth adding that you very likely have a moral obligation to attend to the logical consequence of your answer for your own society now. That obligation may well follow from your reasoning in connection with the decent society, the principle or principles on which you depend.

The question of the justification of punishment, then, has no existence independently of the question of the decent society. It has no existence when it is taken as generally it has been taken. Understood as independent of the fundamental question in political and indeed moral philosophy, the question of the justification of punishment is a non-question, a non-existent question. A proper book about punishment in general would begin here. A book not constrained by the mistake of the past, the mistake of a long line of philosophers, jurisprudents and the like, would begin here. It would begin at this point reached at the end of our improper inquiry. What you must put up with instead is a sketch of such a book, a kind of impression.

THE PRINCIPLE OF HUMANITY

Some contemplate that the decent society is the society that realizes the ambition of the conservative tradition in politics. They are then contemplating the societies for which, primarily, this book is being revised, those of the United States and the United Kingdom and similar countries in 2005. I myself put aside the idea that the conservative society is the decent society, by way of a proposition reported on already. It is not that the tradition of conservatism is unique in selfishness or self-interest, an idea that can indeed arise in the course of an inquiry into it. Conservatism is no more self-interested than other political traditions. Rather, conservatism is the tradition whose self-interest has the support of no other rationale, no moral principle.

You may contemplate, differently, that the decent society is the society of liberalism, or communitarianism, or, as you have heard, the liberal political community. I am among the great majority of humankind who do not join you. Our reason is that facts of such societies, such as how long the lives are of people in different socio-economic classes, overwhelm the recommendations so obscurely claimed for the societies. Liberalism has long been and remains a politics of some concern, some conscience, but without an edge of definition and resolution.[10]

To glance back at its history, liberalism began with John Stuart Mill saying that the decent society is the one where everyone is to be left alone in the running of his life so long as he does not cause harm to anybody else. Liberalism began, as well, with Mill not reflecting to any clear effect on what harm is. To come up to date, Duff's struggles, and the struggles of the political and legal philosophers of liberalism, are no closer to effective definition. Rawls, their leader, for all his talk of equality, should be notorious for a certain thing. That is his declaring that there is to be no more inequality than is necessary in order to raise up the worst-off, and then not question-ing and not judging claims by the well-off as to what is necessary. That makes his theory of justice into a kind of servant.[11]

It may be as well to eschew certain political traditions of the left as well. Having myself been no Marxist before or after the wall of a kind of empire fell down, but inclined only to unmetaphysical thinking about rich and poor attached to no mechanical philosophy of history, I have no problem with this eschewing.[12] It cannot be, however, that the principle that underlies those traditions and others of the left can be passed by. This principle also has an immeasurably greater recommendation. It is the principle to which virtually all of humanity commits itself when its self-interest is not engaged, when it is not favouring itself or cheating on behalf of itself. It is, further, a principle to which our real human nature commits us. That nature is first that we are desirous of the great goods of life and second that we are rational in the sense of having reasons, the latter by *their* nature being general.

The Principle of Humanity is known in a way to all of us. As remarked, it is depended on with confidence by all of us to judge disputes and conflicts where our own interests are not engaged and we do not identify with a party to the dispute or conflict. The principle has to do with the great goods of life. They have been conceived in various ways but not in arguable ways that make them fundamentally different. In one central conception, there are six of them. Quickly and very inadequately stated, without proper and full reality, they are as follows.

A decent length of life, say 75 years rather than 35, the existence that is the lasting of a personal world for that time.[13] Secondly, bodily well-being, including not being in pain and having more to eat than what merely sustains life. Freedom and power, in a living place and maybe in a family, and in the larger setting of a society and a homeland. Respect and self-respect, as against denigration and inferiority. The goods of relationship with others, narrower and wider. Finally, the goods of culture, just one of them being knowledge rather than ignorance.

The Principle of Humanity has to do, more immediately, with the results of having and of lacking the great goods. These are good lives and bad lives. Good lives have these goods to some considerable extent. Bad lives lack them to some considerable extent. Both extents are open to definition, this definition of course being a matter of decision as well as attention to fact. Bad lives are thus lives of frustration, deprivation, suffering, misery or agony.

The Principle of Humanity also has to do with rationality in a sense as fundamental as the different one mentioned above. This rationality is the policy of taking or adopting means to an end that can actually be judged to be effective and economical – they will achieve the end and will not do so, so to speak, at too great a cost in the currency of that end. The Principle of Humanity, reassuringly open to simple and concise statement, is that *we are to take what are best judged to be rational steps to get or keep people out of bad lives*. The means in question are not those thought at a time, as a result of ignorant convention, to be the only possible ones, or the only reasonable ones, or the only effective ones. We are to avoid pretences that are much of the stuff of our societies, we are not to invent a difference in rightness between fatal acts and fatal omissions, we are not to persist in ignorance of what we do, not to suppose we can rely on the pushers who are most of our politicians.

The Principle of Humanity, if open to clear and concise statement, does of course have further content. This is given, first, by specifying *policies* in which it issues. Some of these have to do with the means, at bottom the material means, to the great goods and good lives. Such policies, about the means to well-being, are central but not alone. Another policy of the principle, in need of being added to previous lists, is a commitment to a struggle for conceptual adequacy, consistency above all, and for truth. That is struggle, most importantly, against what is rightly described as the moral stupidity of our societies, a stupidity owed to a managed ignorance. A further policy is the assertiveness of plain speaking and of judgement not made quiet or hesitant by deference, and an aversion to the abstraction that leaves out human facts.

The Principle of Humanity is also to be understood in terms of certain *practices*. Some important ones are practices of equality. Among them is a practice of what can properly be called democracy, and distinguished thereby from what we have, which is merely hierarchic democracy.[14] That is not to say that the end of the principle is an equality, a relationship. It is about bad lives, the alleviation and prevention of distress, which distress of course stands in several connections with equality and inequality.

This is but a glance at a principle, for me the principle of the decent society and thus the only principle for punishment.[15] But it is within your own ready capability, very likely, to do more than supplement the glance, to see and contemplate more of the Principle of Humanity. It is no factitious thing, but a thing common to us all, including those of us, almost all, who do not serve it in all circumstances. It does indeed arise out of our natures. As remarked already, it is what we use to decide what is right when we are not distracted by our departures in our own minds from our own rationality – or rather our two rationalities.

This is the occasion to return to a question left hanging. That was the question of the actual reason as distinct from the hopeless official reasons against victimization in the tradition of retributivism. It seems to me that this decency in retributivism is indeed mainly recoil from pointless distress, in fact a response inseparable from our common commitment to humanity. An impulse to theoretical consistency on the part of retribution theorists, a mistaken one, has had much to do with the mistake of supposing that a reason against victimization is in fact just the same as the reason for punishment. Also, that the strength of the objection to victimization has had the effect of buttressing their argument for punishment cannot have been unwelcome to retributivists. Still, it remains the case that retributivism has had something right in it.

OUR SOCIETIES

Punishment is justified in societies generally if it is in accordance with the Principle of Humanity. That is the fourth last proposition of this book. Punishment is right when it can be judged to be a rational means to getting or keeping people out of bad lives. It is right when it somehow contributes to that end, somehow moves any society in that direction. All punishments are wrong which are not such rational means to the end. This is a proposition that has the strength and weight of the Principle of Humanity itself. That is a strength and weight that overwhelms the viciousness of conservatism, the weakness of liberalism, and the many related moralities of mere association – those that take what is right to be what is good for one's own family, class, people, race, or other group.

The third last proposition of this book, which needs or at any rate will get little attention, is that at least usually there is a harder question about the actual practice of punishment in a particular society than the question of its proper end. What is harder is not the moral side of the question, so to speak. The answer to this is the Principle of Humanity. What is harder is seeing whether a particular practice of punishment, say the one in your society, *is* a rational means to the end. The harder question is that question of fact, that question of judgement as to fact. It has counterparts of several kinds, one now to the fore being the question of terrorism. None of these questions becomes much easier when you see that proponents of particular principles and politics constantly engage in distortions of fact in order to support their principles and politics. Nothing is more common than arguing, about what in fact you do not want someone else to do, that it will not work or will certainly have this or that bad effect.

Despite the difficulty, the second last and related proposition of this book must have to do with whether our punishments as we have them, say in the United States and the United Kingdom and like places now, *are* rational with respect to the end having to do with bad lives. Can our punishments be judged to be in accord with the Principle of Humanity? Or, which of our punishments can be? A proper book about punishment in general, as you have already heard, would be a book about the decent society, a book about the Principle of Humanity. *Another* book could begin here, at this sentence. It would be about our existing punishment, facts about punishment itself as well as related and greater facts. If the factual question is harder, it could surely be given a full and proper answer owed to evidence, reflection and argument. Some of that evidence etc. can be ancipated here.

The wealthy societies of the West, societies largely subject to the wealthy within them, also have in them men whose lives are short because they have not had the wherewithal to arrange to make them long. They die before they want to go. These millions of men, those in certain fractions of populations with least income, lose about six or seven years of seeing people and places they like, having a drink. There are related differences among women. Our societies and their leaders in particular have arranged, as well, through omission and commission, greatly shorter lives elsewhere. One sample of Africans, the poorest tenths in Malawi, Mozambique, Sierra Leone and Zambia now alive, have very much shorter average life-expectancies and so lose 20 million years of living time.[16] They would have done a lot in it.

In our wealthy societies many of us, when we fall into pain, distress, awful conditions or into our final straits, cannot have the help that others have from that primary profession, the doctors. So we do not see very well, or breathe very well. Talk of having and not having health insurance, or of a society not being able to afford a full health-care system, passes by means of self-deception over the top of human facts of suffering. It is of interest that for some of us, if we get cancer and are impoverished, it is better for the purposes of treatment of it to be in jail. A society cannot ignore someone in jail so effectively.

In our societies we have democracies defended and praised as giving us freedom and power. Our societies are said to give us the great good of freedom and power in what is perhaps its most important form to all of us, the political one. Our politicians, most of them not the best and brightest among us, being only student politicians grown up, are unaware of much. Let us have a simple example. Freedom and power are most importantly relative goods. That is, how much you have depends on how much somebody else has.

How much you have depends on my gun or my money or my family or social or business connections. Everybody else knows that. With decreasing equality, increasing inequality, the freedom and power of those with less decreases down to zero.

The inequality in political freedom and power in our societies is such that some of us, a large fraction, have hundreds or thousands of times as much political freedom and power as another fraction.[17] This fact, about influence before, during and after elections, is quite untouched by the fact of one person, one vote. Our hierarchic democracy, too kindly named, this denial of the great good of freedom, contributes to the first denial, of decent lengths of life.

In our societies, to pass on to the matter of respect and self-respect, some live lives that are among other things a continuing awareness of their inferiority. The people in question are not only aware of being treated as inferiors. They know that in plain ways they and their lives *are* inferior, say in terms of political and other freedom and power, to which can be added the other great goods. They live, then, without the respect and self-respect that depends not on dismal pieces of rhetoric about all of us being equal, equal in the eyes of God as used to be said, but on realities of our existence together. They live, too, with the knowledge that these realities are arranged or made by others to an overwhelming extent rather than ordained by nature.

Some of us, as would be expected from all this, have no human connection with the others around us. We are not in their community. In a way we live alone. Some of us are denied that important kind of another great good, relationship. It may be because we are black, and not lucky in attributes that make for the success that gives actual membership in a society, accreditation. We are denied the good mainly because of the parents we did not choose.

Some of us, finally, are not far from living as if the great history of culture had not happened. It is not so much that we know only lower as against higher pleasures, say pornography or a degrading newspaper, as John Stuart Mill said with reason. It is that we are deprived and vulnerable. We are ignorant, and in this ignorance we are used by others. They can actually get us on their side, which is not ours. We vote for them.

To such judgements about our rich societies, mainly denied by way of brazen resistance to the uncomfortable, more need to be added about other societies. Our rich societies do not only arrange, through omission and commission, that millions of Africans have half-lives and quarter-lives. We arrange that people are sickly and blind, in suffering. We arrange their being unfree and weak. We arrange inferiority, and being outside the greater world of men and women, and not knowing what is known. These are other contributions of the societies into whose systems of punishment we are for a few minutes inquiring.[18]

These human facts of our own indecent societies are given further definition by some facts of wealth and income within them, these facts being good measures of the human ones despite obvious qualifications – the best-known qualification being the slight one that some of the poor are happy and some of the rich are unhappy. The qualification has not issued, presumably paradoxically, in any noticeable number of the rich setting out to become poor. The former facts of our indecent societies are also in principal ways explained rather than given further definition by the facts of wealth and income. This remains true despite evident complexity about levels and directions of explanation – for example, what is secondary rather than primary as an explanation, and, again for example, whether X is in a way explanatory of Y but Y in a different way explanatory of X.

The facts of wealth and income I have in mind are that the best-off hundredth of population in the United Kingdom in recent years had 22 per cent and then nearly 25 per cent of the total wealth. The best-off tenth of population had well over half the total. The top half of population had 93 per cent rising to 95 per cent. The bottom tenth had no wealth at all to speak of or less than none – negative wealth, otherwise known as debt. The top tenth thus had at least some thousands of times as much wealth as the bottom tenth. In America, the best-off tenth has recently had over 70 per cent of the wealth.[19]

In terms of income or consumption, the worst-off tenth of population in the United Kingdom has recently had about 2.6 per cent of the total. The best-off tenth of popualtion has had about 27.3 per cent. The figures for America have been about 1.8 per cent and 30.5 per cent. So, in America, those on top had about 17 times as much of ongoing income and consumption.[20]

There has been an increase in these wealth and income inequalities in America in recent years, and either an increase or no significant decrease in the United Kingdom inequalities under New Labour governments.[21] With this sort of distribution of wealth and income goes a distribution of political freedom and power in particular – the one of which you have heard. In the simplest case, it is true to say that votes are purchased by immense investments in election campaigns. The political power of the top tenths in our societies is indeed thousands of times greater than that of the bottom tenths. This is so partly because the richer have large advantages of every kind, most of which can be purchased.

So much for differences in possession of the great goods in our societies, and the further definition and large explanation of them in terms of economic facts. In thinking of the economic facts, it is essential to keep in mind what they are measures of, which is lives. The figure of over 50 per cent of the wealth as against none and the figure of 27.3 per cent of the income as against 2.6 per cent, like many other figures, is about numbers of children who will remain stupid because of ignorance and will also be sickly, men who spend half their years without work and thus in resentment, women in wretched jobs suitable to their skin colour rather than their intelligence, old people in discomfort or worse, bad deaths.

We now need some reminder of something else, the existing criminal law of our societies. Only a yet more cursory glance is possible. The criminal law is such a thing, of course, a structure of rules covering so much of life, with such connected and related parts and sides, that systematic summary of it, summary into categories, is difficult indeed. Lawyers and jurisprudents disagree. Certainly there is no single and obvious summary, and certainly categories in any summary overlap. An additional difficulty is that summaries by jurisprudents and lawyers depend too much on conventions of law and vocabulary that are historical and internal to their professions. A few of the offences below lack prominence and definition in the criminal law of some of the societies in question.

(1) The category of *offences against private property* in a narrow sense includes robbery, theft, kinds of deception and wrongful appropriation, damage to property, trespass, arson, desecration, and vandalism. The category is concerned with not only material property but also patented and copyrighted things, perhaps life-saving drugs, and so on.

(2) *Financial and commercial offences*, most of them offences against private property in a wider sense, include forgery, fraud, deception, offences to do with inheritance and wills, diverting funds, banking offences, share-dealing and market offences,

blackmail, and counterfeiting. The category also includes false advertising and other trade offences, costs of loans, pension fund appropriations, and tax evasion.

(3) Offences having to do with *business and work* include those having to do with monopolies, cartels, restraint of trade, corporate responsibility, minimum wages, employee pensions, discrimination in work, unfair dismissal, trade unions, strikes, and child labour.

(4) *Offences having to do with the administration of justice and punishment* include those having to do with contempt of court, perverting the course of justice, legal representation, perjury, bribery, falsification of evidence, law governing the police, obstructing officers in the course of their duty, and aiding escape from prison.

(5) Another category consists in *offences against public order, safety, health, amenity and property*. It includes riot, obstructing authorities and officers in the performance of their duties, possessing firearms, mob law and lynch law, drug offences, prohibited medical and scientific practices, hazardous manufacturing, food safety, pollution, destruction of the environment, and various kinds of appropriation of public property. Also road traffic offences, the largest enforced sub-category of criminal offences.

(6) *Offences against the constitution, government and elections* include revolution, treason, sedition, denying the authority of the state, revealing official secrets, flag-burning, ballot fraud, political corruption, forms of effective civil disobedience, and terrorism. Also denials of freedom of speech and political rights.

(7) *Offences against the person or crimes of violence* include murder, manslaughter, wounding, torture, domestic violence, organized crime, hostage-taking, false arrest, intimidation and harassment, and, under some description, abuse of the old. Also in the category, as in others, will be soliciting or conspiring with respect to the actions mentioned, and also attempts.

(8) Not wholly separable is the category of *sexual offences* – rape against women and men, other violation and degradation, prostitution, brothel-keeping, incest, sexual abuse of children, enticement, some pornography and obscenity, some public indecency.

(9) *Offences to do with the family and other social institutions and relations* include bigamy, some abortion, infanticide, abandoning or neglecting children, wills and inheritance, blasphemy and other offences against religion, criminal libel, invasion of privacy, incitement of hatred, and gambling.

OUR UNJUSTIFIED PUNISHMENTS

The Principle of Humanity and the sketches of the denials of human goods in our societies, of the further definition and measured extent of these denials, and of our existing criminal law issue in ideas as to a full and proper answer to the question of the justification of punishment in our wealthy societies.

The answer will have to do, first, with our societies conceived in terms of the great human goods and the means to getting them, importantly wealth and income and also the means to these. Here already there are problems or anyway complexities about explanation, notably directions of explanation, since possession of the human goods itself serves as means to the end of wealth and income. Neither possession of any of the great goods nor of wealth or income is a single thing, a particular, or anything whatever at a time, as distinct from something continuing and changing over time. Thus some parts of the fact of wealth and income explain some parts of the fact of having the great goods, and other parts of the latter explain other parts of the former, which causal processes make up a history of both facts. All this deals with the seeming paradox of saying both that X is explanatory with respect to Y and Y explanatory with respect to X – explanatory to some extent.

Our societies conceived in terms of possession of the human goods and the economic means to them, and also in political terms, including political power, and also in social terms, such as respect, evidently stand in relation to law and punishment. One part of that relationship is that our societies so conceived are to a great extent owed to punishment – owed to what gives existence and reality to our criminal law. Our societies are more owed to punishment than they are owed to another great determinant, convention in thought and emotion.[22] Further, our societies are indecent ones, wrong. The conclusion follows immediately that it is as good as inconceivable that punishment as we have it can have anything like a full moral justification, that all of our punishment is right.

This is not a matter of miscarriages of justice, of course, despite their importance, but of of its carriage, its intended working. What is surely the principal means to an indecent society cannot possibly even in general or for the most part be right. It cannot be such because it is what mainly has the effect of keeping people in bad lives.

The greater difficulty of making, elaborating and qualifying this factual judgement, as against arriving at a general moral principle, does not seem to me to leave the factual judgement uncertain. It is possible to drift along half-supposing that our systems of punishment have support from some social truth or theory or outlook, or something about human nature, no doubt about iron necessity, that half-succeeds in making our societies morally respectable. It is not possible when actually thinking, as it seems to me, not possible when we actually try to get up to a level of moral intelligence, to believe that our law, our police, our courts and our prisons and execution chambers can be judged on the whole to be rational means of getting or keeping people out of bad lives.

What our law, police, courts and prisons now do, in general, is to create, maintain, strengthen or defend an economic, political and social system and indeed a conventional morality that does more for the improvement of already good lives than for the prevention of bad lives. Our law, police, courts, prisons and electric chairs are not directed to lengthening the lives of the impoverished, to offering to men and women the freedom of decent work, to raising up those who are denigrated, to making all of us full members of communities and societies and the human race, to rescuing those victimized by ignorance. Surely you agree that we do not actually have to look into the categories of crimes and thus of punishments in order to know the fact?

Do you want to put this aside as somehow merely political declamation? Well, the merely political may be in the ear of the hearer. There is rant, if that is what it is, that is true. In any case, there simply can be no sense in denying that our law, police, courts and prisons support our societies as they are. In fact no one doubts it when not engaged in contention about the justification of punishment. The rare and vanishing moments of the independence of the law from the facts of power in our societies stand against its record of conformity. As for the other premise of the argument, moral standing of our societies, how can it be escaped? The ludicrous affirmations and praisings of American society by its politicians, and such essays in the hypocrisy of self-deception as those of the wretched Blair, are made trivial by the ongoing reality of their policies, which have death in them.[23]

It was remarked at the beginning of this whole inquiry that justification is needed for punishment because it is an intentional infliction of suffering, and it deprives not only offenders of freedoms, and it affects the character of the rest of life in a society. Those considerations, it was said, whether or not others existed, were enough to raise the question of justification. We now have clear that there is another consideration, at any rate about our actual punishments. Our punishments make what is surely the principal contribution to the ongoing existence of indecent societies. It is reasonable to judge, I think, that what above all raises the question of the justification of our punishment is the consequence to which it contributes so greatly, our indecent societies. This is a consequence more in need of justification than the distress caused to offenders.

You may be inclined to make a response to the proposition that our punishment cannot even in general or for the most part be right – indeed the proposition that for the most part it is wrong. Despite a hope of mine expressed above, you may ask for a clarification and defence of that judgement. You may want to know more of what punishment is wrong and what remainder is not, or anyway what can be said for and against particular categories of punishment. Only a little can be said here.

The first category of offences, those against private property in a narrow sense, plainly do not serve the end of a decent society, but rather the end of what can be called self-profiting power and influence in a society. That is no novel proposition, but one with whole histories of elaboration behind it. It did not fall down with a wall. It is not something that has been heard only in morals and politics or only from the left in politics. Nor does the proposition get no sympathy from those untheoretical persons who do not share or declare it. Most defenders of our punishment systems have less confidence, to say the least, about punishing offences against property as against offences against the person, certainly offences against property committed in circumstances of deprivation.

Do you say that a society must have *some* punishment of offences against property, some defence of some property rights? Very likely that is true. Who denies it? But there is no reason, is there, to confuse that truth with the idea that whatever punishment a society has for private property offences is right? Do you agree with Nozick about private property and the family without it that is starving to death?

The second category of offences, financial and commercial ones, has less but a good deal to do with the end of protecting self-profiting power and influence. Is it important that the offenders who may come to mind here are unlikely to include any in circumstances of need? Well, a resistance to punishment for property certainly does not rest on the mad illusion that all punishments are of criminals who were in need, maybe the deserving poor. Nor does it rest on the illusion that all of or most of the victims of property offences are the well-off. If there is some redistribution of that kind, redistribution that can bring to mind a distinction between the criminal and the cowed, the main point is that our punishment, of whoever, defends law of an indecent society. It defends law, to speak quickly, that does indeed deprive those in need of great goods that we all desire.

It will be apparent that others of the nine categories of crimes, whatever else can be said of them, also serve the end in question. Convictions having to do with strikes come to mind with the third category of offences, those having to do with business and work. Offences against the constitution, government and elections are indeed offences that include actions and campaigns against the society largely owed to the constitution and government, the society that denies decent lives to many of its members. But there is no need to hunt around in the categories for offences against laws objected to by traditional left-wing activists or members of unions or the like. A general point about our criminal codes or our uncodified systems of punishments needs making in this connection.

The point applies to all nine categories of offences. It is that our codes and systems evidently need to be considered not only in terms of what they positively *do* with respect to a part or side of life, but also in terms of what they *do not do* – what they leave outside the jurisdiction of the law, what things they leave outside the reach of punishment that might instead be within it. The category of offences having to do with property in a narrow sense might have included, of course, offences whose punishment would have served the general end of preventing what we have been labelling self-profiting power and influence. The category of offences might have included profiteering. It might have included the offence of politicians that is the profitizing of what was public property, which offence has been in existence before now. In several ways that is no unheard of or novel idea. The category of offences might have included what New Labour governments pretended at moments to consider, offences of executives enriching themselves in ways that even those governments could not say they could swallow. There is no limit within the nature of criminal law as to what it can prohibit.

It is not as if our existing offences against property in a narrow sense were not already and in themselves absolutely a matter of establishing and maintaining a certain distribution of property. It is not as if the offences were, so to speak, outside of the political world of the distribution of the great goods and the means to having those great goods. Maybe that needs saying. The chosen offences, rather, are internal to that world. They are means by which possession of the great goods and the means to them is governed and, more important, not governed. The illusion that omission are not causes, that they do not have effects, is perhaps at its most absurd in connection with punishment and the law.[24]

Leaving aside the application of this proposition about omission to (2) financial and commercial offences, thereby passing by the important matter of the inheritance of property, what of the categories so far unconsidered? Might it be that (4) offences having to do with the administration of justice and punishment itself are offences of which it can safely be said that they would have to be offences in any society whatever? And so with (5) offences against public order, safety, health, amenity and property? And the categories to do with (6) offences against the constitution, government and elections, and (7) offences against the person, (8) sexual offences, and (9) offences to do with the family and other social institutions and relations?

Plainly there are omissions in each of these categories of offences that can be shown to be or argued to serve the end, whatever other end they also serve, of self-profiting power and influence. There are omissions with respect to offences against public health, amenity and property. Bhopal, that industrial massacre, comes to mind, as do coastlines ruined by oil, and the matter of corporate responsibility in general.[25] In connection with offences against the constitution, government and elections, one that is omitted is what may occur to you as the greatest perjury, a prime minister's lying about the necessity of war, lying about the necessity of deaths and maimings for his fellow-citizens.

There are also omissions in the categories in another sense, at least as important. These are not things actually left out, not mentioned in any way, but things included that from the point of view of an argued morality are none the less weak and insufficient. The offence of false advertising is no effective prohibition on false advertising. Offences of corporate responsibility do not actually make for effective responsibility by corporations for the deaths they cause. So with other offences in the category having to do with business and work, and the category of offences against public order, safety, health, amenity and property.

These considerations of several kinds about our punishments give some clarification and defence to saying that they do not have anything like a full moral justification, that for the most part they are wrong. These considerations also go some small way towards a distinction between indefensible and defensible punishments. As you will anticipate, there can of course be argument from the Principle of Humanity to the conclusion that offences against the person and sexual offences *are* indeed to be punished, as are certain offences to do with the family, notably the care of children. These offences are to be prevented for the reason that these offences do themselves make for bad lives. They do so in the most visible of ways.

So much for the fact of the general consequence of our punishments, a kind of society, and its upshot for the question of justification. We leave behind such items as the weak idea that the result of our reflections, properly speaking, is not that punishment is mainly wrong but that we must change society. Not changing punishment *is* not changing society. We leave behind too the truth that unfair societies are doubly so. They deprive by the use of law that is obeyed and then deprive further by punishment when it is not. Also the truth that offences against property make for offences against the person – that indefensible punishments give rise to and make for actions rightly punished.

There are other ways of reflecting on our punishments in our societies, ways that do not have to do in the same way with general consequences. These ways concern not only punishments having to do directly or indirectly with private property, which have mainly been our concern so far. These other reflections have to do with those of our punishments that are defensible, that are of kinds that may be necessary in any society. What is to be said here, so far short of proper inquiry, will have to be brief indeed.

It was a habit of the New Labour government in Britain led by Blair and Brown, from its first election in 1997 up to the terrorist attack on America on 11 September 2001, to declare a certain policy in connection with law and order, not that the policy was ever acted upon in both its parts. The policy was 'Tough on crime, tough on the causes of crime.' No doubt it was the likelihood of hearing a response about being not only tough on terrorism but also on its causes that ended the use of the statement of policy about crime. The present point, however, is that even governments of conservative kinds in effect come close to recognizing that crime does have causes that are not, so to speak, within the offenders.

What we have here, as anticipated, is causation and explanation running from our societies to our systems of punishment rather than in the other direction. What we have is the fact of our inhuman societies giving rise to crime and hence to punishment. Our societies are perfectly rightly spoken of as larger causes of offences and punishment than the offenders themselves. Here, in place of many other bodies of evidence and statistics, is a simple reason for saying so. The United States is now the most inhuman among at least the principal societies of the world. The poor are poorer and the rich richer than elsewhere. It is also true that America has a twentieth of the world's population, but a quarter of the world's prisoners in its prisons. It is a stunning fact, half of a stunning connection.[26]

The conclusion to be drawn from the fact that the greater causes of offences are not within offenders, indeed not offenders, is of course that we are wrong to seek to prevent crime by concentrating on punishment. We are wrong not to concentrate on our own omissions and commissions, on bodies of law and on conventions of thought and feeling that are indeed offences against humanity, social criminality that is rightly judged by the Principle of Humanity.

This second ground for condemning our punishment systems can be expressed differently, indeed more forcefully. America with its privatized prisons can again serve as an example. In June 2004, when there were 2,131,180 individuals in American prisons, there were 726 per 100,000 of population in the society. That statistic was the result of others: 376 per 100,000 of whites in the population, 997 per 100,000 of Latinos, and 2,526 per 100,000 of blacks. For males the figures were 717, 1,717, and 4,919 per 100,000 of the male population.[27]

This second way of thinking of our punishments is connected with a third. It too has to do with the larger causes of crime, the realities of our indecent societies, the injustice and unfairness that consists in moral offences against the Principle of Humanity, moral offences of all of us but above all our democratic politicians and those who have most influence over them. The denials of great goods to large numbers of people can rightly be regarded as issuing in unsatisfied needs of human nature, compulsion, constraint, compelling desires, senses of deprivation, well-based grievance, properly elaborated convictions of injustice, rage, and hatred. It is no illusion on the part of those towards the bottoms of our societies that the rules are to the benefit of others. In a word, these are pressures in the direction of offences.[28]

What we come to is thinking of the larger causes of crime in terms of freedom and responsibility, in fact diminished responsibility. The kind of responsibility is not the one put in question by determinism, the kind whose nonexistence makes for a further destructive objection to retributive theories of punishment – the kind of holding people responsible that has in it an assumption of free will or origination. Rather, this matter of responsibility has to do with holding people responsible to different extents on account of the extents to which their actions were owed to their own unconflicting desires and their own natures as against other things, including the desires of others, compulsion and constraint by others. What is in question is the freedom not of origination but of voluntariness (p. 144).

Courts are to a very great extent taken up with their own practice of fixing different degrees of responsibility, as noted earlier, certainly including degrees of compulsion and constraint. This is a practice, so to speak, of looking at individuals as individuals. In Hart's view, this endeavour has to do with rules having to do with justification, as in the case of a man's action of self-defence, and excuse, having to do with his voluntariness in a narrower sense, and mitigation, having to do with his special difficulties in abiding by the law. These differentiations in voluntariness more generally conceived, however, are made against a large background assumption. It is an assumption of *general equality* or at any rate an approximation to general equality. It is the assumption that the responsibility of a defendant is not in general and to a significant or considerable extent a function, to speak in too abstract a way, of being a member of an economic and social class or group, perhaps a racial group. That the assumption does not rule absolutely, that admittedly there are exceptions where a judge *does* take into account an existing background of deprivation, evidently does not touch the fact that they are what they are, which is exceptions.

What this comes to is that large numbers of us are less voluntary than others in the commission of both indefensible and defensible offences. We are at least constrained to offend, subject to pressures in that direction. We are made less voluntary by those around us, their arrangements. The familiar and extreme case is stealing food in the case of hunger. That we are made less voluntary is unfair and unjust, against the Principle of Humanity. There is a still larger point, however. It follows from the involuntariness of an offence, as you have heard before now, despite the proposition being open to some dispute, that there is no point or only a lesser point in punishing the offender for a preventive purpose. A man out of jail but still with hungry children is likely to steal again. Prevention is unlikely to happen.

Certainly you have to think of extending this idea of at least a reduced general voluntariness from offences against private property to other offences. Despite our rational and right determination to act on offences against the person, we have to think about extending the idea exactly to offences against the person. To bite the bullet, one thought here is that rape is an offence of those with less freedom and power to gratify their sexual desires or power-over-others desires. My newspaper has not misled me in having given no details of wealthy or well-off rapists. Something the same is true of murder. The wealthy murderers in my paper, in my recollection, are relatively few as against the rest of the murderers. Perhaps the evidence for this line of thought about good and bad lives and violence is on the way to being as strong as statistics correlating money and violence.[29]

Further, we can think of, and indeed cannot resist, an explanation of why the connection between wealth and rape must be as presumed. That explanation is that those of greater freedom and power have more than one means of securing an end or satisfying a desire. They need not choose the dangerous one, and will not. The point is of course a general one. If we well-heeled persons find ourselves troubled by a neighbour who is worsening our lives, perhaps by taunting our children, we can do something other than attack him. We can set the law on him effectively. We can move away to another good house if necessary.

Insufficiently careful as I am about the danger of being reported as a sympathizer with rape, murder and maiming, which I am not, I leave behind the mistake we make in supposing that our punishments do in general serve the Principle of Humanity when considered in terms not of their general effect but in terms of the voluntariness and responsibility of offenders and hence the preventive effects of the punishments. I leave complexities unconsidered, and the mistake of thinking that none of the rest of us share the moral responsibility for offences of our criminals.[30] A few more separate matters having to do with the justification of our punishments need mentioning. They have to do with special involuntariness, the working of our justice or penal systems, and retributive penalties.

There is the large and grim fact noticed earlier that a very large proportion of all offenders, certainly including many offenders against the person and many sexual offenders, are mentally disordered or the like. They are not the 'ordinary' offenders of whom you were very likely thinking a moment ago. As you will recall, it has become clear that a majority of prisoners in British prisons, maybe as many as 70 per cent, have mental health disorders (p. 119). They were therefore in this special way less than fully voluntary in their offences. Such offenders are being treated especially unfairly and unjustly. Moreover, such offenders cannot be prevented from committing offences in the future in the way that we suppose more rational offenders can be prevented. They are being subjected to the distress of punishment without the extent of justification that can be supposed in connection with a minority of prisoners – those not somehow mentally disordered or the like.

If our justice system does not in general serve the end of the Principle of Humanity, but in large part supports laws and conventions antithetical to it, and thus to a large extent is without justification, is it also the case that the working of the justice system itself, the working of our courts and indeed prisons, has the nature of the society it supports? It is impossible to deny it. The system has that nature with respect to all punishment. It not only serves a society whose good lives rest on bad lives, but in its own operation makes its own contribution. There are conceivable systems of punishment that are fair in the way that they serve the end of an unfair or indecent society. Such a system, even if it serves an end other than a human one, holds to rules of true justice in its operation, perhaps true rules of justification, excuse and mitigation. To some small extent, such a conceivable system goes against its own rationale. There are jurisprudents, judges and lawyers who wish to suppose that our own existing systems of punishment have this little recommendation.

There is little realism in this attitude, more desire to think well of a line of life. The deprivations marked by the material inequalities of our societies are not by some astonishing barrier kept from having effects in the operation of our machine of justice. Lawyers cost money, some of us get very good ones, and judges are not impervious to the influence of good lives in their power and standing. They are certainly not impervious to politicians. Courts reward the capabilities and resources of those who have been given those capabilities and resources by a society that has deprived others of those things. To my mind, there can only be the effrontery of ideology in claiming otherwise.

A last consideration, about retribution, has to do with the severity of our punishments for offences against the person, sexual offences and some other offences. It has readily been granted by me that there is indeed reason for some punishment with respect to these offences. You have heard, too, that right punishment is the punishment that is rational – effective and economical – with respect to the aim of the Principle of Humanity, getting or keeping people out of bad lives. Do all our punishments for the given offences actually have the given recommendation?

Very often they lack it. They lack it since they are punishments in some considerable degree owed to theories of punishment and attitudes that are indefensible. Both legislators and judges have been and are subject to the influence of retributive theories of punishment. Not a few judges remain in the grip of such illusions. Most judges, true to the analysis of retribution to which we have come, are partly engaged in providing satisfaction for grievance desires. To these facts need to be added another one. It too is large. This grievance punishing is done under the assumption that offenders had a certain freedom and responsibility in the committing of their offences, freedom of origination rather than voluntariness. Given the truth of determinism, there is no such freedom. It is hardly too much to say that the law is in this respect mediaeval.

We have been looking at the propositions that punishment in general can be justified only by the Principle of Humanity, that questions of fact about systems of punishment are harder than the question of morality strictly speaking, and that the punishments in such societies as those of the United States and the United Kingdom are in general unjustified.[31] The last of four propositions is about what we are to do. Are we to remember the storming of the Bastille, that beginning of the French Revolution? Are we to hope that it will somehow come about that we can go to our prisons and open the doors to let out many selected persons inside? Since for the most part we are wrong in our punishment, should we not have this dream? The dream forgets much, including the connection of punishment with a whole society and those who benefit most from it, not to mention their army.[32]

My last proposition is that what we are obliged to do is to take forward in any rational way we can the reformation of our societies, indeed a revolution of their natures. More than our Bastilles need to be overturned. We need more disrespect, above all disrespect for law. We need to make clear that good law is used to protect vicious law. We need disrespect, indeed disdain, for hierarchic democracy. We need to try to raise up human nature from a level to which conservative politicians under several names have dragged it down. We need to do more against moral stupidity owed to arranged ignorance. We need to rely on and get a hearing for clear truth, that adversary of an army on another battlefield. We need to do what is required by the moral principle most true to our own human natures. It is a principle to which we all commit ourselves without significant doubt when we are not merely looking out for ourselves.

It is not a principle that you can know to be without chance of more realization. The world is more contingent than that. If it is a world of cause and effect, it is not really a simple world, with only simple, persistent effects. It is not as our politicians take it to be. Things happen in it that can make for a little hope and resolution. One is mass civil disobedience, which has lately changed some governments. Other means of change are boycotts and divestment, say with respect to any company that deals with Corrections Corporation of America. Tens of thousands of us can refuse to pay taxes. We also need new rational ways of getting or keeping people out of bad lives.[33]

Acknowledgements

The first edition of the book owed a good deal to table-talk with John Honderich and also Kiaran and Pauline Honderich. Comments were made on the manuscript by Richard Wollheim, and there was good advice from the first publisher's reader, P. H. Nowell-Smith. At the PhD oral examination on the-book-as-thesis, the agreeable and Wittgensteinian Peter Winch, with strong views on the difficulty of understanding alien societies, said he agreed with no single proposition in the thesis, and so discussion would be pointless, and so we should just go to lunch, which we did. At it, the other examiner, Nigel Walker, made useful criminological comments. The second and third editions of the book were improved by the good editor Jonathan Riley. Along the way, there has also been help and advice from John Finnis, Nicola Lacey, Peter Morriss and Carlos Nino. This fifth edition is better for the judgements of Ingrid Coggin Honderich, who also made the labour on it tolerable. The edition is also better for the useful and kind help of Michael Neumann and Leo Zaibert in particular and also Lindsay Clark, Nick Davies, Peter Goodrich, Kiaran Honderich, Ed Kent and Julian Pike. To none of these advisers can be assigned responsibility for the judgements and conclusions.

The first edition was *Punishment: The Supposed Justifications* (Hutchinson, 1969; Harcourt, Brace & World, 1970). The second and third editions, under the same title, the third being an enlarged edition, were Penguin and Peregrine books (1971, 1976). The fourth edition, also under the same title, was by Polity Press in 1989.

Notes

INTRODUCTION

1. For an account of the sociology of punishment, including the meaning of punishment, see David Garland, *Punishment and Modern Society* (Oxford University Press, 1990).
2. As will transpire, mainly in Chapter 6, there are two fundamental kinds of freedom, origination and voluntariness, and hence two ways in which people can be responsible and held responsible.
3. For an account of the change in the United States and Britain, since about 1970, see Garland, *The Culture of Control* (Oxford University Press, 2001).
4. *How Free Are You?* (Oxford University Press, revised edition, 2002); *On Determinism and Freedom* (Edinburgh University Press, 2005).
5. If no really new doctrine of punishment has arrived on the scene, something else has, or at any rate something has come back onto it. That is terrorism and thinking about it. This does not get into this book, which is about ordinary apolitical crime. For my own reflections on terrorism, see *After the Terror* (Edinburgh University Press, enlarged edition, 2003), *Terrorism for Humanity: Inquiries in Political Philosophy* (Pluto Press, 2003), and a forthcoming book provisionally titled *Palestine, 9/11, Iraq, 7/7*.

CHAPTER 1

1. J. D. Mabbott, 'Professor Flew on Punishment', *Philosophy*, 1955, pp. 257–8. As is well known, the French sociologist and philosopher Michel Foucault makes a theoretical meal of the historical progress from torture and the like to more restrained punishments – *Discipline and Punish: The Birth of the Prison* (Penguin, 1979). For a good attempt to deal with his self-contradictions etc., see Sara Mills, *Michel Foucault* (Routledge, 2003).
2. Nicola Lacey, *State Punishment* (Routledge, 1988), pp. xiv–xv; R. A. Duff, 'Legal Punishment', p. 1, *The Stanford Encyclopedia of Philosophy* (Spring 2004 edition), ed. Edward N. Zalta, <http://plato.stanford.edu/archives/spr2004/entries/legal-punishment/>. Cf. Duff's book *Punishment, Communication and Community* (Oxford University Press, 2001). I do not imply that Professors Lacey and Duff much underestimate the distress of penalties. Both have felt the necessity to give an inclusive account of the nature of penalties.
3. In the three years during which Mr David Blunkett was our British government's man on prisons, in the second New Labour government, about 232 people took their own lives in them, including 25 women and five children (Frances Crook, 'Blunkett's Real Failure', *Guardian*, 3 December 2004). Some did this as a result of being raped in prison.

4. Dr Stephen Ladyman, in evidence to a parliamentary committee. See Nick Davies, 'Scandal of Society's Misfits Dumpted in Jail', *Guardian*, 6 December 2004.

5. Mortimer Adler (ed.), *The Idea of Freedom* (Doubleday, 1961).

6. The contention that punishment in general, as distinct from punishment by the state, cannot be effectively distinguished from revenge is argued interestingly by Leo Zaibert in *Punishment and Retribution* (Ashgate, 2005). The distinction, he maintains, is mostly rhetorical. See also John Kleinig, *Punishment and Desert* (Martinus Nijhoff, 1973) and C. L. Ten, *Crime, Guilt and Punishment* (Oxford University Press, 1987).

7. This book cannot get down to differences in punishment in different places and times. In particular, it cannot consider the weakening of offenders' rights in Britain after the terrorism of 9/11 but certainly not shown to be made necessary by 9/11. See Helena Kennedy, *Just Law* (Chatto & Windus, 2004).

8. The matters of moral responsibility, intention and negligence are not so clear as is sometimes supposed. There are two ways of being morally responsible, as remarked in note 2 to the Introduction, and they are related in several ways to intention and negligence. The subject gets more attention, mainly in Chapter 6.

9. Duff, *Punishment, Communication and Community*, e.g. pp. 60–4; 'Legal Punishment'.

10. David Garland, The Culture of Control (Oxford University Press, 2001), ch. 1; Hugo Adam Bedau, 'Punishment', *The Stanford Encyclopedia of Philosophy* (Summer 2003 edition), ed. Edward N. Zalta, <http://plato. stanford.edu/archives/sum2003/entries/punishment/>.

11. The nature of conservatism, and the course of recent British politics, is considered in Honderich, *Conservatism: Burke, Nozick, Bush, Blair?* (Pluto Press, 2005).

12. Zaibert in *Punishment and Retribution* notes the fact of interest that punishment is now often defined in some or other retributivist way, but rarely if ever defined as being directed to certain consequences. No doubt this indicates some actual fact of retributivism in our thinking and feeling and our practice of punishment. As in the case of desert, there would be no gain for moral inquiry in writing deterrence or whatever into a definition of punishment.

13. John Rawls's definition of punishment is that '. . . a person is said to suffer punishment whenever he is legally deprived of some of the normal rights of a citizen on the ground that he has violated a rule of law, the violation having been established by trial according to the due process of law, provided that the deprivation is carried out by the recognised legal authorities of the state, that the rule of law clearly specifies both the offence and the attached penalty, that the courts construe statutes strictly, and that the statute was on the books prior to the time of the offence' ('Two Concepts of Rules', *Philosophical Review*, 1955, p. 10). Nicola Lacey writes that legal punishment is 'the principled infliction by a state-constituted institution of what are generally regarded as unpleasant consequences upon individuals or groups adjudicated, in accordance with publicly and legally recognized criteria and procedures,

correctly applied, to have breached the law, as a response to that breach, as an enforcement of the law and where that response is not inflicted solely as a means of providing compensation for the harm caused by the offence' (*State Punishment*, pp. 11–12). For Hugo Adam Bedau, punishment under law is 'the authorized imposition of deprivations – of freedom or privacy or other goods to which the person otherwise has a right, or the imposition of special burdens – because the person has been found guilty of some criminal violation, typically (though not invariably), involving harm to the innocent' ('Punishment'). Antony Duff writes that 'punishment is, typically, something intended to be burdensome or painful, imposed on a (supposed) offender for a (supposed) offence by someone with (supposedly) the authority to do so' (*Punishment, Communication and Community*, pp. xiv–xv). I suspect none of these definitions intends actually to exclude anything in another definition.

CHAPTER 2

1. The matter is returned to, on p. 53.
2. *The Philosophy of Law: An Exposition of the Fundamental Principles of Jurisprudence as the Science of Right*, trans. W. Hastie (Clark, 1887), pp. 195–8.
3. Compare a strong book which at first appears to suggest that to require an offence as a necessary condition of punishment is already to be engaged in retributivism – J. Angelo Corlett, *Responsibility and Punishment* (Kluwer, 2004). In fact another analysis of desert is provided subsequently, most fully in Chapter 5.
4. For a sympathetic discussion of Kant's retributivism, see Corlett, *Responsibility and Punishment*.
5. John Rawls, 'Two Concepts of Rules', *Philosophical Review*, 1955, p. 7. I do note the word 'first' in the first of the passages from Kant. That passage thus may fight with the other two. See also Rawls's *A Theory of Justice* (Oxford University Press, 1971).
6. Cf. Michael Moore, *Placing Blame* (Oxford University Press, 1997).
7. One good survey of retribution theories is given by John Cottingham in 'Varieties of Retributivism', *Philosophical Quarterly*, 1979.
8. See 'retribution theories' in the index of this book for a list of them.
9. Lawrence H. Davis, in 'They Deserve to Suffer', *Analysis*, 1972. Davis reported I was in error and confusion because I say that sometimes people use *He deserves the penalty* to mean *It's right that he get the penalty*, and hence that they cannot give the first as a reason for the second. The main presumed error, although Davis is not sufficiently explicit, must be the failure to see what is presumed to be true, and discussed below, that the first claim and like ones are standardly used only to mean a third thing, *there is intrinsic good in his suffering, he being guilty*. The second presumed error is thus supposing that the first does not provide a reason for the second. The presumed confusion, also owed to failing to see that the first claim is equivalent to the third, is running together the first and second. My reply is that there is no error and no confusion since it is not true, but

false, that the first claim and like ones are standardly used to mean only the third. Rather, there is a use of them which makes them equivalent to the second, commoner than its use as equivalent to the third. What I say depends only on the use of the first claim as equivalent to the second.

10. Davis, 'They Deserve to Suffer', p. 139.

11. Jeffrie G. Murphy, 'Marxism and Retribution', *Philosophy and Public Affairs*, 1973, reprinted in Patricia Smith (ed.), *The Nature and Process of Law* (Oxford University Press, 1993); John Finnis, 'The Restoration of Retribution', *Analysis*, 1972, and *Natural Law and Natural Rights* (Oxford University Press, 1980), pp. 260–6.

12. It can be argued that by our human nature, which may be taken to be a matter of fundamental desires and our having reasons, the latter being general, we are committed to the Principle of Humanity, of which more will be said in the last chapter of this book.

13. Michael Neumann makes the strong point to me that even if it is granted that something has intrinsic value, it doesn't follow that it has a lot of it – say enough to make some price worth it.

14. There is a discussion of mercy, forgiveness and retributivism in Corlett, *Responsibility and Punishment*, ch. 6.

15. Cf. P. F. Strawson, 'Ethical Intuitionism', in W. Sellars and J. Hospers, *Readings in Ethical Theory* (Appleton Century Crofts, 1952). For discussions and defences of what may seem in some respects a successor to moral intuitionism – moral realism – see Honderich (ed.), *Morality and Objectivity, A Tribute to John Mackie* (Routledge, 1985).

16. Leo Zaibert in *Punishment and Retribution* (Ashgate, 2005) makes an attempt to defend something close to intrinsic-good retributivism by means of the idea of organic wholes, found in the work of G. G. Moore and several other philosophers. For Moore an organic whole is something that has an intrinsic value different in amount from the sum of the value of its parts. See also Michael Moore, *Placing Blame* (Oxford University Press, 1997), and David Dolinko, 'Some Thoughts About Retributivism', *Ethics*, 1991.

17. Michael Neumann points out to me that such a view has a kind of premoral appeal, involving *balance*, that may lie behind a lot of other less primitive ideas.

18. Alan H. Goldman, 'The Paradox of Punishment', *Philosophy and Public Affairs*, 1979.

19. It is the burden of Goldman's paper that while his proposition about rights does indeed give one of the necessary reasons for punishment, a part of a justification, it is in conflict with the other part, concerning prevention. Hence the paradox of his title.

20. A reader of earlier editions of this book will know I gave this sort of argument a kind of puzzled credence.

21. Hyman Gross, 'Culpability and Desert', in R. A. Duff and N. E. Simmonds (eds), *Philosophy and the Criminal Law* (Archiv für Rechts und Sozialphilosophie, 1984). Cf. Prof. Gross's book, *A Theory of Criminal Justice* (New York, 1979).

22. Gross, 'Culpability and Desert', p. 60.

23. Ibid., p. 59.

24. Ibid., p. 61.

25. Chapter 6.
26. Gross, 'Culpability and Desert', p. 65.
27. Ibid., p. 66.
28. Ibid.
29. Ibid.
30. Ibid., p. 67.
31. Hugo Adam Bedau, 'Punishment', *The Stanford Encyclopedia of Philosophy* (Summer 2003 edition), ed. Edward N. Zalta, <http://plato. stanford.edu/ archives/sum2003/entries/punishment/>.
32. G. W. Hegel, *The Philosophy of Right*, trans. T. M. Knox (Oxford University Press, 1942), p. 69.
33. Ibid., pp. 69–70.
34. Bernard Bosanquet, *Some Suggestions in Ethics* (Macmillan, 1918), pp. 190–6.
35. We can contemplate the infamous old idea, indeed, that it makes no sense of the most important kind to engage in these metaphysical speculations, that in fact they are not propositions, not utterances with truth values. That is, it is possible to suppose there was something in the old doctrine of logical positivism. We cannot go into that now. Interested parties could make their way to an admiring introduction to the work of a philosopher who counts as great in the tradition of David Hume – my introduction to the eight volumes republished as *A. J. Ayer: Writings on Philosophy* (Palgrave Macmillan Archive Press, 2004).
36. Ernest Barker, *Principles of Social and Political Theory* (Oxford University Press, 1951), p. 179.
37. Hegel, *Philosophy of Right*, p. 70.
38. J. M. E. McTaggart, *Studies in Hegelian Cosmology* (Cambridge University Press, 1901), p. 137.
39. This is one of several lines of thought in Murphy's 'Marxism and Retribution', mentioned above. For clarity, I treat it separately. Cf. Rawls, *A Theory of Justice*.
40. Immanuel Kant, *The Metaphysical Elements of Justice*, trans. John Ladd (Hackett, 1965, 1999), pp. 55 ff. Cited by Murphy, 'Marxism and Retribution', p. 225.
41. Murphy, 'Marxism and Retribution', p. 225.
42. 'Concerning the Common Saying: This May be True in Theory but Does not Apply in Practice', in *The Philosophy of Kant*, ed. and trans. Carl J. Friedrich (Random House, 1949), pp. 421–2. Cited by Murphy, 'Marxism and Retribution', p. 226.
43. 'The Contract Argument in *A Theory of Justice*', in *On Political Means and Social Ends* (Edinburgh University Press, 2003).
44. C. S. Nino, 'A Consensual Theory of Punishment', *Philosophy and Public Affairs*, 1983.
45. Ibid., p. 306.
46. Ibid., p. 302.
47. Ibid., pp. 302–3.
48. Ibid., p. 293.
49. Nino does write that following out this suggestion as to the justification of punishment 'would lead to a discussion of the extent to which the

consent of the person affected can justify measures and political arrangements which may imply inequitable burdens upon him. I shall not
develop this theme here; but I venture to say that the discussion of the
justification of punishment could be considerably expanded and illumi-
nated if it embraced this topic' (ibid., p. 305).

50. A view of this kind is defended, although not separated from other
    things, in Herbert Morris, 'Persons and Punishment', in *On Guilt and
    Innocence: Essays in Legal Philosophy and Moral Psychology* (University of
    California Press, 1976). The same is true of Murphy, 'Marxism and
    Retribution', and also Murphy, 'Three Mistakes About Retributivism',
    Analysis, 1971. See also Finnis, 'Restoration of Retribution' and *Natural
    Law*, pp. 260–6.

51. Finnis makes the point clearly.

52. Murphy develops his conclusion most fully in 'Marxism and
    Retribution'. There is also a related concession, to my mind given insuf-
    ficient attention, in Morris, 'Persons and Punishment'. Finnis touches
    on the question and appears to want to have it both ways: that the
    theory does and does not apply to other than 'an imaginary "well-
    ordered" society' – *Natural Law*, pp. 264–5.

CHAPTER 3

1. His papers are collected in two volumes, *Logic and Knowledge* and *Persons
   and Values* (both Oxford University Press, 1985). See also *Ethics: Inventing
   Right and Wrong* (Penguin, 1977) and *Hume's Moral Theory* (Routledge,
   1980).

2. J. L. Mackie, 'Morality and the Retributive Emotions', *Criminal Justice
   Ethics*, 1982, pp. 3, 6. Anthony Kenny, *Free Will and Responsibility*
   (Routledge, 1978, pp. 69 ff.) has the related view that retributivism is
   incoherent.

3. Mackie, 'Morality and the Retributive Emotions', p. 3.

4. Michael Moore, *Placing Blame* (Oxford University Press, 1997), p. 89,
   rightly insists that a retributivist may support a punishment even if the
   victim of an offence lacks a grievance desire, as of course can happen.
   See also Leo Zaibert's discussion of the grievance theory in *Punishment
   and Retribution* (Ashgate, 2005), ch. 4, and John Cottingham's article,
   'Varieties of Retributivism', *Philosophical Quarterly*, 1979.

5. It does not seem to me, as David Garland suggests of all attempted justifications of punishment or understandings of such things, that this conclusion must depend on sociology or on an improved sociology. See
   Punishment and Modern Society (Oxford University Press, 1990), p. 1,
   pp. 9–10, and also Antony Duff and David Garland, 'Introduction:
   Thinking About Punishment', in *A Reader on Punishment* (Oxford
   University Press, 1994). However, the grievance-satisfaction theory is in
   kinds of accord with at least sides of the sociological theories of
   Durkheim, certain Marxists, and Foucault. Further, maybe there is the
   possibility of giving more content to the theory by way of a sceptical
   attention to the sociological theories. The beginning of Garland's

summary of Foucault: 'The essence of punishment is not rationality or instrumental control – though these ends are superimposed upon it – the essence of punishment is irrational, unthinking emotion fixed by a sense of the sacred and its violation' (*Punishment and Modern Society*, p. 32). Nor does my view depend on anything like the general psychology of the philosopher Friedrich Nietzsche or its application to punishment. 'To behold suffering gives us pleasure, but to cause another to suffer affords even greater pleasure. This severe statement expresses an old, powerful, human, all too human sentiment' – *The Birth of Tragedy and the Genealogy of Morals* (Random House, 1956), p. 198. For Nietzsche, as Garland remarks (p. 63), 'To punish another is to gratify the impulses of sadism and cruelty which a will to power over others produces in the human psyche.'

6. Hermann Lotze, *Outlines of Practical Philosophy*, trans. George T. Ladd (Ginn, 1885), p. 98.

7. Stephen, *Liberty, Equality, Fraternity* (Smith Elder, 1873), pp. 161–2. (Also, New York, 1968.)

8. Nigel Walker, in 'Symposium: Predicting Dangerousness', *Criminal Justice Ethics*, 1983.

9. *General View of the Criminal Law of England* (London, 1863), p. 99. Cf. Henry Sidgwick, *The Methods of Ethics* (Hackett, 1981)), bk. 3, ch. 5.

10. Jeffrie G. Murphy, 'Three Mistakes About Retributivism', *Analysis*, 1971, p. 169.

11. Michael Neumann has pressed the point that despite all this there is enough variation in feelings of grievance, and in satisfactions of them, to make difficulty for the theory. Not enough, to my mind, to stand in the way of coming to judgements on what can be called standard grievances. Leo Zaibert has supposed that what must be in question is a reasonable grievance, in such a sense as to require another reason or principle of right punishment. I do not see that. In depending on judgements of standardness or normality, the theory does not move in the direction of being an 'ideal observer' or 'ideal participant' theory.

12. Honderich, *Conservatism: Burke, Nozick, Bush, Blair?* (Pluto, 2005), ch. 8.

13. There is a bit more on revenge later in connection with Nozick's retribution theory, which also moves in the direction of being a reform theory. There are reflections on revenge of strong interest in Zaibert's *Punishment and Retribution* (Ashgate, 2005), ch. 3.

14. K. G. Armstrong, 'The Retributivist Hits Back', *Mind*, 1961.

15. See Duff and Garland, 'Introduction', David Dolinko, 'Some Thoughts About Retributivism', *Ethics*, 1991, and Hugo Adam Bedau, 'Punishment', *The Stanford Encyclopedia of Philosophy* (Summer 2003 edition), ed. Edward N. Zalta, <http://plato.stanford.edu/archives/sum2003/entries/punishment/>.

CHAPTER 4

1. Consequentialisms, of course, are said to be moralities or theories that take the rightness of an action or whatever to be a matter of its

consequences or effects. Are there really any other moralities? For a minority viewpoint on the supposed distinction between consequentialism and non-consequentialism, see 'Consequentialism, Moralities of Concern, and Selfishness', in the collection of my papers *On Political Means and Social Ends* (Edinburgh University Press, 2003). The paper is a revision of the one published under that title in the journal *Philosophy*, 1996.

2. A little more will be said of these feelings, having to do with holding the offender responsible, in Chapter 6.

3. For more thoughts on this tradition see my *Conservatism: Burke, Nozick, Bush, Blair?* (Pluto Press, 2005) and several papers in *On Political Means and Social Ends*.

4. Jeremy Bentham, 'Principles of Penal Law', p. 383, in *The Works of Jeremy Bentham*, vol. 1, ed. John Bowing. p. 396. Reprinted New York, 1962.

5. Eli Lehrer, 'The Most Silent Crime', *National Review Online*, 29 April 2003.

6. Patrick A. Langan and David J. Levin, 'Recidivism of Prisoners Released in 1994', Bureau of Justice Statistics, <http://www.ojp.usdoj.gov/bjs/pub/pdf/rpr94.pdf>.

7. John Simmons and Tricia Dodd, *Crime in England and Wales, 2002/2003* (Home Office, 2003).

8. 'Homicide Trends in the U.S.: Age Trends', Bureau of Justice Statistics, 2003.

9. Howard Jones, *Crime and the Penal System* (University Tutorial Press, 1956), p. 140.

10. Ibid., pp. 141–2.

11. It is possible to think, about punishment and a lot else, that reflection on it would be much improved if participants spent a little time on the general subject of causation. My own views on it, uncontroversial with respect to the point in question, are in the first chapters of both *Mind and Brain* (Oxford University Press, 1990) and *A Theory of Determinism: The Mind, Neuroscience and Life-Hopes* (Oxford University Press, 1988, 1990). They are summarized in ch. 1 of *How Free Are You?* (Oxford University Press, 2002).

12. In a good deal of sociology, by the way, there is the idea, curious to me, that because punishment is less than successful by some test in the aim of prevention, it must have some other aim, role or the like. See David Garland, *Punishment and Modern Society* (Oxford University Press, 1990), ch. 1. The conclusion certainly doesn't follow from the premise, and is unlikely to turn out to follow when much theory is added. Some success in an aim, even very little success, may keep us doing something, without our also having another aim. Consider research into the cause of cancer. Another unconnected point is also worth making in this note. To speak up for prevention of offences by punishment is of course not necessarily to speak up for the death penalty. There is no real evidence that the death penalty is more effective in preventing offences than other punishments.

13. I mainly have in mind the well-known work of Bernard Williams in *Utilitarianism: For and Against* (Cambridge University Press, 1973) having

to do with integrity and negative responsibility. For my reaction, see *Terrorism for Humanity: Inquiries in Political Philosophy* (Pluto Press, 2003), ch. 1, or earlier editions of the book under other titles.

14. K. G. Armstrong, 'The Retributivist Hits Back', *Mind*, 1961.

15. Bentham, 'Principles of Penal Law', p. 397.

16. 'In point of utility apparent justice is everything, real justice, abstractedly from apparent justice, is a useless abstraction, not worth pursuing and, supposing it contrary to apparent justice, such as ought not to be pursued' – Bentham, 'Principles of Judicial Procedure', *Works*, vol. 2, p. 21.

17. Clare Dyer, Michael White, Alan Travis, 'Judges' Verdict on Terror Laws Provokes Constitutional Crisis', *Guardian*, 7 December 2004.

18. Anthony Quinton, 'On Punishment', *Analysis*, 1954. For a view similar in some respects, see John Rawls, 'Two Concepts of Rules', *Philosophical Review*, 1955.

19. Rawls, 'Two Concepts of Rules', p. 11. The argument I am considering is combined with several others in this paper. I treat them separately.

20. Robert Verkaik and Andrew Grice, 'Day 1: Resignation, Day 2: Humiliation', *Independent*, 17 December, 2004.

21. H. L. A. Hart, 'Prolegomenon to the Principles of Punishment', *Proceedings of the Aristotelian Society*, 1959–60. See also Richard Brandt, *Ethical Theory* (Prentice Hall, 1959), ch. 19. Notice, incidentally, that the kinds of victimization now in question (as against knowingly penalizing the wholly innocent) also count as punishments.

22. See also Hart, 'Prolegomenon'.

23. Hart, 'Prolegomenon', argues that it is impossible to explain the rules of excuse and mitigation by reference to prevention and then goes on to explain them by the consideration, for example, that they increase 'the power of individuals to identify beforehand periods when the law's punishment will not interfere with them'.

24. T. L. S. Sprigge, 'A Utilitarian Reply to Dr McCloskey', *Inquiry*, 1965, p. 274.

25. First, to philosophers, by Hart, 'Prolegomenon'.

26. See J. O. Urmson, 'The Interpretation of the Moral Philosophy of J. S. Mill', *Philosophical Quarterly*, 1953.

27. It is true, certainly, that traditional utilitarianism also makes use, rather puzzling use, of rules. What is certain is that the rules are guides and we are not enjoined to stick to them in all cases, no matter the consequences. For discussions of rule utilitarianism, see Urmson, 'The Interpretation of the Moral Philosophy of J. S. Mill' and Rawls, 'Two Concepts'. Richard Brandt presents a justification of punishment in terms of rule utilitarianism in *Ethical Theory* (Prentice Hall, 1969), ch. 19.

CHAPTER 5

1. A. C. Ewing considered and defended such a view in *The Morality of Punishment* (Kegan Paul, Trench, Trubner, 1929). It was more briefly stated in 'Punishment as a Moral Agency', *Mind*, 1927. Related accounts

were given by J. M. E. McTaggart, *Studies in Hegelian Cosmology* (Cambridge University Press, 1901), ch. 5, by Hastings Rashdall, *The Theory of Good and Evil* (Oxford University Press, 1907), vol. 1, ch. 9, and by E. F. Carritt, *The Theory of Morals* (Oxford University Press, 1928), pp. 108–13. McTaggart, as mentioned in an earlier chapter, supposed Hegel to have held the view in question.

2. Ewing, *The Morality of Punishment*, p. 97. Compare the view and the quoted passage, by the way, with the thought of Robert Nozick (pp. 176–84).

3. Ibid., p. 96. Ewing's optimistic claim, by the way, is certainly different from my claim (p. 84) about punishment and unreflective obedience to law.

4. Ewing attempted some rejoinders to the traditional claims about victimization. His rejoinders rest, in my view, on a happy choice of cases. See *Morality of Punishment*, pp. 90 ff.

5. An early analysis was by Antony Flew, 'Crime of Disease', *British Journal of Sociology*, 1954.

6. It is no surprise that Prof. Flew was not only a hammer of critics of punishment and advocates of treatment but also a hammer of unconservatives in politics. See my *Conservatism: Burke, Nozick, Bush, Blair?* (Pluto, 2005).

7. Nick Davies, 'Scandal of Society's Misfits Dumped in Jail', *Guardian*, 6 December 2004.

8. One influential book was Kate Friedlander's *The Psycho-Analytical Approach to Juvenile Delinquency* (Routledge & Kegan Paul, 1947, 1960).

9. For a careful discussion of these theories, see Barbara Wootton, *Social Science and Social Pathology* (Allen & Unwin, 1959), ch. 4.

10. See H. J. Eysenck, *Crime and Personality* (Routledge, 1964).

11. Ibid., p. 177.

12. Edwin H. Sutherland, *Principles of Criminology* (Lippincott, 1955), p. 78.

13. See Wootton, *Social Science*, ch. 7.

14. A valuable essay on general theories of crime and their weaknesses, and an argument for particularized research, was given by Wootton in *Crime and the Criminal Law* (Stevens, 1963), ch. 1.

15. Eysenck, *Crime and Personality*, p. 163.

16. Ibid., p. 173.

CHAPTER 6

1. For fuller accounts of the large subject, in line with the sketch to follow here, you could begin with *On Determinism and Freedom* (Edinburgh University Press, 2005), a collection of my papers. There is also *How Free Are You?* (Oxford University Press, 2nd edition, 2002). The latter, except for its last chapter, is mainly an abbreviation of the 644 pages of *A Theory of Determinism: The Mind, Neuroscience, and Life-Hopes* (Oxford University Press, 1988), subsequently published in halves as the paperbacks *Mind and Brain* and *The Consequences of Determinism*. The sketch that follows here is mainly lifted from ch. 2 of *On Determinism and Freedom*.

2. See *How Free Are You?*, ch. 8. Also, for more, *A Theory of Determinism*, ch. 7 or *Consequences of Determinism*, ch. 1.

3. For related discussions of causation, see *On Determinism*, ch. 1, or *How Free Are You?*, ch. 1, or, for a full account, either *A Theory of Determinism* or *Mind and Brain*, ch. 1.

4. For this and other accounts of the nature of conscious or mental events, including choices and decisions, and also of the mind–body problem, see my *On Consciousness* (Edinburgh University Press, 2004), or *A Theory of Determinism*, ch. 2.

5. Galen Strawson regards indeterminist views of the mind as in a way incoherent. See his *Freedom and Belief* (Oxford University Press, 1986).

6. 'Freedom and Resentment', in his *Studies in the Philosophy of Thought and Action* (Oxford University Press, 1968), p. 211.

7. The outstanding example of neuroscience on holiday is *The Self and Its Brain* (Springer, 1977) by Karl Popper and J. C. Eccles. There is also the thinking of Benjamin Libet, considered in 'Is the Mind Before the Brain? After It?', in *On Consciousness*. See also 'Mind the Guff', on John Searle, in that volume.

8. John Earman, 'Determinism: What We Have Learned and What We Still Don't Know', in *Freedom and Determinism*, ed. Joseph Keim Campbell, Michael O'Rourke, and David Shier (MIT Press, 2004).

9. It is also supposed of these events of true chance, of course, that they may have been very probable. They may have had a probability of 95 per cent, whatever this talk of probability is taken to mean. Does this reassure many people who are rightly averse to imposing mystery on reality? It should not, as already indicated several times. To the question of why the events *actually occurred*, their having had a probability of 95 per cent is of course no answer at all. To assign them a probability of 95 per cent is precisely not to claim they had to happen or could not have failed to happen. It is exactly to hold open the possibility that they might not have happened at all. In fact, on the assumption about true chance being made, there is *no* answer to look for as to why in the fundamental sense they happened. To the question of why in the fundamental sense they actually occurred, there is no relevant fact to be known, no relevant fact of the matter at all. This is very clear because, *ex hypothesi*, everything might have been just the same without their occurring at all. You can miss this little proof of the absolute exclusion of explanatory fact in what we are contemplating, but it is not a good idea to do so.

10. Thomas Hobbes, *Of Liberty and Necessity* and *Leviathan*, in *Works*, ed. W. Molesworth (Bohn, 1839–45, originally c. 1650); David Hume, *A Treatise of Human Nature*, ed. L. A. Selby-Bigge (Oxford University Press, 1888 [1739]); *An Enquiry Concerning Human Nature*, ed. L. A. Selby-Bigge (Oxford University Press, 1963 [1748]).

11. Immanuel Kant, *Critique of Pure Reason*, trans. N. Kemp-Smith (Macmillan, 1950 [1781]), p. 477; *Critique of Practical Reason*, trans. L. W. Beck (University of Chicago Press, 1949 [1748]), pp. 97–8. J. Bramhall, 'A Defence of True Liberty', in his *Works* (Dublin, 1676).

12. *A Theory of Determinism*, ch. 7, *How Free Are You?* ch. 8.

13. Peter van Inwagen, *An Essay on Free Will* (Oxford University Press, 1983).

14. Daniel Dennett, *Elbow Room* (MIT Press, 1984).
15. Harry Frankfurt, 'Freedom of the Will and the Concept of a Person', *Journal of Philosophy*, 1971; *Necessity, Volition and Love* (Cambridge University Press, 1999).
16. *The Open Universe*, ed. W. W. Bartley (Hutchinson, 1982), p. xix. See also Popper and Eccles, *The Self and Its Brain*, the most numbing of speculations about free will.
17. There has been, by the way, another philosophical reaction to compatibilism and incomptibilism. Suppose (as in *How Free Are You?* pp. 115–21) you are about to make up your mind. If you are going to decide on the good thing rather than the bad, a neuroscientist will affect your brain so that you decide to do the bad thing. However, you on your own decide to do the bad thing. So, it is said, you are morally responsible for doing it even though you could not have done otherwise. Such examples have led some philosophers to say that moral responsibility does not require freedom, that it is consistent with determinism. They add, however, that freedom itself is *inconsistent* with determinism. This is called semi-compatibilism, but plainly might as well be called semi-incompatibilism. Philosophical time not well spent, in my opinion. It is pointless to try to detach the given examples from the fact of our attitudes of voluntariness and origination, in terms of which they are easily explained. *Any* moral responsibility continues to include *some* kind of freedom. Above all, the examples do not come near to showing we have only one conception of freedom and one conception of responsibility. Nor, as is also said despite what you have heard, some conception of freedom for moral responsibility and another one for our personal dignity etc. See Laura Waddell Ekstrom, *Free Will* (Westview, 2000) and the works cited there of Harry Frankfurt and John Fischer.
18. *A Theory of Determinism*, p. 613.
19. Leo Zaibert, who kindly read the first draft of this revised edition, pressed the question of whether some retributivism can rest on the idea of freedom of voluntariness alone. I remain convinced that retributivism as we have had it has presupposed origination, and that to give up the presupposition would transform it, indeed as good as destroy it. Zaibert has also noted that if determinism affects retributivism, it also affects a lot more. Indeed it does – which is not the conclusion that determinism does not affect retributivism.
20. I do not now hold to the theory of determinism that has been sketched, but am inclined to another one as deterministic, the product of a certain general theory of the nature of consciousness, known as Consciousness as Existence. See *On Consciousness*, and in particular, with respect to the present point, p. 218.
21. See *How Free Are You?* ch. 12, added to the second edition of the book, and also *On Determinism*, ch. 12.

CHAPTER 7

1. H. L. A. Hart, 'A Prolegomenon to the Principles of Punishment', in his *Punishment and Responsibility: Essays in the Philosophy of Law* (Oxford

University Press, 1963); John Rawls, 'Two Concepts of Rules', *The Philosophical Review*, 1955.

2. 'Prolegomenon', pp. 1–4.
3. 'Two Concepts'.
4. 'Prolegomenon', pp. 17–21.
5. Ibid., p. 1.
6. Ibid., p. 9.
7. Hart, 'Punishment and the Elimination of Responsibility', in *Punishment and Responsibility*, pp. 182–3.
8. Robert Nozick, *Philosophical Explanations* (Oxford University Press, 1981), p. 363.
9. Ibid., p. 366.
10. As remarked earlier, however, Leo Zaibert maintains that no effective distinction can be made between punishment in general, as distinct from punishment by the state, and revenge. See his *Punishment and Retribution* (Ashgate, 2005).
11. H. P. Grice, *Studies in the Ways of Words* (Harvard University Press, 1989).
12. *Philosophical Explanations*, pp. 370–1.
13. There is much earlier thought on punishment as communication, some in the work of the sociologist Emile Durkheim. On Durkheim, see David Garland, *Punishment and Modern Society* (Oxford University Press, 1990), ch. 2, especially p. 45. See also Jean Hampton, 'The Moral Education Theory of Punishment', *Philosophy and Public Affairs*, 1984, Anthony Skillen, 'How To Say Things With Walls', *Philosophy*, 1980 and Igor Primoratz, 'Punishment as Language', *Philosophy*, 1989.
14. *Philosophical Explanations*, p. 374.
15. Ibid., p. 375.
16. Ibid., pp. 372, 373.
17. Ibid., p. 373, cf. pp. 378–9.
18. Nozick's setting aside of actual moral reformation by punishment sets his view aside from A. C. Ewing's reform theory, noted earlier, despite very notable similarities about punishment as communication. See above pp. 114–18.
19. *Philosophical Explanations*, pp. 375–6.
20. Ibid., p. 373.
21. *Anarchy, State and Utopia* (Blackwell, 1974).
22. Honderich, *On Political Means and Social Ends* (Edinburgh University Press, 2003), pp. 31–3, 164.
23. Duff, *Punishment, Communication and Community* (Oxford University Press, 2001).
24. Ibid., p. xvii.
25. Ibid., p. xix.
26. Ibid., p. 88, cf. p. 129.
27. J. Feinberg, 'The Expressive Function of Punishment', in his *Doing and Deserving* (Princeton University Press, 1970); I. Primoratz, 'Punishment as Language', *Philosophy*, 1989, and also *Justifying Legal Punishment* (Humanities Press, 1989).
28. *Punishment, Communication and Community*, p. 79.
29. Ibid., pp. 81–2, cf. p. 123.

30. *Punishment, Communication and Community*, pp. 121–5.
31. Ibid., p. 131.
32. Ibid., p. 137.
33. Ibid., pp. 11–12, 131–4.
34. Ibid., p. 134.
35. Ibid., p. 35.
36. Nicola Lacey, *State Punishment: Political Principles and Community Values* (Routledge, 1988).
37. See, for a start, 'Liberalism' by Will Kymlicka, in *The Oxford Companion to Philosophy*, ed. Honderich (Oxford University Press, 2005). For something on a liberal theory of punishment, see Hugo Adam Bedau, 'Punishment', *The Stanford Encyclopedia of Philosophy* (Summer 2003 edition), ed. Edward N. Zalta, <http://plato.stanford.edu/archives/sum2003/entries/punishment/>.
38. *Punishment, Communication and Community*, p. 42.
39. Elizabeth Fraser, 'Communitarianism', in *The Oxford Companion to Philosophy*.
40. *Punishment, Communication and Community*, p. 47.
41. Ibid., pp. 47–8.
42. *On Political Means and Social Ends*, mainly the papers on Mill and Rawls.
43. *Punishment, Communication and Community*, ch. 5.

CHAPTER 8

1. I have had recourse to it myself, however, mainly in connection with Palestinian terrorism against neo-Zionist ethnic cleansing, which was said by me to be the moral right of the Palestinians, as I remain convinced it has been – *After the Terror* (Edinburgh University Press, expanded edition, 2003), pp. 151, 155–86; *On Political Means and Social Ends* (Edinburgh University Press, 2003), pp. 155–76; *Terrorism for Humanity: Inquiries in Political Philosophy* (Pluto Press, 2003), p. 199.
2. This analysis of conservatism is given in *Conservatism: Burke, Nozick, Bush, Blair?* (Pluto Press, 2005).
3. In that conviction, by the way, there is an additional objection to intrinsic retributivism (p. 24).
4. For reflection on desert in general, not only with respect to punishment, see *Conservatism*, ch. 8.
5. A different view of a sociological kind also brings together moral and political facts in reflection on the justification of punishment. It is to be found in David Garland's *Punishment and Modern Society* (Oxford University Press, 1990). He speaks (pp. 1–2) of his 'attempt to shift the sociology of punishment away from its recent tendency – engendered by Foucault and the Marxists – to view the penal system more or less exclusively as an apparatus of power and control, and to recognize that criminal laws and penal institutions usually encapsulate moral values and sensibilities that are widely shared – even if the older Durkheimian tradition overstates the extent to which this is true'.

6. For my examination of these ideas of Bernard Williams, as remarked before, *see Terrorism for Humanity*, pp. 29–35.

7. *Punishment, Communication and Community* (Oxford University Press, 2001), pp. 3–14.

8. *After the Terror*, pp. 8–9.

9. Certainly this view is now held by others, and no doubt if it was not much heard it was held prior to the original edition of this book. For a recent exposition of it, see Hugo Adam Bedau, 'Punishment', *The Stanford Encyclopedia of Philosophy* (Summer 2003 edition), ed. Edward N. Zalta, <http://plato.stanford.edu/archives/sum2003/entries/punishment/>.

10. Leo Zaibert, in *Punishment and Retribution* (Ashgate, 2005) makes an attempt to clarify liberalism in connection with punishment.

11. For more of my views of liberalism, Mill and Rawls, see *On Political Means and Social Ends*.

12. On the philosophy of history, see 'Trying to Save Marx's Theory of History, by Teleology, and Failing', in *On Political Means and Social Ends*. It is possible, as it turns out, to have a far better view of Marx as what he said he was not, which is a social moralist. There is a good account of Marxist theory of punishment, and in particular of *Punishment and Social Structures* (Platt & Takagi, 1980) by Georg Rusche and Otto Kirchheimer, in David Garland, *Punishment and Modern Society* (Oxford University Press, 1990), chs. 4 and 5.

13. It seems to me possible that some of us would be still more moved by a life cut short if we were more aware of, so to speak, the immensity of what is lost – according to an arguable view of the nature of perceptual consciousness. See my *On Consciousness* (Edinburgh University Press, 2004).

14. 'Hierarchic Democracy and the Necessity of Mass Civil Disobedience and Non-Cooperation', in *On Political Means and Social Ends*.

15. There is more on the Principle of Humanity, if not enough, in *On Political Means and Social Ends*, *After the Terror*, and *Terrorism for Humanity*. Certainly it faces problems – fewer, to my mind, than the mysterious philosophical moralities to which it is opposed. For some thoughts along these lines, see in particular 'Consequentialism, Moralities of Concern, and Selfishness', in *On Political Means and Social Ends*.

16. *After the Terror*, pp. 18–20.

17. Cf. Robert Dahl, *A Preface to Democratic Theory* (University of Chicago Press, 1956), p. 211.

18. It is a shortcoming of the present book that it does not consider the matter of the collective responsibility of societies for offences against other peoples, notably native or aboriginal peoples, and the question of reparation and compensation. See J. Angelo Corlett, *Responsibility and Punishment* (Kluwer, 2004), chs. 6–10.

19. *Conservatism*, pp. 30, 191, 217; *After the Terror*, pp. 110–15.

20. *After the Terror*, pp. 8–9.

21. *Conservatism*, the sections on Britain's New Labour governments at the ends of the chapters.

22. There is no need to withdraw from or much hesitate about this judgement on account of a surprising lacuna in philosophy, science and much else. That is the absence of thinking on the weighting of causes and conditions in general – the assigning of greater or lesser explanatory power, different degrees of explanation, to different conditions within a full cause or causal circumstance or a sequence of such causes. Certainly there is a theoretical problem here, one that may require philosophically radical thinking – but it is a problem of explaining judgements that sometimes can be confident.

23. See the poverty statistics in *Conservatism*.

24. *Terrorism for Humanity*, pp. 109–47; *After the Terror*, pp. 73–88.

25. Corporate responsibility is discussed in ch. 8 of Corlett's *Responsibility and Punishment*.

26. Peter G. Herman, *American Prisons and Imprisonment* (Wilson, 2001).

27. *Prison and Jail Inmates at Midyear 2004; Bureau of Justice Statistics, Prisoners in 2003; Prison and Jail Inmates at Midyear 2003*; Census Bureau Population estimates for 2003.

28. Cf. Pat Carlen, 'Crime, Inequality and Sentencing', in Antony Duff and David Garland (eds), *A Reader on Punishment* (Oxford University Press, 1994).

29. As Kiaran Honderich points out, some rape statistics would be more useful than conjectures. Is it the case that rape does not correlate with less money but rather that conviction for rape does? In effect that matter is considered below.

30. For a consideration of the idea of Bernard Williams that the rest of us are only 'negatively responsible' for what others do, see my *Terrorism for Humanity*.

31. For views related to the proposition that punishments in our societies are in general unjustified see W. A. Bonger, *Criminality and Economic Conditions* (Little Brown, 1916); I. Taylor, P. Walton and J. Young, *The New Criminology* (Routledge & Kegan Paul, 1973); Jeffrey Reiman, *The Rich Get Richer and the Poor Get Prison* (Allyn & Bacon, 1979); Elliott Currie, *Confronting Crime* (Pantheon Press, 1986); J. G. Murphy, 'Marxism and Retribution', in Duff and Garland, *A Reader on Punishment*.

32. For a consideration of alternatives to punishment, see Hugo Adam Bedau's 'Punitive Violence and Its Alternatives', in James B. Brady and Newton Garver (eds), *Justice, Law and Violence* (Temple University Press, 1991).

33. As remarked earlier, this book is about ordinary crime, and does not consider terrorism. Also, this edition was completed before 7 July 2005, when more than 50 people were killed in an attack on London. Terrorism is considered in my *After the Terror* and in *Terrorism for Humanity: Inquiries in Political Philosophy*, and also in a forthcoming book provisionally titled *Palestine, 9/11, Iraq, 7/7*.

Index

Absolute, the 43
Adler 230
agreement *see* consent theories
annulment 41–3
annulment theory *see* retribution
    theories: annulment
Armstrong 237
authority 8, 9, 11

backward-looking theories 17–57,
    46, 109, 163 *see also* retribution
    theories, rational contract
    theory, consensual theory *cf*
    compromise theories
Barker 233
Bartley 240
Bedau 231, 233
behaviour therapy 122–3
Bentham 75 *see also* utilitarianism,
    utilitarian prevention theory
Blair 220, 221
Blunkett 239
Bonger 244
Bosanquet 43
Brand 237
Brown 221
burdens 54

Carlen 244
Carritt 238
causal explanation 84, 134, 236
chance 143, 239
circular retributivism *see* retribution
    theories: circular
civil disobedience 227, 243
collective responsibility 243
commensurate penalty 22 *see also*
    desert
communication 7, 176–84, 181,
    184–94, 241
communitarianism 189
compatibilism *see* determinism and
    freedom: compatibilism

compromise theories 2, 3, 7, 93,
    164–5, 204
  correct-values retributivism
    176–84
  free and responsible offence
    170–6
  liberal community retributivism
    184–93
consciousness 240, 243
consent theories 6, 17, 46–53
consequentialism 74, 200,
    235–6
conservatism, political 3, 15, 62,
    118, 197–8, 227, 235, 236 *see
    also* Nozick
contractors, imaginable 47
contract theory 17 *see also* rational
    contract theory
contract, social 47
control 16, 153
Corlett 231, 232, 243, 244
Cottingham 231, 234
crime 16, 79, 188, 194, 202,
    214–15, 219
criminology 1
Crook 229
culpability 30–1, 36
Currie 244

Dahl 243
Davies 119, 238
Davis 24, 231, 232
death penalty 236
definition of punishment 8–14, 15,
    16, 230–1
definitions 8, 9, 12
democracy 227
Dennett 239
desert 2–3, 13, 14–15, 17, 20, 22–3,
    36, 59–60, 70, 178, 183, 185,
    192–3, 231–2 *see also*
    retribution theories *cf*
    compromise theories

determinism and freedom 2, 68,
131–3, 172–6, 201, 211, 238,
240
  affirmation 158
  attitudinism 145, 150, 156
  compatibilism 144, 153, 155, 240
  freedom as origination 25–6, 136,
137
  freedom as voluntariness 4, 5, 25,
144, 223
  free will 26 *see also* freedom as
origination
  incompatibilism 145, 151, 155
  responsibility, kinds of 145–51
deterrence *see* prevention
Duff 4, 112, 184–93, 200, 229, 230
see also retributivism: liberal
community
Durkheim 234
Dyer 237

Earman 239
Eccles 239
economical prevention *see*
prevention, economical
Ekstrom 240
ends, not only means, treat people
as 49, 89
equality 53, 69, 107, 110, 223
equivalent penalty 22, 31, 35, 178
see also desert, retribution
theories
Ewing 114–16, 237–8, 238
excuse, rule of 98
exemplary penalties 104–5
explanation 239
explanation of punishment 1–2
Eysenck 122–3

fairness owed to consent *see*
consent theories
Feinberg 241
Finnis 232
fittingness 42 *see also* desert
Flew 156, 238
Foucault 234
Frankfurt 240
freedom *see* determinism and
freedom

Freud 121, 125, 132
Friedlander 238

Garland 229, 234–5, 241, 242
Garver 244
Goldman 232
goods 72, 208, 214, 216 *see also*
Humanity, Principle of
Grice 237
grievance 60, 160
grievance-satisfaction 60 *see also*
retribution theories: grievance-
satisfaction, systematic
Gross 35–41, 67, 232
guilt 60 *see* responsibility, legal
guilty, finding 10, 12, 15

Hampton 241
Hart 165–76, 237 *see also*
retribution theories: free and
responsible offence
Hegel 42
Herman 244
Hobbes 144
Honderich, Kiaran 244
Humanity, Principle of 43, 107,
111, 206–10
Hume 58, 144, 233

illness, crime as 118
immunity loss *see* consensual
theory
incapacitation *see* prevention
incompatibilism *see* determinism
and freedom
indoctrination 128, 141
inequality 210–14 *see also* equality
innocence 39, 91
intrinsic-good retributivism *see*
retribution theories: intrinsic
good
intuitionism, moral 28

Jones 236
justice 65–6, 111, 183, 202, 237 *see
also* equality, Humanity,
Principle of, retribution theories
justification, rule of 98 *see also*
excuse, mitigation

Kant 17–21, 46, 49, 89, 145, 170, 202
Kennedy 230
Kirchheimer 243
Kleinig 230
Kymlicka 242

Lacey 4, 229, 230
Ladyman 230
law 85, 117 *see also* crime
legal retributivism *see* retribution theories
Lehrer 236
Levin 236
lex talionis 20, 29, 177
liberalism 3, 21, 189, 207 *see also* Duff, Rawls
logic 1
logical positivism 233
Lotze 63

Mabbott 4, 229
Mackie 58, 64, 234
Marx 207, 232, 234, 243
McNaghten rules 120
McTaggart 228, 233
meaning of punishment 2, 229
mental disorder 119 *see also* McNaghten Rules
Mill 87, 107, 207
mitigation, rule of 98
mixed theories *see* compromise theories
Moore 231, 234
moral responsibility *see* responsibility, moral
Morris 234
Murphy 232, 233, 234

Nagel 195
need to justify punishment *see* punishment, moral problem of
Neumann 232, 235
neuroscience 139, 239
New Labour Party 221
Nino 48–53, 233
Nozick 7, 112, 176–84, 238, 241

offence 9, 13–15
offender 8–14, 15

paradox of retributivism *see* retributivism, paradox of
philosophy 1, 166
politics and punishment 2–3, 15, 75, 87, 217 *see also* conservatism, liberalism, Duff, Nozick
Popper 156, 239
prevention 75–6 *see also* utilitarian prevention theory
  deterrence 3, 6, 75, 77–84
  economical 87–9
  factual question 76–86
  incapacitation 6, 75–7
  unreflective law-abidingness 83–6, 238
prevention theories 75 *see also* utilitarian prevention theory
Primoratz 241
prisons 4–5, 222
property 214–15, 218
proportion 22, 36, 37, 187 *see also* desert
public good 87
punishment, moral problem of 4–6, 217–18

quantum theory 138–44
questions, separate, about punishment 166–70 *see also* Hart
Quinton 237

rape 224
rape in prison 5, 77
Rashdall 238
rational contract theory 46–8
Rawls 21, 47, 94, 165, 230, 231
recidivism 78
reciprocal penalty 22 *see also* desert, retribution theories
reform theories 6–7, 75, 112–29 *see also* compromise theories, correct values retributivism
  punishment as opportunity to reform 113

reform theories – *continued*
  punishment itself as reformative
    6–7, 114
  punishment as condemnation
    114–15
rehabilitation 3, 7 *see also* reform
  theories
Reiman 244
responsibility, legal 19–20
responsibility, moral 11, 18–21, 68,
    130, 144–62, 146, 240 *see also*
    determinism and freedom
restoration 53
retribution 6 *see also* desert
retribution theories 3, 6, 13, 58, 159,
    163, 195–200, 201, 202,
    203 *see also* desert, negative
    retributivism *cf* compromise
    theories
  annulment 41–3
  bare system 65–7 *cf* system
  circular 24, 25, 31, 36, 41, 110
  consistency 45
  distress 196
  distress-culpability 29, 30–1
  forfeited-rights 31–2
  grievance-satisfaction, systematic
    3, 58–73, 164, 197–9, 234–5,
    235
  indifference 32–3
  innocence-system 35–41
  intrinsic-good 24–9
  jurisprudential *see* system
  legal 18–19, 23
  offender's rights 44
  restorative *see* satisfactions-in-
    acting
  rights *see* forfeited rights,
    offenders' rights
  same-action 30
  same distress 30
  satisfaction-in-acting 53–7
  system 35–41
retributive emotion 148, 160 *see
    also* grievance-satisfaction,
    systematic *cf* revenge
retributivism, negative 20 1, 198
retributivism, paradox of 58
revenge 8, 177, 180, 235

rights 31, 33–5, 46, 242 *see also*
  retribution theories
rule, rules 96–101, 237
rule-breaking 12–13
rule-utilitarianism *see* utilitarianism,
  rule
Rusche 243

satisfactions *see also* grievance-
    satisfactions, retribution
    theories: grievance satisfaction,
    systematic
satisfactions-in-acting 17
Simmons 236
Skillen 241
social emotion 62
social theory 1
society, decent 202, 204–5, 211
sociology 1, 2, 4, 126, 229,
    236, 242
Sprigge 102, 237
Stephen 63, 65
Strawson, G. 239
Strawson, P.F. 232, 239
strict liability 10–11, 12, 104
suffering 4
Sutherland 238
system 35, 65 *see also* retribution
    theories: system

Taylor 244
Ten 230
terrorism 1, 14, 94, 229, 242, 244
theories of punishment 2, 7
Todd 236
Travis 237
treatment 8, 118–25

unreflective law-abidingness *see*
  prevention
Urmson 237
utilitarianism 6, 48, 51, 86, 172,
    200, 237
utilitarianism-related doctrines,
    attitudes 87
utilitarianism, rule 107
utilitarian prevention theory
    86–111, 164, 203 *see also*
    prevention

van Inwagen 239
Verkaik 237
vicarious liability 11, 12, 13
victimization 89–109, 110, 127
voluntariness *see* determinism and
    freedom: freedom as
    voluntariness

Walker 234
Walton 244

White 237
Williams 236–7, 244
Wootton 238
wrong act necessary for
    punishment 14

Young 244

Zaibert 230, 232, 234, 235, 240,
    241, 243